MULTILITERACIES, MULTIMODALITY AND TEACHER PROFESSIONAL LEARNING

ANNE CLOONAN

MULTILITERACIES, MULTIMODALITY AND TEACHER PROFESSIONAL LEARNING

ANNE CLOONAN

Common Ground

First published in Australia in 2010
by Common Ground Publishing
at TheLearner.com
a series imprint of TheUniversityPress

Copyright ©Anne Cloonan 2010

All rights reserved. Apart from fair dealing for the purposes of study, research, criticism or review as permitted under the Copyright Act, no part of this book may be reproduced by any process without written permission from the publisher.

The National Library of Australia Cataloguing–in–Publication data:

Multiliteracies, Multimodality and Teacher Professional Learning Cloonan, Anne
Bibliography.
978 1 86335 712 8 (pbk.)
978 1 86335 713 5 (pdf)

1. Literacy--Study and teaching
372.6

Table of Contents

Acknowledgments xiv

Preface xv

Chapter 1: Introduction to the Research Project 1
    1.1: The Issue in Context 1
    1.2: Significance of This Research 8
    1.3: Overview of the Book 8

Chapter 2: Literature Review 11
    2.1: New Millennium Communication Affordances and Educational
        Responses 11
    2.1.1: Multiliteracies, Multimodality and the Development of a
          Metalanguage 17
    2.2: New Millennium Pedagogy 22
    2.2.1: Multiliteracies Pedagogy 25
    2.2.2: Learning By Design 28
    2.3: New Millennium Teacher Professional Learning 30
    2.3.1: Teacher Impact: Changing Teacher Roles; Changing Teacher
          Learning 31
    2.3.2: Professional Learning for Quality Teaching and Renewed
          Professionalism 35

Chapter 3: Methodology and Procedures 39
    3.1: Research Paradigm: Victorian Early Literacy Policy 40
    3.1.1: The Early Literacy Research Project 40
    3.1.2: The Early Years Literacy Strategy 42
    3.1.2.1: Schools Television and the Early Years Literacy Strategy .. 43
    3.1.2.2: The Work of the Statewide Early Years Literacy Team 45
    3.1.2.3: Victorian Early Years Literacy Policy in Transition 47
    3.1.2.4: The Emerging Influence of Multiliteracies Theory 49
    3.1.2.5: Victorian Essential Learning Standards: A Victorian Literacy
           Policy Addendum 50
    3.2: The Evolution of a Research Project 54
    3.2.1: Transition from Policy and Project Officer to Participatory
          Researcher 54
    3.2.2: Emergence of a Research Project 54
    3.3: The Research Design 56

    3.3.1: Participatory Research and the Researcher's Role 58
    3.3.2: Deployment of Research Interventions 63
    3.3.3: Participant Selection 65
    3.3.4: Ethical Procedures 66
    3.3.5: Data Collection Methods 67
    3.3.5.1: Interviews 67
    3.3.5.2: Participant Observations 68
    3.3.5.3: Artefacts 68
    3.3.5.4: Professional Learning Interventions within the participatory
         Action Research Spiral of Cycles 70

Chapter 4: The Research Project's Case Study Narratives 75
    4.1: Participating Teachers' School and Classroom Contexts 75
    4.2: Rachel: Profile, Project Interests, Knowledge of Multiliteracies
        and Starting Points 76
    4.3: Kim and Meredith: Profile, Project Interests, Knowledge of
        Multiliteracies and Starting Points 81
    4.4: Pip: Profile, Project Interests, Knowledge of Multiliteracies and
        Starting Points 84

Chapter 5: Breakthrough to New Practices 89
    5.1: Introduction 89
    5.2: Rachel: Meaning-making in Narratives 91
    5.2.1: Rachel Summary 101
    5.2.1.1: Addressing Multimodality 101
    5.2.1.2: Deployment of Pedagogical Knowledge Processes 103
    5.3: Kim and Meredith: Multicultural Festivals and Celebrations 105
    5.3.1: Kim and Meredith Summary 113
    5.3.1.1: Addressing Multimodality 113
    5.3.1.2: Deployment of Pedagogical Knowledge Processes 114
    5.4: Pip: Researching Personal Passions for a Class Website 115
    5.4.1: Pip Summary 124
    5.4.1.1: Addressing Multimodality 124
    5.4.1.2: Deployment of Pedagogical Knowledge Processes 126
    5.5: Generalising from the Data 127

Chapter 6: Towards a Metalanguage for
Multimodal Literacies 131
    6.1: Analysing Teacher Language for a Multimodal Metalanguage 131
    6.1.1: Issues in the Analysis of Prompts and Emerging
         Teacher-intended Lexicon 134

6.2: Teaching Multimodality and Mode; Teaching through Multimodality and Mode; and Teaching about Multimodality and Mode 137
6.3: Teaching Emphasis: Modes and Dimensions of Meaning 140
6.3.1: The Gestural Mode: Discussion of Dimensions/Pedagogy 142
6.3.2: The Visual Mode: Discussion of Dimensions/Pedagogy 148
6.3.3: The Audio Mode: Discussion of Dimensions/Pedagogy 153
6.3.4: The Linguistic Mode: Discussion of Dimensions/Pedagogy 156
6.3.5: The Spatial Mode 160
6.4: Deployment of Pedagogical Knowledge Processes to Address Teaching of Modes 161
6.5: Generalising from the Data 164

Chapter 7: Developing Teacher Professionalism 169
7.1: Rachel's Impact Story 169
7.1.1: On Multimodality 170
7.1.2: On Pedagogy 176
7.1.3: On Professional Repertoires 178
7.2: Kim and Meredith's Impact Story 186
7.2.1: On Multimodality 186
7.2.2: On Pedagogy 192
7.2.3: On Professional Repertoires 194
7.3: Pip's Impact Story 203
7.3.1: On Multimodality 203
7.3.2: On Pedagogy 207
7.3.3: On Professional Repertoires 208

Chapter 8: Conclusions 217
8.1: Role and Impact of Researcher as Educational Consultant 217
8.1.1: Findings and Recommendations: Educational Consultants 218
8.2: Role of the Film Co-production between Early Years Branch and Schools Television Unit 219
8.2.1: Findings and Recommendations: Future Filming 221
8.3: Role of the Victorian Early Years Literacy Program 221
8.3.1: Findings and Recommendations: Literacy Policy Development 222
8.4: Role of the 'Multimodal Schema' 222
8.4.1: Findings and Recommendations: Multimodality 225
8.5: Role of 'Pedagogical Knowledge Processes Schema' 226
8.5.1: Findings and Recommendations: Pedagogical Knowledge Processes 228
8.6: Role of Participatory Action Research Methodology 229

    8.6.1: Findings and Recommendations: Participatory Action Research
        Methodology 230
    8.7: Recommendations: Future Research Agendas 231

Bibliography **233**

List Of Figures

Figure 1.1: Aspect of Multiliteracies and Schemas for Realising Renewal of Literacy Education 6

Figure 5.1: Rachel's Knowledge Objectives in Learning Element 92

Figure 5.2: Rachel's Knowledge Processes in Learning Element 92

Figure 5.3: Rachel's Student Artefacts, Lesson 4 98

Figure 5.4: Rachel's Student Artefacts from Language Experience Approach 100

Figure 5.5: Kim and Meredith's Data Categories for Discussion of Breakthrough Multiliteracies Practices 106

Figure 5.6: Kim and Meredith's Student Artefacts, Student Developed Cards 111

Figure 5.7: Pip's Knowledge Objectives in Learning Element 116

Figure 5.8: Pip's Student Artefacts from Unit of Work on 'Web Passion' . 122

List of Tables

Table 3.1: Example of the Standards Set for English Level 1 51

Table 3.2: Action Research Cycle and Professional Learning Interventions . 61

Table 3.3: Alignment of Research Interests and Assumptions Underpinning Professional Learning 64

Table 5.1: Rachel's Data Categories for Discussing Breakthrough Multiliteracies Practices 93

Table 5.2: Rachel's Teaching Focus—Mode 101

Table 5.3: Rachel's Deployment of Pedagogical Knowledge Processes 103

Table 5.4: Kim and Meredith's Data Categories for Discussion of Breakthrough Multiliteracies Practices 107

Table 5.5: Kim and Meredith's Teaching Focus—Mode 113

Table 5.7: Pip's Data Categories for Discussion of Breakthrough Multiliteracies Practices 117

Table 5.8: Pip's Teaching Focus—Mode 124

Table 5.9: Pip's Deployment of Pedagogical Knowledge Processes 126

Table 5.10: Rachel-Pip's Teaching Focus—Mode 127

Table 5.11: Rachel-Pip's Deployment of Pedagogical Knowledge Processes by Documented Lessons 129

Table 6.1: Teaching Focus on Mode Based on Prompt/Lesson 141

Table 6.2: Focus of Teaching Prompts: Dimension of Meaning 141

Table 6.3: Focus of Teaching Prompts: Dimension of Mode 142

Table 6.4: Teacher Prompts Classified According to the Mode of Meaning 161

Table 6.5: Teacher Prompts Classified According to Pedagogical Effect on Mode 161

Table 6.6: Summary of Pedagogical Effect on Mode 162

Table 7.1: Rachel: Addressing of Dimensions of Meaning in Each Mode of Meaning. Teaching Sequence 1 175

Table 7.2: Rachel: Deployment of Pedagogical Knowledge Processes in Teaching Multimodality (Predominant mode of focus is shown by print size) Teaching Sequence 1 (Body Talk) 178

Table 7.3: Rachel: Deployment of Pedagogical Knowledge Processes in Two Teaching Sequences 181

Table 7.4: Rachel: Addressing of Mode and Deployment of Pedagogical Knowledge Processes (Predominant mode of focus is shown in italics) Teaching Sequence 1 182

Table 7.5: Kim and Meredith: Deployment of Pedagogical Knowledge Processes in Teaching Multimodality (Predominant mode of focus is shown by print size) Teaching Sequence 1 194

Table 7.6: Kim and Meredith: Deployment of Pedagogical Knowledge Processes in Two Teaching Sequences 196

Table 7.7: Kim and Meredith: Addressing of Mode and Deployment of Pedagogical Knowledge Processes (Predominant mode of focus is shown in italics) Teaching Sequence 1 198

Table 7.8: Pip: Deployment of Pedagogical Knowledge Processes in Teaching Multimodality (Predominant mode of focus is shown by print size) Teaching Sequence 1 209

Table 7.9: Pip: Deployment of Pedagogical Knowledge Processes in Two Teaching Sequences 211

Table 7.10: Pip: Addressing of Mode and Deployment of Pedagogical Knowledge Processes (Predominant mode of focus is shown in italics) Teaching Sequence 1 212

Table 8.1: Teaching Focus: Mode Rachel-Pip (% of lessons) 223

Table 8.2: Focus of Teaching Prompts: Dimension of Mode Teaching Sequence 1 225

Table 8.3: Teacher Deployment of Pedagogical Knowledge Processes 226

Acknowledgments

There are many people and institutions whose support made this book possible.

Firstly, thanks must go to the four teachers who allowed me to bring a camera into their classrooms and who tirelessly discussed their practices and understandings. Thanks also to the students in their classes and their school communities for their patience and support.

I remain indebted to my colleagues at the Catholic Education Office, Melbourne, and at the Department of Education, Victoria for the opportunity and resources to innovate and research.

The continued interest and encouragement of many wonderful colleagues from Deakin University, RMIT University, and the University of Illinois at Urbana-Champaign is truly appreciated. Particular thanks for intellectual engagement must go to Mary Kalantzis, Bill Cope, Helen Smith and Peter Burrows. I warmly acknowledge the support of my employer, Deakin University, particularly the financial support granted by Diane Mayer and the temporal support which Chris Bigum approved.

Finally I wish to thank my circle of understanding family and friends. To Peter Davis and Teresa Cannon whose interest and encouragement never faltered. Above all, love and thanks to Steve, Helen, Danny and Sinead for your daily inspiration and tolerance of it all.

Preface

Personal Narrative, Purpose and Journey

In the writing of this book the question of voice has presented an issue, prompted by my positioning as participant researcher. The following statement is offered to explain how this issue has been resolved.

The origin of this research described in this book was a workplace-based task I was required to undertake in my role as a literacy policy and project officer in an Australian government department.

The research was conducted in a transitionary time: a time of major policy development and consultation. In the vacuum created by the imminence of policy renewal, the bureaucracy was in an exploratory mood. My task was to develop a resource for literacy teachers—a resource which would stimulate professional dialogue around multiliteracies. I undertook to develop a series of videos presenting the views of multiliteracies theorists and the multiliteracies practices of classroom teachers.

Traditional project management practices would have positioned this as a relatively straightforward task—a studio-based film shoot capturing the expertise of the talking heads and school-based film shoots capturing the practical applications of the teachers. Crisp coherence would be gained through the process of film editing, with distribution and use of the videos within the existing statewide train-the-trainer infrastructure ensuring that the films' purpose would be fulfilled as teachers would be prompted to engage in professional dialogue. In this way the project outcomes would have been accounted for completely.

But reduction of the complexities presented by the multiliteracies argument into easy answers would have been tantamount to a denial of the transformation wrought on text and meaning relationships by the shift from print-based to digital communications. It would also have been a denial of the transformation wrought on social dynamics and the balance of agency by shifts in the production and consumption of knowledge. It would have presupposed answers where questions were more appropriate. It would have suggested replicable, rather than locally situated, responses. It would have encouraged a theorist-to-teacher flow of knowledge. For these reasons, I decided to depart from the traditional model for developing professional learning artefacts.

The starting point of the journey of the book can be traced back to my approaching Professors Mary Kalantzis and Bill Cope, members of the *New London Group* and developers of Multiliteracies Theory, to ask them if they would contribute to the project. But its genesis was founded in my rejection of the use of formulas for teacher learning and literacy teaching and learning which no longer resonated adequately with the lifeworlds of teachers, students and bureaucrats: the world in which our work is, after all, situated. From within the set of values that intertwine and define my sensibilities, I found that some were jostling for greater recognition; demanding a more active, less passive positioning of the literacy practitioner I was, as well as those practitioners I worked with and for; and necessitating an embracing of, rather than a denial of, the importance of the affordances of the emergent communications in this problematic called literacy education.

I rejected the prevailing norms and proposed and developed a project somewhat radical in nature: a participatory, exploratory project involving theorists, teachers and myself in my role as bureaucrat.

I have adopted various roles in relation to the work of Professors Kalantzis and Cope—from bureaucratic representative to academic consultant working in a broader team of people involved in testing, challenging and developing multiliteracies and Learning by Design. These roles have involved me in a changing set of relationships with the theorists and their work. The position of insider, however, has presented issues in the development of this book: issues of objectivity, and issues of referencing, particularly in discussing the context of participatory research.

My roles within the government education department also positioned me as an insider, and subsequently I have embodied knowledge of policy, projects, and resources on which I worked. I also continue to have strong relationships with former work colleagues through my role as consultant to schools and regional offices. My insider position has presented me with issues of referencing—unpublished knowledge that has been difficult to fully reference and citing from publications which are only partial in the knowledge presented.

In some respects, the challenges embedded in this moveable set of social relations reflect those presented by the new communications environment. These challenges are, in part, technically related, clearly exemplified in the capacities afforded to users of the internet. Internet users have immediate and global information, communication and technological access and dissemination capacities. Capacities involve a range of meaning-making resources enabled by ever-emerging new technologies and opportunities to engage in, and transform, new and continuously changing literacy practices.

But the changes are not only technical, as egalitarian access to formerly specialised literacy affordances differentially impact on sensibilities or mindsets, perhaps part of broader challenges in social dynamics of agency. Just as the communications environment of the early days of the twenty-first century in Western countries enables new systems for producing and sharing knowledge, it also enables new producers and sharers of knowledge; new flows of knowledge and new relationships, challenging hierarchical and authoritative flows of knowledge, the kinds of flows evident in many bureaucracies, schools and universities.

The interface between theoretical suggestions and actual workplace practices continues to present a problematic gap as well. While work such as the examples produced by the teachers and students in this research and the associated professional learning project present possibilities for relevant and rigorous learning, the interface between existing practices and theoretical possibilities remains tense and unresolved.

This book is part of the resolution of the problem that started me on this journey: a disjuncture between the changing communications environment and existing organisational practices concerning professional learning and literacy education. It is a vehicle for the story of my learnings. The knowledge is a contribution back to the original problem, a problem of changing social dynamics and shifts in agency as much as it is a problem of a changing communications environment.

Finding language to adequately reflect the relationships between the participants in this professional learning project and associated research has been a challenge and I have opted to lay the issues open to scrutiny by means of this preface. Hereafter, I have adopted a more traditional tone.

Glossary of terms

To enhance readability, explanations of key terms used within the context of the book are offered here. References in the body of the text are not always followed by full referencing details.

Dimensions of meaning schema: A framework of five dimensions of meaning— representational, social, organisational, contextual and ideological meaning (Cope and Kalantzis, 2000a; Kalantzis and Cope, unpublished paper;)—used as a schema for the purpose of data analysis.

Early Years Literacy Team, Department of Education Victoria: the work-based team to which the researcher belonged, and which was also, at times, known as the Keys to Life Project Team, the Early Years Literacy and Numeracy Project Team, and the Early and Middle Years Branch.

Learning Element: teacher developed and documented teaching and learning sequences using the Learning Element template.

Learning Element template: template providing a documentation scaffold for teacher consideration when developing teaching and learning. Designed to be accessed by other teachers (Teacher Resource) and learners (Student Resource), this integrates with digital publishing technologies to offer educators collaborative spaces to design learning choices (Kalantzis and Cope, 2004; Kalantzis et al., 2005).

Multiliteracies pedagogies schema: Four-part framework of pedagogy, consisting of situated practice, overt instruction, critical framing and transformed practice (New London Group, 1996, 2000).

Multiliteracies schemas: frameworks to support expansion and transformation of conceptions of literacy to reflect the changes brought about by technology and globalisation (Cope and Kalantzis, 2000b; New London Group, 1996, 2000).

Multimodal schema: A framework of six modes of meaning-making—linguistic, visual, audio, gestural, spatial and multimodal (New London Group, 1996, 2000)—used in this research as a schema for professional learning and data analysis purposes.

Pedagogical knowledge processes schema: Learning by Design framework (Kalantzis and Cope, 2004; Kalantzis et al., 2005) articulating the multiliteracies four-part pedagogy as eight detailed pedagogical knowledge processes—experiencing the known and new; conceptualising by naming and by theorising; analysing functionally or critically; and applying appropriately or creatively. The schema is used in this research for the purposes of professional learning and for data analysis.

Research project or **my research:** A case study investigation of a professional learning initiative introducing to school teachers a multiliteracies approach to literacy. The goal was to gauge the ways in which the participating teachers generated a metalanguage across the various meaning-making modes (linguistic, visual, audio, gestural and spatial) as they made pedagogical choices (experiential, analytical, conceptual and applied). The case study used a participatory action research methodology, with the four teachers in the roles of participatory action researchers. The study recursively deployed professional learning interventions to support both the collection of data and to advance the goals of the work-based professional learning project (see below).

Work-based professional learning project: A workplace-based professional learning project initiated by the researcher in the role of Early Years Literacy Policy and Project Officer at the Department of Education, to facilitate the production of a series of films, *Multiliteracies in the Early Years*. The goal of these films was to serve as a professional learning resource for classroom teachers to enable them to enhance the literacy learning of their students. The film project thus took on a double role. It engaged in the transformation of the teachers as it captured and recorded their practice. A participatory action research approach was used to engage the four teachers with the tenets of multiliteracies theory, and, through a series of other interventions, to support professional learning about multiliteracies in order to enhance their classroom practices.

Chapter 1
Introduction to the Research Project

Chapter One will describe the issue which prompted this research project and the context in which it arose. The scope and interests of the research will be foregrounded and the research questions presented. The context is literacy teaching and learning of students in their early years of primary schooling (aged approximately 5–10 years) in a changing communications context. The research questions relate to reform of teacher professional learning, literacy pedagogy and literacy metalanguage within this context.

1.1: The Issue in Context

This research emerged from a workplace-based project designed and undertaken by the researcher in her role as Early Years Literacy Project and Policy Officer with the Victorian Department of Education in Australia. Developed in the context of a communications environment rapidly changing as a result of the increased digitisation and networking of technologies, the project saw the researcher undertake a staged filming project in which four early years teachers were required to engage with issues surrounding the changing nature of literacy and progressively modify classroom applications as a result of their engagement. This research project has adopted the terminology of the Victorian Department of Education, referring to students in their first five years of schooling (students aged approximately 5–10 years) as 'early years'.

In 2003, at the inception of this research, Departmental early years literacy policies and programs assumed that literacy simply referred to reading, writing, speaking and listening to linguistic resources—in other words, they were print-focused (Education Victoria, 1999b, 1997h, 1998b). However, theoretical cases for reconsidering this view of literacy, allowing it to acknowledge and address modes of meaning other than linguistic as literacy meaning-making resources, were being persuasively argued (Alvermann and Hagood, 2000; New London Group, 2000; Reinking, et al., 1998; Unsworth, 2001). Within the Department of Education, Victoria, such arguments were being considered, in part because of the rapid developments in digital communications. Pressure was mounted for a broad policy renewal which acknowledged the changing social, historical and political context. Prevailing state models of curriculum, organised around eight key learning areas, were increasingly seen as inadequate. Within the context of these influences, the researcher's workplace professional learning project evolved into an exploration of 'theory in practice' (Department of Education and Training, 2003b) and an examination of the ways in which profession-wide dialogue and innovation could be promoted through the development of grounded, classroom-based examples of early years literacy pedagogy which responded to the changing communications landscape.

The aim of the workplace professional learning project was to consider the design of the kind of professional learning that would enable sustained energy by early years teachers in the changing communications environment; professional learning which positioned teachers as knowledge collaborators and creators rather than as technicians. To this end the researcher invited four early years teachers and two theorists to collaborate in a series of interventions designed to develop and capture knowledge of classroom-based multiliteracies pedagogical understandings and practices. Four teachers drawn from two Victorian state schools—one in inner-urban Melbourne, the other from a small regional town—agreed to participate and Professor Mary Kalantzis and Dr Bill Cope, members of the *New London Group* and developers of multiliteracies theory, also agreed to collaborate in the research dimension of the project, sharing their expertise in workshops and in filmed interviews. Both schools had a high proportion of students from low socio-economic backgrounds. The four teachers collectively had teaching responsibilities for students from Years Prep to 4.

While many teachers have been found to be reticent about adopting new technologies and developing digital literacies in classrooms, students have tended to be enthusiastic adopters of digital practices, particularly in out-of-school contexts (Lankshear, 1999; Prensky, 2001; Snyder, 1996). This research project explored teacher interaction with specific conceptual resources, utilising the schemas which multiliteracies theory offers for exploring issues of meaning-making. These conceptual resources gave the potential for classroom explorations of multimodal textual designs such as those enabled by digitisation. Developing proficiency in the heritage practices of the three 'Rs' has long been central to the role of early years literacy teachers. Current syllabus documents continue to expect that teachers will develop student reading and writing literacy proficiency but require that they also develop student proficiency in the new technologies (Victorian Curriculum and Assessment Authority, 2005b). Unfortunately these curriculum documents do not extend to advice on how teaching related to multimodal meaning-making enabled by digitisation might be addressed.

The proposition of the research which forms the basis of this book was that a contemporary literacy teacher need be concerned not only with developing proficiency in reading, writing and the use of technologies but also with developing literacies in the multimodal designs enabled by technologies. The workplace professional learning project was designed to avoid superficial discussion of literacy teaching practices using dichotomies such as monomodal and multimodal or digital and non-digital. Rather it sought to explore the complexities faced by early years teachers positioned at the intersection of old and new literacy practices.

Schemas arising from multiliteracies theory were used as tools to stimulate professional learning. Multiliteracies theory addresses two aspects of language use affected by the changing communications environment: the variability of meaning-making in different cultural, social or professional contexts and the nature and impact of new communications technologies. Multiliteracies theory argues that contemporary literacy pedagogy needs to engage diverse, multilayered learners' identities so as to experience belonging and transformation in their capacities and subjectivities (New London Group, 1996, 2000). Becoming 'multiliterate' involves students in developing proficiency in modal and multimodal meaning-making design, and linguistic, visual, audio, gestural, spatial and multimodal designs, with multimodal being a combination of the other modes (New London Group, 1996, 2000). These six modes of meaning-making will be referred to as a 'multimodal schema' throughout this thesis. A pedagogy of multiliteracies, featuring teacher integration of four key pedagogical orientations—situated practice, overt instruction, critical framing and transformed practice—was developed to support the development of students' multiliterate capacities (New London Group, 1996, 2000). Considered to be problematic when deployed in isolation (Kalantzis and Cope, 2000), when used in combination, the four aspects of the multiliteracies pedagogy 'represent epistemological orientations, four ways of knowing, four 'takes' on the meanings of meaning' (Kalantzis and Cope, 2000, p. 241).

'Learning by Design' (Kalantzis and Cope, 2004, 2005; Kalantzis et al., 2005), re-frames the four-part pedagogy of multiliteracies as student-centred knowledge processes, a union of epistemology and pedagogy in which 'knowing is a form of action and to know in this sense is to learn' (Kalantzis et al., 2005, p. 70). Pedagogy is a 'knowledge process' employing 'ways of knowing that are capable of drawing the knower closer to the knowable' (Kalantzis et al., 2005, p. 71). Learning by Design's epistemological positioning of the multiliteracies pedagogies as pedagogical knowledge processes can be summarised as follows:

- situated practice is described as student experiencing, be that experiencing the known or the new;
- overt instruction is described as student conceptualising, be that conceptualising by naming or by theorising;
- critical framing is described as student analysing, be that analysing functionally or critically; and
- transformed practice is described as student applying, be that applying appropriately or creatively (Kalantzis and Cope, 2004; Kalantzis et al., 2005).

In this book the four-dimensional pedagogy of multiliteracies with be referred to as the 'multiliteracies pedagogy schema' and its further articulation as pedagogical knowledge processes in Learning by Design will be referred to as a 'pedagogical knowledge processes schema'. Learning by Design also presents a 'Learning Element template', a template for the purpose of documenting pedagogy which can be published for public sharing (Kalantzis and Cope, 2004; Kalantzis et al., 2005; New London Group, 1996, 2000). The Learning Element template contains a series of prompts for teacher consideration when developing teaching and learning sequences. These include a 'Learning Focus'; 'Knowledge Objectives'; 'Knowledge Processes' (as outlined above); 'Knowledge Outcomes'; and 'Learner Pathways' (Kalantzis and Cope, 2004; Kalantzis et al., 2005).

Responses to the case made by the New London Group include Australian educational policy initiatives (Education Queensland, 2002, 2005; Luke and Freebody, 2000); pedagogically-focused research (Bond, 2000; Newfield and Stein, 2000); and exploration of teacher multimodal metalanguage (Jewitt and Kress, 2003; Kress, et al., 2001; Unsworth, 2001; van Leeuwen, 1999). The teachers participating in this research project were amongst the first to enact Learning by Design by incorporating multiliteracies ideas and practices in their classrooms. While fledgling projects were concurrently under development (Neville, 2005, 2006; Pandian and Balraj, 2005; van Haren, 2005), articulated precedents were scarce, with only two early years examples available at the time of the research: one undertaken by the researcher in the year prior to this research project (Cloonan, 2005; Kalantzis and Cope, 2004) and the other from Bamaga, Queensland (Kalantzis and Cope, 2004; Kalantzis et al., 2005).

Multiliteracies theory is presented as a 'programmatic manifesto which necessarily remains open and unfinished' (Cope and Kalantzis, 2000b, p. 8). As part of the unfinished work relates to teacher accessibility to the potential of the theoretical arguments and tools, there is still a need existing for examples of multiliteracies theory enacted in classrooms (Unsworth, 2001, 2002). Also unfinished is the development of a multimodal metalanguage, accessible to both teachers and students, which will be 'capable of supporting a sophisticated critical analysis of language and other semiotic systems, yet at the same time not make unrealistic demands on teacher and learner knowledge, or conjure teachers' accumulated and often justified antipathies towards formalism' (New London Group, 2000, p. 24).

An accessible and generative multimodal metalanguage, a means by which students and teachers can articulate the functions of components of multimodal designs, is seen as a gaping need in the task of developing students' multiliteracies capacities (Unsworth, 2001). Metalanguage enables strengthened capacity to explore and analyse, through articulation, the constructed nature of designs. Multimodal metalanguage enables the exploration and analysis of the constructedness of linguistic, visual, audio, gestural, spatial and multimodal designs. Literacy teaching has long emphasised a metalanguage for articulating linguistic resources, be that a formal grammar or a functional grammar based on systemic functional linguistics (Unsworth, 2006b).

Systemic functional linguistics offers frameworks for the development of multimodal metalanguage through its positioning of language as just one of many interconnected semiotic systems, with meaning-making functions related to social contexts (Halliday and Hasan, 1985; Unsworth, 2006b). In systemic functional linguistics, the clause is the core unit of meaning and texts can be analysed according to three metafunctions: the ideational, the interpersonal and the textual. The ideational involves analysing the text in terms of participants, processes and circumstances; the interpersonal involves approaching the text as a dialogue (including monologue) and interacting with it in the form of an argument; and the textual involves a temporal organising approach (Halliday, 1994; Martin et al., 1997). The metafunctional basis has been used in the development of grammars or metalanguages of other modes of meaning: modes which include the visual Kress and van Leeuwen, 1996), action (Martinec, 1999, 2000a, 2000b) and audio (van Leeuwen, 1999), the last two of which were more problematic, perhaps because as modes they are relatively unexplored as systemic semiotic resources in comparison to language and, to a lesser extent, images.

Extrapolating from the metafunctional basis of systemic functional linguistics, Cope and Kalantzis (2000a) proposed the consideration of five dimensions of meaning-making—representational, social, organisational, contextual and ideological dimensions—across modes of meaning in the development of a multimodal metalanguage. It is argued that in order to promote an intermodal, generative metalanguage, specific questions be addressed to the modes of meaning, as follows:

- Representational: To what do the meanings refer?
- Social: How do the meanings connect the persons they involve?
- Organisational: How do the meanings hang together?
- Contextual: How do meanings fit into the larger world of meaning?
- Ideological: Whose interests are meanings skewed to serve?

The five dimensions of meaning to which these questions relate will be referred to as a 'dimensions of meaning schema' throughout this work.

The various aspects that contribute to multiliteracies theory have been described as the 'why'; the 'what' and the 'how' of multiliteracies (New London Group, 1996, 2000). The 'why' of multiliteracies is a rationale for a renewal of literacy education. The 'what' and the 'how' of multiliteracies suggest schemas which can support renewal. Figure 1.1 below shows the alignment between the 'what' and the 'how' of multiliteracies theory and schemas for realising literacy renewal.

The primary aims of this research project were to explore the outcomes of a case study investigation of agentive, knowledge-collaborating teacher professional learning of multiliteracies and, in particular, the generation by teachers of a multimodal metalanguage developed within these teachers' pedagogical choices. Deploying a methodology of participatory action research, with four teachers in the roles of participatory action researchers, the study recursively deployed professional learning interventions to support both the collection of data and the sustaining of teacher professional learning which positioned teachers as knowledge collaborators and creators.

Figure 1.1: Aspect of Multiliteracies and Schemas for Realising Renewal of Literacy Education

Aspect of multiliteracies theory (New London Group, 1996, 2000)	Schemas for realising the renewal of literacy education.
The 'what' of multiliteracies	'Multimodal schema' refers to a framework of six modes of meaning-making: linguistic, visual, audio, gestural, spatial and multimodal (New London Group, 1996, 2000). 'Dimensions of meaning schema' refers to a framework of five dimensions of meaning: representational, social, organisational, contextual and ideological meaning (Cope and Kalantzis, 2000a).
The 'how' of multiliteracies	'Multiliteracies pedagogies schema' refers to a four-part framework of pedagogy: situated practice, overt instruction, critical framing and transformed practice (New London Group, 1996, 2000). 'Pedagogical knowledge processes schema' refers to the Learning by Design framework (Kalantzis and Cope, 2004; Kalantzis et al., 2005) of eight pedagogical knowledge processes: experiencing the known and experiencing the new; conceptualising by naming and conceptualising by theorising; analysing functionally or analysing critically; and applying appropriately or applying creatively.

| | Learning Element template refers to a Microsoft Word template providing a documentation scaffold for teacher consideration when developing teaching and learning. It can integrate with digital publishing technologies to offer educators collaborative spaces to design learning choices (Kalantzis and Cope, 2004; Kalantzis et al., 2005) |
| | Learning Element refers to teacher developed and documented teaching and learning sequences using the Learning Element template. |

The following research questions were posed in relation to case study teachers' learning:
1. How was the professional learning of teachers enhanced through interventions designed to operationalise multiliteracies theory?
2. What elements of a metalanguage can be gleaned to inform emergent theories of multimodal meaning?

The first research question addressed the effectiveness of professional learning interventions designed to develop and analyse early years teachers' multiliteracies-influenced teaching practices. The interventions position teachers as participatory, agentive, knowledge creators in the public sphere (Cochran-Smith and Lytle, 1993; Kemmis and McTaggart, 2005). The tools are in the form of a 'multimodal schema' (Cope and Kalantzis, 2000b; New London Group, 1996, 2000) and a 'pedagogical knowledge processes schema' (Kalantzis and Cope, 2004; Kalantzis et al., 2005).

The second research question was addressed through the research project's use of the 'dimensions of meaning schema' (Cope and Kalantzis, 2000a) as an analytical lens for gleaning aspects of a teacher-generated metalanguage of modes of meaning (New London Group, 1996, 2000). The research data under discussion occurred in the planning, documentation and enactment resulting from engagement in the workplace professional learning project.

This research project used early years teachers multiliteracies planning, enactments and reflections to illuminate the way teachers approach multimodal metalanguage; and to discern patterns, and emphases in relation to existing multimodal metalanguage frameworks (Cope and Kalantzis, 2000a; Kalantzis and Cope, unpublished paper; Kress and van Leeuwen, 1996; Martinec, 1999; Unsworth, 2001, 2006a; van Leeuwen, 1999).

1.2: Significance of This Research

During the life of this research there remain tensions between the early years literacy policy and programs within the Department of Education, Victoria Education Victoria, 1999b; Education Victoria, 1997h, 1998b) and the new opportunities presented by the rapidly changing communications environment, with prevailing policies and programs taking a narrow view of literacy (Luke, 2003a). The current school syllabus (Victorian Curriculum and Assessment Authority, 2004a, 2004b, 2005b) advises teachers to engage students with digital texts in the earliest years of schooling but does not provide advice on developing meaning-making capacities in the multiple modes of meaning present in such designs. Given an inertia on the part of many early years teachers to focus student attention on digital rhetorics, under the current curriculum model and in the absence of an explicitly multimodal pedagogy, student engagement with multimodal designs can remain at a functional level that consistently falls short of an exploration of the deep, complex, combining modes of meaning presented by digital texts.

This research, therefore, is located in the transitionary moment in which questions about multimodal affordances are pressuring practitioners, requiring exploration and knowledge building. This book seeks to inform the gap between policy, which requires teachers to teach through and about digital texts, and school syllabi, which fail to address the literacy-related, meaning-making affordances of semiotic resources—linguistic, visual, audio, gestural and spatial—whose easy combination and distribution characterise the contemporary communications environment. Research findings, therefore, will crucially inform literacy, pedagogy and professional learning theory, practice and policy.

1.3: Overview of the Book

Chapter One outlines a rationale for the research project: an investigative case study of teacher professional learning of multiliteracies as a means of meeting the literacy learning needs of contemporary learners. The research questions and their particular interests are outlined: interests in teacher professional learning of multiliteracies, with a view to gleaning teacher-generated multimodal metalanguage within teachers' pedagogical choices. The relationship between the research project and a workplace professional learning project initiated and undertaken by the researcher in the role of Early Years literacy Policy and Project Officer is outlined. The workplace professional learning project, involving a group of four early years teachers in a series of recursive interventions designed to enable teacher learning and classroom applications of multiliteracies theory through teacher engagement with multiliteracies schemas, set out to investigate the efficacy of the professional learning interventions in enhancing teacher professional learning.

Chapter Two explores the literature relating to new affordances of multimodal design and related social changes enabled by developments in digitisation and networking of information and communications technologies and the inadequacies of educative responses which fail to appreciate the affordances. Renewed pedagogical approaches to literacy education for contemporary learners are suggested through teacher engagement with schemas emanating from multiliteracies theory: a 'multimodal schema' (New London Group, 1996, 2000); a 'pedagogical knowledge processes schema' (Kalantzis and Cope, 2004; Kalantzis et al., 2005; New London Group, 1996, 2000); and a prompt for teacher-documentation, a Learning Element template (Kalantzis and Cope, 2004; Kalantzis et al., 2005). A social semiotics-influenced 'dimensions of meaning schema' is identified as an analytical tool for a teacher-generated multimodal metalanguage (Cope and Kalantzis, 2000a). Literature relating to effective teacher learning indicates trends towards an expansion in teachers' roles to encompass a new professionalism that positions teachers as increasingly agentive, inquiring and collaborating in knowledge generation. Features of effective professional learning which resonate with the affordances of digitisation and networking of information and communications technologies are discussed.

Chapter Three describes the research context, the prevailing Victorian government literacy policy, programs and models of professional teacher learning and contextual influences for policy and program renewal that gave rise to the work-based professional learning project that became the subject of this research project. More recent literacy policy advice, in which the meaning-making potentials of modes other than language remain unaddressed as meaning-making resources, is also detailed. The research design is described: a case study investigation (Yin, 2003) of a work-based professional learning project, informed by multiliteracies research findings, implemented with four teachers in the role of participatory action researchers (Kemmis and McTaggart, 2005). The inter-relationship between data collection, research design and teacher professional learning is acknowledged. The context, parameters and processes of data collection and analysis for insights into addressing the research questions within a work-based professional learning project are detailed.

Chapter Four describes the case study participants, including their professional background, interests and strengths; school community and classroom teaching contexts; experience in deploying the Early Years Literacy Program, the recognised literacy program of the Department of Education, Victoria; knowledge of multiliteracies at the commencement of the research; and starting points for classroom applications.

Chapter Five explores the interface between case study teachers' existing literacy practices articulated in the Early Years Literacy Program and their emerging practices resulting from engagement with schemas emanating from multiliteracies theory: the 'multimodal schema', the 'pedagogical knowledge processes schema' and its associated documentation tool, the Learning Element template. Three case study teacher responses to this engagement with the multiliteracies schemas are described with an emphasis on classroom applications designed to meet locally contextualised needs.

Chapter Six analyses teacher prompts and a teacher-generated lexicon intended to support multimodality teaching in order to gain insight into teacher-generated multimodal metalanguage. Through deployment of the 'multimodal schema' and the 'dimensions of meaning schema', the research project analysis discerned patterns, emphases and inattentions in teacher planning and teaching of dimensions of the modes of meaning. The emergent teacher-generated lexicon is discussed in light of theoretical developments of multimodal metalanguage. Through deployment of the 'pedagogical knowledge processes schema', influences of pedagogical choices on multimodal teaching are discerned and discussed.

Chapter Seven evaluates the efficacy of the research project's interventions in enhancing teachers' professionalism in the operationalisation of multiliteracies. It examines the effect of teacher engagement with the multiliteracies schemas ('multimodal schema' and 'pedagogical knowledge processes schema') on professional knowledge, practice and identity.

Chapter Eight presents the study's findings and recommendations in six main areas of intervention: 1) the researcher's role as an educational consultant; 2) the role of the filming co-production; 3) the role of the Early Years Literacy Program; 4) the role of the 'multimodal schema'; 5) the role of the 'pedagogical knowledge processes schema'; and 6) the role of participatory action research methodology. Five future research agendas indicated by the findings of this research project are also presented.

Chapter 2
Literature Review

Chapter Two presents a literature review which locates the research project within a theoretical frame of reference and builds a framework for the subsequent analysis of the research data. The theoretical framing for this research project identifies trends in three fields of literature:
- New Millennium Communication Affordances and Educational Responses
- New Millennium Pedagogy
- New Millennium Teacher Professional Learning

Within the review, these three fields will, as far as is practical, be treated separately, although in the context of the research project they serve as three inter-related and overlapping aspects of the one inquiry.

2.1: New Millennium Communication Affordances and Educational Responses

A panoramic view of the broad societal communications context of the first decade of the twenty-first century, the context in which contemporary literacy education resides, shows a complex combination of rapid and continuously changing communications and meaning-making resources and practices. Textual designs and user practices afforded by the globalised, digitised communications environment are features of a post-typographical age

(Reinking, et al., 1998) which stand in marked contrast to those of an earlier typographical age. The post-typographical age is characterised by transformations in what constitutes texts; of the contexts in which texts are created and used; and by shifting relationships between textual creators and textual users.

The mark of a literate person has always been context specific, shifting according to the opportunities, demands and availability of temporally and culturally situated technologies. In early human societies:

> [t]he nature of ... literacy... is closely tied to the available technologies of oral sounds, drums and flutes, gestures, facial expressions, petroglyphs, or the display of artefacts. As with the internet today, there is a strong emphasis on visual images, icons, and brief sound segments (Bruce, 2003, p. 15).

The advent of emerging technologies such as mediated communication, hypertext, the Web, virtual reality and interactive agents present far reaching social consequences across many communities; consequences not unlike earlier transitions from oral communication to writing; from manuscript to print; and from print to radio, movies and television (Bruce, 2003).

Ten years before the completion of this book, frontier technologically-enabled practices in the social realms of work and citizenship included virtual workplaces, telecommuting, globalised workflows, 24-hour teleshopping, access to school websites and international libraries, participation in interest-based virtual communities such as chatrooms and bulletin boards (Luke, 2000). In offering these examples the reader was alerted that such:

> ...frontier media practices and content will be commonplace in the near future, and will generate new text-place social repertoires, communication styles and symbolic systems for accessing and participating in new knowledge and cultural configurations (Luke, 2000, p. 73).

The prophecy that such practices would lose their pioneering quality and take on more of a 'commonplace' positioning, has come to fruition for many. The speed and scale of internet access has reached a point where one sixth of the world's population has access to the internet, with half of the world's population due to be online by 2012 if the current rate of uptake continues (Internet World Stats, 2006). While uptake is variable amongst regions, countries and age groups, the speed and scale of growth in internet access in regions with the lowest current access rates, such as Africa, Asia, Latin America and the Middle East, suggests ubiquitous access in the near future (Internet World Stats, 2006).

Of course, discussion of 'new' literate practices is accompanied by a rider that 'new' is a fleeting term when used in relation to digitised technologies and associated practices. These include tools for knowledge and inquiry; social networking tools such as blogs and instant messaging; video and music dissemination tools such as You Tube, which have effects on popular culture, community and citizenship, as well as what constitutes literacy (Coiro et al., 2007).

The development of literate abilities across the breadth of each and every new emerging technology is increasingly unlikely due to their rapid introduction. For this reason, literacy in the new media age is more productively approached as considering affordances of modes of meaning and their multimodal combination which are enabled by the digital communications (Kress, 2000a, 2000b, 2003). Clearly, identifying connections among ideas and practices is more important than mastering particular practices or software in itself (Luke, 2000).

Print, meaning-making and mass schooling are co-joined by historical circumstance and teachers' practices reflect this long-maintained interdependency. However, truths which have been chiefly expressed as language-based propositions, particularly since the invention of the printing press, are now finding form, simultaneously and interactively, in multiple media (Lankshear and Knobel, 2003 after Heim 1999). A major change in meaning-making afforded by the digitised networked environment is that from the unimodal or linguistic print-based textual resources to the multi-directionally linked, multimodal designs in which meaning-making draws concurrently on the resources of language and other modes including the visual, audio, gestural and spatial modes of meaning (New London Group, 1996, 2000).

That the impact of digital technologies is literacy-related as well as technology-related has been long argued (Atkinson and Hansen, 1966–1967). Reconceptualising computers as symbol machines (Labbo, 2003) acknowledges that meaning is presented by an increasing number of co-deployed semiotic modes, or multimodal meanings. For example:

> ... laterally connected, multi-embedded and further hot-linked information sources variously coded in animation, symbols, print text, photos, movie clips, or three-dimensional and manoeuvrable graphics (Luke and Freebody, 2000, p. 73).

To be fully literate, young students born into this complex communications environment require an interplay of literacy practices to read and produce textual designs and, 'to be digitally literate will mean to learn skills necessary to navigate, locate, communicate online and participate in digital, virtual and physical communities' (Labbo, 2000, p. 6).

As a result of the impact of these post-typographical affordances, not only are the nature and context of textual design affected but also the dynamics of social power and agency. The impact of the changes in the communications environment also includes shifting relationships between textual creators and textual users. The affordances of interactivity of textual design in networked spaces challenge the previous relationship of the 'uni-directionality' of knowledge in textual designs flowing from author to reader. In the digitised world, uni-directionality has been replaced, or at least joined by, relationships of 'bi-directionality' in which users interact with textual designs (Kress, 2003). Authorship, in the form of blogs (web-logs), vlogs (video-logs) and interactive websites reliant on social software, heralds opportunities for user interaction as well as user creation of unique navigational experiences through multiple non-linear hypertext pathways, all within environments featuring co-deployed semiotic modes. Unlike the stable textual order of authorship within the print-based publishing industry, an environment of ready access to inexpensive, enabling networked technologies no longer positions authorship as rarefied, but offers a 'promise of great democracy ... accompanied by a levelling of power' (Kress, 2003, p. 146).

Affordances of interactivity involving multi-directional linkages and changes in social dynamics pressure traditional concepts of textual literacy.

> As literacy is redefined by the protean capacities of electronic verbal and visual text generation, questions are raised about virtually all our current concepts of text: of authorship and authority; of ownership, intellectual property, creativity, originality and identity; of reading and writing, production and reception, making and consuming; of access and power (Beavis, 1997, p.243).

Social identity is affected in the changed environment as, 'we no longer have roots, we have aerials; we constantly download culture' (Wark, 1994, p. 55). Global networks impact on the relational aspects of meaning-making, which emphasise cross-cultural understandings and sensitivity to various discourses—for example, 'netiquette' when engaged in practices such as visiting a museum online, joining a newsgroup or navigating an international website (Luke, 2000).

Attitudes to such changes in social power and agency can be seen through the application of the concept of comparative 'mindsets' to the question of the impact of new technologies (Bigum and Lankshear, 1998; Lankshear and Knobel, 2003; Lankshear and Knobel, 2006). The mindset still constrained by the typographical or 'bookspace' world sees the impact of the changed communications environment as simply technologically-related—the product of a more sophisticated technologised world. This mindset maintains an industrial view of production: a stable textual order wherein those with expertise and authority produce material artefacts, supported by the infrastructure of company-owned production units in purpose specific spaces. The value is in commodity scarcity in industrial terms with value given to control and influence. In another mindset, however, the emergence and uptake of digital inter-networked technologies has resulted in a post-industrial view of production wherein products enable unrestricted user participation, mediation, and social relating. There is a focus on collective intelligence with expertise and authority distributed in open, fluid spaces and value is in the dispersal of information by hybrid experts and textual change (Bigum and Lankshear, 1998; Lankshear and Knobel, 2003, 2006).

Varied terminology and definitions have been deployed in distinguishing between mindsets forged in physical space and the mechanical age and those forged in cyberspace and the digital age. A digital outsider mindset frames the world as similar to the world before digitisation but more technologised; and the digital insider frames the world as radically altered as a result of the development and uptake of digital electronic inter-networked technologies. A digital newcomer is one who moves from a pre-digital outsider mindset towards an insider mindset. A critical difference between these positions has to do with controlling such things as values, morals, knowledge and competence (Bigum and Lankshear, 1998; Lankshear and Knobel, 2003). The concept of mindset can also be applied to the apparent disjuncture between most students' enthusiastic adoption of multimodal designs and practices and many teachers' reticence towards or avoidance of their adoption.

> We must now also take seriously the idea that the sensitivities of very many young people who are 'insiders' to Discourses associated with having grown up within (and only within) the contemporary information technology revolution can be marginalised when formal learning is dominated by outsider mindsets (Lankshear and Knobel, 2003, p.78).

This link between the concept of insider and outsider, or even the outsider–newcomer mindsets to notions of Discourse acts as a warning about the implications for student 'insider' engagement and success if these differences go unattended.

Differences between the 'net' generation (Tapscott, 1998) and their teachers have also been described in terms of the former as 'digital natives' growing up speaking computer language and at ease with the digital practices entailed with technologies such as the internet, a range of software and mobile phones, while the latter must necessarily be only 'digital immigrants'. Having been introduced to these technologies later in life, they will always be influenced by those practices used prior to digitalisation, despite attempts to understand and use such technologies (Prensky, 2001).

Digital native students have learning needs which differ greatly from those of their predecessors.

> Today's students are no longer the people our education system was designed to teach. Today's students have not just changed incrementally from those of the past, not simply changed their slang, clothes, body adornments, or styles ...[but a] really big discontinuity has taken place. One might even call it a "singularity"—an event which changes things so fundamentally that there is absolutely no going back. This so-called singularity is the arrival and rapid dissemination of digital technology in the last decades of the 20th century (Prensky, 2001, p. 1).

It is clearly simplistic and stereotypical to suggest that the mindset division cuts cleanly along generational lines: that all students are comfortable and knowledgeable with technologies and the affordances they offer, and that all teachers are not. Just as clearly, however, the response of some public institutions to the rapidly changing, digitised, globalised, communications environment can only be described as inadequate, particularly in comparison with the uptake and transformation in the private sphere of lifeworlds. In the words of historian Eric Hobsbawm, although globalisation can be seen to have 'already transformed... important aspects of private life, mainly by the unimaginable acceleration of communication and transport':

> ... the most striking characteristic of the end of the twentieth century is the tension between this accelerating process of globalisation and the inability of both public institutions and the collective behaviour of human beings to come to terms with it (Hobsbawm, 1994, p. 15).

Certainly, there does seem to be a polarising set of trends between children's and teachers' responses to the changing communications environment. Children display high levels of identification, engagement and purposeful knowledge creation, including engagement with television and media texts (Buckingham, 2002; Buckingham and Sefton-Green, 1994); capacities as screen audiences (Buckingham, 1996); and as media producers (Buckingham, 2000; Buckingham et al., 1995). These findings are paralleled in recent Australian research into the multiliterate practices of children aged four to eight years of age, which found eager adoption of, and competence in, technologically literate practices. Such research revealed young children who:

> ... switched effortlessly between genres, scanning material for information, following procedures, searching by scrolling through menus, and interpreting icons and written instructions on tool bars. ... although reading, writing, listening and speaking are paramount, today's students must be able to do more, as they decipher, code break, achieve meaning and express ideas through a range of media incorporating design, layout, colour, graphics and animation (University of South Australia and South Australian Department of Education and Children's Services, 2005 p. viii).

Teachers, however, have been found to regard media, multimedia and digital literacies as rivals to conventional print text, or to dismiss the importance of digital literacies in school curriculum offerings, suggesting that this area of learning is adequately developed in students' out of school lives (Snyder, 1996).

This disjuncture can result in digitally-savvy students being positioned as 'aliens in the classroom' (Durrant and Green, 2000; Green and Bigum, 1993) by teachers who, themselves alienated by the new technologies, feel threatened by the electronic incursions into their print literacy domains of expertise and may have trouble reconceptualising literacy (Luke, 1995). A continued print-focused approach to literacy teaching and learning within the changed communications context represents a paucity of intellectual rigor in curriculum offerings, since reducing:

> ... literacy to the mechanics of encoding and decoding print during the early—let alone middle or later—years would amount to a conspiracy against the proper intellectual development of learners (Lankshear, 1999, p. 3).

Given the imperative for literacy practices to be responsive to the technologies available to a society, the emergence of technologies which enable the non-specialist to produce and manipulate a range of semiotic resources, a focus on print without complementary attention to other modes enabled by the technologies reduces the possibilities for expression (Cope and Kalantzis, 2000b). The complementarity of traditional print-focused and multimodal designs requires consideration by literacy educators since:

> ...multimedia, electronic information sources are quickly taking up the communication of much information previously presented solely in traditional text formats, [and] rather than being displaced by computer text, conventional literacies are maintaining a complementary role as well as being both co-opted and adapted in the evolution of our textual habitat (Unsworth, 2002, p. 63).

Educational responses involving the integration of computer-based technologies into existing approaches to curriculum often fail to acknowledge the affordances of the new technologies, resulting in 'digital makeover' responses (Lankshear et al., 2000). School-based implementation of curriculum reform can thus offer 'pretence' of change, rather than the dramatic shifts of mindsets and practices that genuine reform requires.

> Despite the systemic concern and the adoption of 'new basics' and 'essential learnings' proclaiming the importance of 'multi-media', communication, futures and relationships, the role of CCTs [computing and communication technologies] in all of these new initiatives remains true to the current mindset: artificial (Rowan and Bigum, 2004, p. 2).

However, requiring teachers to undertake more than digital makeover practices raises the question of informing theories, tools and schemas. Literacy teachers trained in print-based typographical era pedagogies require tools to reframe teaching to account for changes in multimodal designs and social dynamics. The following section presents multiliteracies schemas, as tools appropriate for supporting teacher reflective learning and teacher classroom enactments which reflect the changes in the context of literacy education.

2.1.1: Multiliteracies, Multimodality and the Development of a Metalanguage

The previous section discussed the affordances of multimodal meaning-making and the social dynamics presented by the changed communications environment and discussed those trends which point to disjunctures between the responses of children and teachers in engagement with the new affordances. This literature review now turns to an exploration of the theory of multiliteracies as an educational response that seeks to take account of the affordances of the digital communications environment. The expanded affordances in multimodal design and the social dynamics of the changed communications environment call for a literacy pedagogy which encourages a sense of student belonging by engaging diverse identities and subjectivities, allowing student transformation through changes to capacities and subjectivities through learning (New London Group, 1996, 2000).

Drawing on the concept of *design,* multiliteracies theory offers a reconceptualisation of what constitutes literacy education in the light of the increasing multimodality of texts. Design can refer both to the way in which a text has been designed, or to the process involved in designing. For this reason this research project uses the term in regard to semiotic activity that involves six design elements: linguistic, audio, visual, gestural, spatial and multimodal resources (New London Group, 1996, 2000). Multiliteracies theory offers the notion of design to describe the codes and conventions of meaning-making modes and posits that these six identified modes of meaning show regularities or grammars. Multiliteracies theory presents:

> ... any semiotic activity, including using language to produce or consume texts, as a matter of Design involving three elements: Available Designs, Designing, and The Redesigned. Together these three elements emphasise the fact that meaning-making is an active and dynamic process, and not something governed by static rules (New London Group, 2000, p. 20).

In a multiliteracies-influenced literacy program, students draw on available designs; existing design elements that can be linguistic, visual, audio, gestural, spatial or multimodal designs. Students are involved in designing by harnessing available designs to make meaning for their own purposes. They produce redesigned meaning or transformations of meaning, which then become available designs for other meaning-makers to draw upon (New London Group, 1996, 2000).

The notion of design is aligned with a social semiotic view of sign-making (Halliday, 1978; van Leeuwen, 2005). In contrast to theories which position people as users of (stable) meaning systems, social semiotics places an emphasis on peoples' social agency, or in terms of multiliteracies theory, as designers of available resources for meaning, which produces a re-designed product as a result of this engagement. A social semiotic approach is one of three semiotic approaches to have applied ideas from the linguistics domain to non-linguistic modes of communication during the last century, the others being the Prague school and the Paris school (Kress and van Leeuwen, 1996). Social semiotics arose from systemic functional linguistics, or systemic functional grammar as it is called by some practitioners (Halliday, 1994; Martin et al., 1997). As part of the field of sociolinguistics, it involves the development of grammar as a means of social interaction to enable text analysis and interpretation. The clause is the core unit of meaning and texts can be analysed according to three metafunctions: the ideational, the interpersonal and the textual.

The ideational metafunction involves analysing the text in terms of participants and processes to discover the construction of representations of 'what goes on in the world'. Grammatical realisations of linguistic ideational meanings include lexis, or terms that represent processes (material, mental, verbal), participants, (material processes involve actors and goals; mental processes involve a sensor and phenomenon), and circumstances (adverbs and adverbial phrases). A system of transitivity enables different relations between participants (Halliday, 1994).

The interpersonal metafunction involves the construction of relationships among participants, using language to do things to, or for, or with others. Grammatical realisations of linguistic interactive meanings include the use of 'person', which can be used for inclusion (we), or exclusion (us and them); and the use of mood, which includes making statements (declarative through subject and finite verb), asking questions, (interrogative through inversion of declarative finite verb and subject), and telling others what to do (imperative). Modal verbs indicate obligation and modal adverbs allow for personal stance. The textual metafunction involves the organisation and cohesion of representational and interactive meanings as whole texts. Grammatical realisations of linguistic textual meanings include the theme/rheme system, the theme being the element in first position, usually the subject, which attracts the most emphasis (Halliday, 1994).

The social semiotic approach to functional grammar has stimulated work on many languages and has been applied in contexts beyond that of a particular language. The linking of social purpose to text structure, seen applied in the Australian 'genre' movement (Cope and Kalantzis, 1993), involved analysis of texts starting with purpose and looking at the structure of the whole text before turning attention to sentences and clauses within the whole text. Social semiotics applied to visual form differs from other (non-linguistic) grammars in that the focus is on the way in which representations are combined meaningfully into an holistic picture, similar to the way linguistic-based grammars describe how words in texts, clauses and sentences combine. The theories and methodologies of linguistics are not imported into the domain of the visual but, rather, position language and visual as modes of meaning which both realise the breadth of cultural meanings but do so through their own forms (Kress and van Leeuwen, 1996).

The three metafunctions are adapted to present the visual as a full system of communication, which can serve communicational and representational requirements (Kress and van Leeuwen, 1996). The representational/ideational metafunction involves how images construct 'narrative' and 'conceptual' representations of what goes on in the world. Narrative images represent participants partaking in actional verbal or mental processes through the use of vectors, speech balloons and thought clouds. Processes can be actional or reactional, which can, in turn be non-transactional (not acting on anyone or anything else), transactional (acting on someone or something else) and can be differentiated from conceptual images which represent classificational (taxonomies), analytical (part-whole) or symbolic (attributive or suggestive) processes (Kress and van Leeuwen, 1996).

The interactive/interpersonal metafunction involves the relations between the producer and the viewer of the image and includes contact (demand or offer depending on gaze), social distance (intimate social or impersonal differentiated by the view of depicted participants—close, medium or long shots) and attitude (levels of involvement dependent on angle as frontal or oblique; and levels of power dependent on high, eye, or low angle). Interactive meaning is also constructed through modality values, the level of realism an image conveys, naturalistic, abstract or scientific/technological. Naturalistic images have high colour saturation, colour diversification and modulation. High modality is also seen in the level of participant features detail as opposed to schematised detail.

The compositional/textual metafunction relates to the information value, salience and framing of the representational and social meanings. Information value refers to the greater/lesser of centre/margin placement; the left/right placement of given/new information in Western cultures; the vertical over/under polarisation of ideal/real value. Salience is achieved by means such as elemental prominence, distinctiveness and contrast. Framing of elements, by borders, and location impacts on the elements' connection or disconnection from one another (Kress and van Leeuwen, 1996).

In applying the metafunctional questions to the audio mode, however, according to van Leeuwen, 'the resources of sound simply did not seem as specialised as those of language and vision, and the mode of sound simply did not seem so clearly structured along metafunctional lines as language and visual communication' (van Leeuwen, 1999, p. 190). Sound resources such as pitch or dynamics were found to be:

> ...used ideationally *and* interpersonally, or both ideationally *and* textually and so on... [and] that different semiotic modes have different *metafunctional configurations*, and that these metafunctional configurations are neither universal, nor a function of the intrinsic nature of the medium, but cultural, a result of the uses to which the semiotic modes have been put and the values that have been attached to them (van Leeuwen, 1999, p. 190).

A systemic-functional semiotics of action has also been outlined and applied as a tool for textual analysis and interpretation of action in video (Martinec, 1999, 2000a, 2000b). Phrases are recognised as the core unit of meaning, and various movements are classified according to their realisations. Ideational classification involves processes, participants and circumstances. Processes are described as 'acts' such as 'doing: realised by movement; state, realised by lack of movement (e.g. standing or sitting); and verbal, realised by the production of language (e.g. speaking or singing)' (Martinec, 2000a, p. 314). Processes can be directed movement, which is directed at another participant; and non-directed movement, which is not (Martinec, 2000b). Directed movement can involve actual or virtual. Circumstances are described as 'aspect' since 'in action these meanings are not realised by constituents separate from the processes...[but] combine with certain types of processes and not others' (Martinec, 2000a, p. 316). Aspect relates to speed and force, with speed being fast or slow and force being more or less forceful. The interpersonal classifications are evidenced by movement, which decreases the distance between two participants' bodies, resulting in increased 'engagement'. Engagement can relate to distance (close or far) and angle (frontal or oblique). Textual classifications may be realised through cohesion created by componential relations of the participants, processes or circumstances (synonymy, antonymy and meronymy); and reference involving successive mentions of the same participant, process or circumstance (Martinec, 2000a)

Modes of meaning, and their deployment in combination or multimodality, are the building blocks of design in a communications context in which modes other than language are prevalent in public communication. However, in recent times, Western societies have privileged print literacy to the neglect of other communication modes (Kress, 2000a). Responding to a multimedia revolution through re-engagement with, and valuing of, a broader range of modes of representation offers opportunities to regain 'cross-modal synaesthesia... from worlds where words and landscapes and iconic religious visual imagery were overlaid in a way comparable to, but perhaps very different from, our own notions of metaphor, mimesis and abstraction' (Cope and Kalantzis, 2000a, p. 223).

The affordances offered by the new communications environment offer 'strong reasons for setting a quite new agenda of human semiosis in the domain of communication and representation' (Kress, 2000a, p. 183). However, a multimodal metalanguage, a means of describing and analysing the meaning-making resources and their interplay is lacking.

> Teachers and students need a language to describe the forms of meaning that are represented in Available designs and the Redesigned. In other words they need a meta-language—a language for talking about language, images, texts and meaning-making interactions (New London Group, 2000, p. 23–4).

The design metalanguage would describe six meaning-making modes—linguistic design, visual design, audio design, gestural design, spatial design and multimodal design; a means for working on semiotic activities, which would 'identify and explain differences between texts, and relate these to the contexts of culture and situation in which they seem to work' (New London Group, 2000, p. 24).

The New London Group initially suggested a detailed elemental structure for the development of a multimodal metalanguage—an analysis of linguistic design which would involve the key elements of delivery, modality, transitivity, vocabulary and metaphor, nominalisation of process, information structures, local and global coherence relations (New London Group, 2000). It was suggested that key elements of the visual mode would include colours, perspective, vectors, foregrounding and backgrounding related to images, page layouts and screen formats. Analysis of the audio would involve elements such as music and sound effects. Analysis of gesture would involve elements such as behaviour, bodily physicality, sensuality, feelings and affect, kinesics, proxemics. And analysis of spatial metalanguage would involve ecosystem and geographic meanings, and architectural/architectonic spaces, as well as multimodal meaning (New London Group, 2000).

Cope and Kalantzis (2000a) suggest an examination of five 'dimensions of meaning' (representational, social, organisational, contextual, and ideological) across five modes of meaning (linguistic, visual, gestural, spatial and audio) to support literacy teachers in their endeavours to describe the interplay and integration of modes of meaning. A series of critical questions which deepens the knowledge of meaning relating to systems and structure and broadens knowledge of cross-cultural dimensions of meanings are suggested for use with students. The five dimensions of meaning to which the questions would be directed are:

- Representational meaning, which is explored through the question, 'What do the meanings refer to?' relating to the participants represented and the being and acting the meanings represent. This dimension prompts a consideration of who and what the design represents; and what's happening in the design.
- Social meaning, which is explored through the question, 'How do the meanings connect the persons they involve?' relating to the roles of par-

ticipants in the communication of meaning; the commitment the producer has to the message; interactivity; and relations between participants and processes. This dimension prompts consideration of the way meaning connects/relates to the producer and the recipient (Cope and Kalantzis, 2000a).
- Organisational meaning, which is explored through the question, 'How do the meanings hang together?' relating to mode of communication; medium; delivery; cohesion and composition. This dimension prompts consideration of the composition or shape of the organisation of the meaning (Cope and Kalantzis, 2000a).
- Contextual meaning, which is explored through the question, 'How do the meanings fit into the larger world of meaning?' relating to reference; cross-reference; and discourse. This prompts consideration of the context of the meaning and how context and meaning inter-relate.
- Ideological meaning, which is explored through the question, 'Whose interests are the meanings skewed to serve?' drawing attention to the possible motivations of the creator and consequent positioning of receiver. Secondary questions relate to indications of interests; attributions of truth value and affinity; space for readership; deception by omission if not commission; and types of transformation (Cope and Kalantzis, 2000a; Gee, 1996).

This research project adopted schemas emanating from multiliteracies theory as its basis for an investigation of professional learning which re-envisions what constitutes literacy in textual and pedagogical approaches, capitalising on the opportunities for complex literacy practices afforded by the changed communications environment. These schemas include both a 'multimodal schema', that frames literacy meaning-making resources as linguistic, visual, audio, gestural, spatial, and multimodal (New London Group, 1996, 2000); as well as a 'dimensions of meaning schema', that refers to representational, social, organisational, contextual, and ideological dimensions of meaning (Cope and Kalantzis, 2000a).

The 'multimodal schema' is a key tool for the development and analysis of teacher capacities in multimodal meaning-making and is also used in conjunction with the 'dimensions of meaning schema' to investigate evidence of teacher-generated multimodal metalanguage. Pedagogical schemas influenced by multiliteracies and Learning by Design theories (Kalantzis and Cope, 2004; Kalantzis et al., 2005) were also adopted in this research project to assist the development of teacher capacities in multimodality teaching and to analyse the influence of pedagogical deployment on multimodality teaching. These will be discussed in the following section.

2.2: New Millennium Pedagogy

As introduced in the previous section, multiliteracies theory argues that teaching increasingly diverse groups of students to deploy multimodal metalanguage and design requires a re-envisioning of design, social dynamics and pedagogy. Section one described the affordances of the changing communications environment and sketched the potential disjunctures discernible between students' and teachers' responses. In that section the semiotic and linguistic theoretical context of multiliteracies theory was discussed and a 'multimodal schema' presented for conceptualising and analysing multiple and intersecting modes of designed meaning (linguistic, visual, gestural, spatial, audio and multimodal); and 'dimensions of meaning schema' (representational, social, organisational, contextual, and ideological) for analysis of a multimodal metalanguage.

Section two builds on the theme, emerging from the literature reviewed in section one, that school literacy practices should be reflective of the practices of the society in which the learners live. This second section addresses the issue of pedagogy: the means by which teachers can effect change in teaching practices; and the sorts of principles and practices that teachers might employ in developing student literacies. This section will begin by contextualising pedagogy within broader social and educative social practices, and then turn to an examination of the multiliteracies pedagogy, including in this the more recent literature on the Learning by Design pedagogical knowledge processes, research that has been undertaken by Kalantzis and Cope (Kalantzis and Cope, 2004, 2005) which has not only developed but enriched the multiliteracies pedagogy.

A century ago, in a book he called *The School in Society*, John Dewey reflected on the inventions that had led to a concentration of people in urban areas to support the rise of manufacturing and communication. The result of all these changes, he believed, had created no less than a social revolution; a revolution that must force profound changes in the field of education.

> One can hardly believe there has been revolution in all history so rapid, so extensive, so complete. Through it the face of earth is making over, even as to its physical forms; political boundaries are wiped out and moved about... That this revolution should not affect education in some other than a formal and superficial fashion is inconceivable (Dewey, 1990).

The scale and rapidity of technological and global changes affecting many aspects of contemporary Western work, civic and personal life are of a magnitude which can be likened to the impact Dewey saw in the sweeping social changes of the industrial era (Castells, 1996a; Casti, 1994; Lash and Urry, 1994). Society is in 'the midst of a major shift in how we work on, and work out, our physical, biological, social and mechanical worlds' (Gee, 2000, p. 44).

Contemporary productive life in western societies has created what has been referred to as a knowledge economy: an economy in which knowledge workers and knowledge management has become a feature of work in contemporary organisations (Stewart, 1998). The knowledge economy is dependent on technologies to assist flows of information amongst enterprises and consumers (Castells, 1996b, 2001) and technology has enabled an unprecedented global flow of information amongst what are now internationally constituted groups, requiring high levels of intercultural communication (Luke, 2000). Increasingly, organisations in the knowledge economy are dependent on the technological and cultural capacities of their workers to achieve commercial viability.

Dewey's concern that schooling must respond to broader social changes finds resonance in the advent of computer-mediated learning. However it is not just the technology, but the nature of the learning experiences, that is of critical importance in supporting students' learning outcomes. This means far more than the deployment of technology in classrooms (Chandler-Olcott and Mahar, 2003; Lankshear, 1999; Reinmann and Goodyear, 2004). Awareness of this is increasingly leading to a renewed focus on pedagogy by education systems (Department of Education and the Arts, 2006; Department of Education and Training, 2006; Ministerial Council on Education Employment Training and Youth Affairs, 2005), as a recently released Australian government policy documents states:

> Making technologies available does not of itself result in changed teaching methods or in the level of outcomes. Effective use of ICT in education requires appropriate pedagogies (Ministerial Council on Education Employment Training and Youth Affairs, 2005, p. 5).

'Effective use' points to the pedagogical decisions made by teachers about what they see as constituting literacy, and how this literacy should be taught. Such decisions exist not only within a broad framework of curriculum offerings but also within the broader framework of education and of society. Inadequate responses in regard to teaching multimodal design have prompted an increased research focus on the limitations of the pedagogies which arose from industrial-model schooling to meet the needs of students engaged in multimodal community literacy practices (Labbo, 2000; Lankshear et al., 1997; Lankshear and Knobel, 2003; Papert, 1993; Snyder, 1998).

The general inadequacy of this response represents a form of inertia: an inertia that mirrors earlier responses to communicative developments, such as the inability of Socratic dialogue circles, medieval monasteries, universities and industrial era schooling to respond to the emerging communications technologies of their respective times—for example, replicable alphabetic writing, the development of typology, mass literacy, and cinema, radio and television (Luke, 2003b). In other words there are historical patterns of the mode of information dominating pedagogy and of pedagogues' resistance to incorporating the opportunities afforded by the new technologies into their practices.

Rather than a universal pedagogical response, the new times require a less linear, more ecological view of pedagogy—a multi-faceted approach that recognises the contributions of past pedagogical movements and the traditions from which they have sprung.

> Profound and sustainable educational change and innovation require that we move beyond a search for a "correct" and accurate meaning and practice of pedagogy—from a less causal and linear model of educational effects to an ecological model that explores the complex embeddings and mediations of

teaching and learning within cultures and discourses, systems and everyday practices (Luke, 2006, p. 3)

The discussion will now examine what can be seen to be an innovative pedagogical response to the new communications environment and consider how pedagogy can be purposefully deployed by teachers in teaching multimodal textual designs.

2.2.1: Multiliteracies Pedagogy

A pedagogy of multiliteracies features the integration of four orientations to learning or pedagogical approaches—situated practice, overt instruction, critical framing and transformed practice (New London Group, 1996, 2000)—four pedagogical orientations which, taken together, support diverse learners by encouraging a sense of belonging and transformation. Such an education:

> ... ought to be seen as a 'Bill of Rights' for all children, but most especially for minority and poor children. These principles seek to produce people who can function in the new capitalism (Gee, 2000, p. 67).

Each of the four orientations has a pedagogical tradition which can be traced to a theoretical base described in the context of its emergence; however, within the context of a pedagogy of multiliteracies, each has been presented in terms of its affordances and limitations within a contemporary educational environment. When deployed in combination, and with an understanding of the limitations of each pedagogy, these can be offset by the strengths of another, providing a kind of pedagogical palette or 'pedagogical knowledge processes schema', to support teachers in the design and enactment of multiliteracies-influenced classroom practices (Cazden, 2000b; Kalantzis and Cope, 2000; Kress, 2000b; New London Group, 2000).

This research project took the view that contemporary school teaching practices will necessarily be found to reflect a range of different pedagogical movements, affiliation to which is dependent on the individual teacher's practices, themselves affected by factors such as personal background, sensibilities and initial training experiences, as well as school ethos and in-service learning opportunities. Such affiliations may not necessarily be explicit in a teacher's work, but underpinning philosophies will be reflected in classroom management practices, some of which may even be oppositional in terms of a school's stated policies. Articulation of these pedagogical assumptions and biases can lead to the development of a conscious theoretical structure that builds on the pedagogical strengths and removes the weaknesses of a previously narrow orientation, creating a more successful learning environment.

The pedagogy of 'overt instruction', for example, may take the form of didactic drills and rote memorisations, which restrict the development of multiple human intelligences (Gardner 2002), leading to students having to try to guess what's in the teacher's head, or spend valuable lesson time in unquestioning rote learning. This means *doing school* rather than being involved in that rich learning which can open opportunities for those students who would otherwise have been denied them (Bernstein, 1971). However, if overt instruction is positioned as an element within a wider teaching and learning experience, creating a classroom environment in which the student is supported and instruction scaffolded to accomplish more difficult tasks than they could accomplish on their own (Bruner, 1983; Vygotsky, 1978), this otherwise limited approach can become a very important part of new millennium pedagogy. Used in this way, overt instruction can be conceptualised as including:

> ... all those active interventions on the part of the teacher and other experts that scaffold learning activities; that focus the learner on the important features of their experiences and activities within the community of learners; and that allow the learner to gain explicit information at times when it can most usefully organise and guide practice, building on and recruiting what the learner already knows and has accomplished (New London Group, 2000, p. 33).

In short, when overt instruction is positioned as just one of the pedagogical approaches deployed in conjunction with its pedagogical counterpoints, such as situated practice and critical framing, shortcomings such as the decontextualised nature of a rigidly didactic education and its inherent failure to take account of the specifics of a group of learners can be readily overcome (New London Group, 2000).

The pedagogical orientation of situated practice, another of the four approaches suggested in a multiliteracies pedagogy, draws on what was originally the attempt of a progressive education to redistribute the balance of agency between learners and teachers. Progressivism placed value on immersion in those authentic experiences which make the necessary connections with the learner's lifeworlds (Gee, 1990). By developing a respect for the lifeworld of the learner, incorporating the learner's primary discourse into the education process, it was argued that the classroom could become a place in which the learner could feel a sense of belonging, not alienation. Progressivism positioned learners as active rather than passive and engaged them in the process of making-meaning, immersing them within a community of learners (Lave and Wegner, 1991; Wertsch, 1985) engaged in authentic versions of the practices in focus (Cazden, 1988; Gee, 2000; Heath, 1983; Street, 1984). Learning could develop that place of commonsense, lived assumptions (Cope and Kalantzis, 2000a).

Situated practice acknowledges the key characteristic of learners as pattern recognisors in sociocultural contexts and the important capacities of acting flexibly in response to data and experience (Gee, 1992; New London Group, 2000). In this type of sociocultural approach:

> ...the focus of learning and education is not children, nor schools, but human lives viewed as trajectories through multiple social practices in various social institutions. If learning is to be efficacious, then what a child or an adult does now as a learner must be connected in meaningful and motivated ways with 'mature' (insider) versions of related social practices (Gee et al., 1996, p. 4).

Allowing social agency forces a consideration of lifeworld-based learner diversity such as those multiple intelligences, identified by Gardner (2002) as linguistic, logical-mathematical, spatial, bodily-kinesthetic, musical, naturalist, intrapersonal and interpersonal.

However, just as situated practice provides a counterpoint for the limitations inherent in overt instruction, so overt instruction also provides a counterpoint for a rigidly deployed progressive pedagogy hinging on situated practice. Examples of a literacy pedagogy in which overt instruction and situated practice are co-deployed include the supplementation of student interests and experience with genre theory's provision of explicit and transparent access to the structures and language choices of texts (Kalantzis and Cope, 2000). Reading Recovery (Clay, 1992) and the community of learners program outlined in the article 'Guided Discovery in a Community of Learners' (Brown and Campione, 1994), which embed overt instruction in some kind of situated practice with the teacher playing an active role with in-depth topics used to teach strategies of inquiry, comprehension and composition (Cazden, 2000a).

A third orientation of the multiliteracies pedagogy is that of critical framing, a concept arising from critical pedagogy traditions in which students learn first to detach from what they have learned, and then proceed to critique it (Fairclough, 1992; Gee, 1992). Through critical framing, teachers support students to denaturalise learnings and make assessments 'in relation to the historical, social, cultural, political, ideological, and value-centred relations of particular systems of knowledge and social practice' (New London Group, 2000, p. 34). This includes learnings gained through situated practice, as well learnings understood as a result of overt instruction. The importance of developing analytical abilities across a range of modal systems will increasingly involve:

> ...developing students' meta-semiotic understanding and the associated metalanguage to facilitate critical understanding of how meaning-making systems are deployed to make different kinds of meanings in texts and how these may be oriented to naturalise the hegemony of particular interests (Unsworth, 2002, p. 73).

However, critique itself also requires critique, as it a response to particular circumstances in a particular period, with the role of critic historically contextualised. In this way:

> ... the intellectual as critic corresponds to social arrangements and distributions of power, rights and responsibilities of certain social arrangements and of certain historical periods namely arrangements in which some individuals and groups set the agenda and others either follow or object (Kress, 2000b, p. 160).

Critique of critique itself is a product of the contemporary textual environment in which the task of text-makers involves complete responsibility for design. However, when critical framing is linked with situated practice and overt instruction, it 'becomes more grounded in everyday human purposes, and less airy-ideological and impossible to achieve in practice' (Kalantzis and Cope, 2000, p. 240). Again, the combination of the pedagogies is seen as enhancing the qualities of the individual pedagogies.

A fourth multiliteracies pedagogy, transformed practice, offsets critique and involves teachers in the development of ways in which their students can demonstrate how they can design and carry out, in a reflective manner, new practices embedded in their own goals and values. When critical framing is used in conjunction with transformed practice, the evaluative characteristics of critical framing assist students in considering the work of others as a means of achieving their own goals and purposes. Critical framing then leads purposefully to transformed practice. For learners, transformed practice is, in a way, a return to situated practice, only this is a return to practice in a reflective way consequent upon having developed understandings through overt instruction and critical framing. Kalantzis et al. (2005) argue that the new social conditions require precisely such a reflexive epistemology: an epistemology in which teacher and learner agency is rebalanced and which is, for this reason, characteristically dialogical. Transformed practice then involves the learner bringing the lifeworld and learnt concepts and theories together, engaging in critical practices and then moving toward some type of creative or appropriate transformation. In this way, the four pedagogical orientations of the multiliteracies pedagogy link directly to major traditions of literacy teaching. Each pedagogy, when used in isolation, can be problematic but, when used in combination, the shortcomings of each of the pedagogies are 'at least softened and, at best, enhanced and transformed by the others' (Kalantzis and Cope, 2000, p. 240).

2.2.2: Learning By Design

Building on this, Learning by Design (Kalantzis and Cope, 2004; Kalantzis et al., 2005) re-frames the four pedagogies as four knowledge processes: four ways of knowing that are a response to the growing importance of knowledge itself (Stewart, 1998) in the shifting conditions of contemporary work and productive life, be it in terms of the knowledge economy, the knowledge worker or knowledge management. Learning by Design is an epistemologically grounded pedagogy which positions knowledge as a social construct (Vygotsky, 1978), rejecting psychological models and focusing on the microdynamics of knowing, or how knowing happens. Highly developed reflexivity is a suggested response to shifting conditions (Beck et al., 1994) and, to this end, pedagogy is re-framed as knowing in action (Kalantzis et al., 2005).

Learning by Design, as a union of epistemology, or theories of knowledge, with pedagogy, or theories of learning, describes four knowledge processes which relate to the orientations in the four part multiliteracies pedagogy. The epistemological positioning of the multiliteracies pedagogies as knowledge processes in this schema is as follows:

- situated practice is described as students experiencing, be that experiencing the known or the new;
- overt instruction is described as students conceptualising, be that conceptualising by naming or by theorising;
- critical framing is described as students analysing, be that analysing functionally or critically; and
- transformed practice is described as students applying, be that applying appropriately or creatively (Kalantzis et al., 2005)

An epistemologically grounded theory is more appropriate for learners in a knowledge society than pedagogies emerging from a psychological/cognitivist view (Kalantzis et al., 2005). Certainly psychology is acknowledged, since it appears humans are 'driven by the mystery of human consciousness', but in terms of educative possibilities 'the critical question is what we do with its drives' (Kalantzis et al., 2005, p. 30). In the tradition of immersion, the multiliteracies pedagogical orientation of situated practice also involves experiencing the known by recruiting learners' knowledge from their lifeworlds (Husserl, 1970). However, experiencing the new also involves immersing students in new information and experiences in the Vygotskian sense of scaffolded instruction, in which the new learning is in the zone of proximal development (Vygotsky, 1978).

The focus of traditional overt instruction, conceptualising by naming, involves defining and applying concepts. This abstract defining applies to the particular at hand and application in general (Luria, 1976; Vygotsky, 1978). Conceptualising by theorising involves the connection of concepts in discipline knowledge through generalising schemas or models (Kalantzis et al., 2005). In the tradition of critical pedagogies, analysing functionally investigates cause and effect; it involves considering the use of any knowledge, action, object or represented meaning. Analysing critically interrogates human purposes and positions, querying the perspectives, interests and consequences of any piece of knowledge, action, object or representation (Kalantzis et al., 2005). As suggested by transformed practice, applying appropriately involves learner application of knowledge in a typical situation, be it in the human or natural worlds. This is in the tradition of applied or competency-based learning (Kalantzis et al., 2005). While this may involve a typical or accepted application, it is never merely replicated but always transformative to some degree (Kress, 2000b). Applying creatively involves learners in innovative applications or use of learning in a different situation, involving original and hybrid possibilities.

Learning by Design offers teachers a heuristic for auditing biases and gaps in current practices as well as a model for curriculum planning which prompts the use of the four knowledge processes. Offering a palette of pedagogies and so avoiding the endless search for a single effective, or culturally appropriate pedagogy (Cole, 1996), Learning by Design directs focus to pedagogical differentiation for contextualised learning. Within a transformative curriculum, teachers knowingly make choices from this range while ensuring three conditions of learning: belonging, engagement and transformation (Kalantzis et al., 2005).

Learning by Design offers a template which can be used to document pedagogical choices: a 'Learning Element' (Kalantzis and Cope, 2004; Kalantzis et al., 2005) containing a series of prompts for consideration when developing teaching and learning sequences—'Learning Focus', 'Knowledge Objectives', 'Knowledge Processes', 'Knowledge Outcomes', and 'Learner Pathways'. 'Learning Focus' includes the knowledge domain, scope of learning, learning level and prior knowledge of students. Knowledge Objectives prompt documentation of the purposes of teaching and learning experiences, differentiating experiential, conceptual, analytical and applied knowledge objectives. Knowledge Processes are the pedagogical enactments used to achieve the Knowledge Objectives in which experiencing, conceptualising, analysing and applying knowledge processes are further differentiated as experiencing the known and new; conceptualising by naming or by theorising; analysing function or interest; and applying appropriately or creatively. Knowledge Outcomes prompt documentation of experiential, conceptual, analytical and applied assessment. And Learner Pathways prompt documentation of opportunities for further, related knowledge development. These Learning Element templates provide for teacher and/or learner oriented text with the opportunity for teacher professional language on one side and a student learning resource on the other (Kalantzis and Cope, 2004; Kalantzis et al., 2005).

Educational theorists have long argued that there is a need for an interconnection between pedagogical deployment and the lifeworlds of the students in the classroom (Dewey, 1956; Montessori, 1964, 1989). For literacy education in the communications environment of the early days of the twenty-first century in Western schooling, this means supporting students' learning of multimodal designs through a combined renewal of design and pedagogy, a shift in focus that is not sufficiently manifested in much contemporary schooling (Lankshear, 1999; Lankshear and Knobel, 2003; New London Group, 2000; Reinking et al., 1998).

2.3: New Millennium Teacher Professional Learning

This literature review began by tracing arguments for a shift from rigid definitions of literacy as entirely print-based to allow the incorporation of the multimodal needs of societies in the new millennium, accepting and adopting the challenges thrown up by changing literacy practices and the types of affordances offered by the new communications environment. It argued that although this debate is now well advanced and that policy can be seen to acknowledge the existence of a changed communications environment, research still indicates that the changed out-of-school literacy practices of both teachers and students still stand in contrast to the literacy orientations and implementation efforts valued by many school-based educators, schools and school-related bureaucracies.

In the second section, multiliteracies theory, that theoretical response to the changed environment adopted by this research project, has been described with particular emphasis given to the 'multimodal' and 'pedagogical knowledge process' schemas that have been deployed in this research project, and the influences which led to their creation and recommendations for use with contemporary literacy teachers.

Section three now turns its attention to the major impact of teachers in affecting student achievement, and the strong influence of professional learning on teacher knowledge, and subsequently, student knowledge. Trained in print-based literacy pedagogies, the teaching profession is increasingly surrounded by a community of literacy practices influenced by the changed communications environment that stands outside the paradigm in which they were trained. The pedagogical implication of this is the need for a shift to multimodal design and associated social dynamics but there are also implications for teachers' roles and teachers' learning in light of changed community and communicative conditions.

2.3.1: Teacher Impact: Changing Teacher Roles; Changing Teacher Learning

Of all the variables that contribute to student achievement, the quality of teaching has been found to be the singly most powerful variant (Chall et al., 1990). Teacher quality has a far greater impact on the variations in student achievement than student background, class sizes and overall spending levels and other effects (Darling-Hammond, 2000). Studies of student outcomes in randomly selected classes have found that substantial variations in student achievement could be largely attributed to the individual teacher rather than to the school as a whole (Nye et al., 2004). This finding supports earlier research that demonstrates that successful student learning can be seen to be directly related to the quality of teacher knowledge and ability (Muijs and Reynolds, 2000; Wenglinsky, 2000).

School effectiveness, therefore, is largely a result of the quality of teaching; the professional development of teachers directly impacts on this teacher quality (Hill and Rowe, 1996; Hill et al., 1996; Rowe, 2003). Positive effects on student achievement in literacy in the primary years include factors such as maintaining student attentiveness and interest. Teacher participation in specialist literacy in-service programs has a marked effect on student outcomes (Hill and Rowe, 1996). The teacher can be described as 'the key determinant of progress made by the student' (Hill et al., 1996, p. 325), with classroom to classroom differences accounting for 36 and 56 percent of variation in student English and mathematics achievement.

It is clear that professional learning directly affects student achievement by improving the quality of teaching practice, fostering those improved teacher pedagogical and content practices which lead to student achievement.

> [H]igh quality professional development will produce superior teaching in classrooms, which will, in turn, translate into higher levels of student achievement (Supovitz, 2001, p. 81).

The positioning of teachers as the most powerful influence on the variability of student achievement and the impact of the level of teacher knowledge on student learning suggests that a pedagogical renewal must be effected through an increased attention to teacher learning. Building on this, the affordances of a changing communications environment call for the development of professional learning that is directly related to increasing the teachers' multimodal literacy and giving them the pedagogical resources to broaden their teaching repertoires in relation to multimodality. The affordances of the changing communications environment relating to social agency and dynamics also beg consideration in relation to teachers' professionalism, including their ongoing learning. Instructional leadership is no longer sufficient and renewed, dynamic, conceptions of teacher leadership are required instead (Crowther et al., 2002).

An historical view of the evolution of the teaching profession demonstrates that conceptions of teacher learning are related to the prevailing needs of the society and that changed notions of what actually constitutes professionalism and a repositioning of the teacher as a learner as well as a teacher is necessary in the knowledge economy of the new millennium (Hargreaves and Fullan, 2000). The prevailing view of the role of teachers in the early days of a mass public education was in the deployment of pedagogies which emphasised recitation, note-taking and question-and-answer routines. The management of teaching was seen as demanding but technically simple, learnt through imitation, with refinements on the job. Mentoring of teacher learning took the form of words of encouragement and management tips from superiors who judged good practice in others as being like their own (Hargreaves and Fullan, 2000), a kind of elitist patronage designed to perpetuate the reproduction of approved ways of operating (Ehrich and Hansford, 1999).

Lengthened teacher pre-service preparation and improved salaries in the 1960s did much to enhance teacher professionalism. Educators were positioned as autonomous professionals, which led to increased individualism, resulting in stagnation in pedagogical practices and an inhibition of innovation due to teacher isolation and conformity. Individuals attended in-service education and returned to unenthusiastic colleagues who had not shared the learning experience. Teacher learning was confined to new teacher inductions and, in a culture of individualism, was associated with correcting technical weaknesses and solving teaching problems (Hargreaves and Fullan, 2000).

The unsustainable nature of a system structured around individual teacher autonomy was highlighted by the demands of a widened curriculum, the rapid pace of change itself, and the increased complexity of teaching in the wake of the knowledge explosion of the mid-1980s. Collegiate professional cultures which would 'develop common purpose, cope with uncertainty and complexity, respond well to rapid change, create a climate of risk-taking and continuous improvement and develop stronger senses of teacher efficacy' (Hargreaves and Fullan, 2000) were proposed as alternatives to autonomy. However, as pressure to create collaborative cultures grew, persistent individualism resulted in uncoordinated efforts. The need for practitioner engagement in an ongoing reflective examination of their practice gained prominence, both as reflection-in-action necessitated when a practitioner's results were found not to be going as expected, requiring immediate adjustments; and as reflection-on-action, involving a retrospective exploration of events, practices and thought patterns (Schön, 1983). Single loop and double loop learning (Argyris and Schön, 1978, 1974; Schön 1983) assisted the differentiation of unexamined and examined practices. Practitioner research paradigms incorporating reflection were proposed as a means of positioning teachers as inquirers into their own practices and maximising teacher agency (Carr and Kemmis, 1986).

The current global social, economic, political and cultural transformations associated with a changing communications environment see the old boundaries of teachers' work dissolving, with roles becoming less segregated and more complex. Teachers increasingly work with the expectations of diverse communities and other social agencies, responding to changed assumptions regarding participation, integration and involvement in research and reform (Hargreaves and Fullan, 2000).

Lifelong learning, which is directly related to job responsibilities and the adaptation of general and particular competencies and knowledge to achieve new tasks, is a key feature of the changing nature of work in the knowledge society (Aspin and Chapman, 2001). However, much of the focus of discussion about lifelong learning in Australia has centred on increasing the capacity of institutional arrangements to encourage and allow flexibility for entry and re-entry into formal education settings at various life and career stages (James and Beckett, 2000). Attention to lifelong learning has to move beyond the institutional arrangements and settings in which learning currently occurs to include ways that influence the roles of all teachers as lifelong learners. However, the climate in many schools remains unconducive to such a positioning of all teachers as lifelong learners, with expectations on teachers to gain the knowledge required for their professional practice during initial teacher education and to develop further practical knowledge predominantly through teaching experience. A prevailing culture wherein the development of teacher practice is not open to the scrutiny of colleagues, combined with under-investment in professional learning, undervalues the teacher's role as a professional learner (Elmore, 2002).

Collaborations of university and classroom teachers on research projects are seen as useful models for the conduct of research into the integration of digital literacies in schools (Labbo, 2000). Teachers as researchers of their own practice (Darling-Hammond and Sykes, 1999; Leu, 2000; Locke and Andrews, 2004; Unsworth, 2006), involved in research which connects to larger issues facing the profession and, therefore, involving the 'rub between theory and practice' (Miller and Silvernail, 1994), is productive when based in the context of students and their work. As the teaching profession undergoes sweeping socio-cultural changes, it needs to be involved in 'theory-busting, theory building and paradigm shift' (Luke, 2003a, p. 61). Yet curriculum reform studies fail to position teachers as knowledge producers (Ladson-Billings, 1991) and teachers lack a voice in debates on curriculum reform and are all too often positioned simply as subjects of change in response to new policies and knowledge (Cormack and Comber, 1996).

A study into ongoing differential literacy outcomes of poor children found that 'disruption of deficit discourses requires serious intellectual engagement by teachers over an extended period of time in ways that foster teacher agency and respect, without celebrating the status quo' (Comber and Kamler, 2004, p. 295). This study offers an example of reciprocal mentorship relationships in which cross-generational teacher pairs, working alongside academic researchers, framed their own research within a wider community of other pairs working towards a collective goal.

A major factor affecting the role of teachers and teacher professionalism is the isolation of the teaching space which presents difficulty in developing shared knowledge and standards of practice (Darling-Hammond, 1998). Considerable pedagogical knowledge is hidden in the teachers' isolated and privatised work (Luke, 2003a). Despite the enormous potential of teacher influence on student learning, classrooms remain largely unexamined and isolating spaces where a professional:

> gently closes the classroom door and performs the teaching act... [and] puts into place the end effects of so many policies, who interprets the policies, and who is alone with students during their 15000 hours of schooling (Hattie, 2003, pp. 2-3).

Teacher professional learning has traditionally been characterised as individualistic, with a focus on the needs of the classroom teacher (Dillon et al., 2000). An alternative role, however, is the teacher as part of a school professional learning community, sharing a common purpose, collective vision and commitments and measurable goals; fostering collaborative action research and inquiry into the big issues of teaching and learning; building continuous improvement cycles into the school routines; and continuously collecting evidence of student learning (DuFour and Eaker, 1998). Achieving a shared understanding of curriculum is essential in developing a community of mind both amongst teachers and between teachers and other stakeholders (Sergiovanni, 1994). The result can be seen in greater changes in practice than those achieved by any teacher working in isolation (Goodrum et al., 2001).

The rise of knowledge management has led to developments in which groups forming communities of practice can make explicit their informal and often implicit knowledge gained through working in organisations (Scarbrough, 2001) and through discussing and documenting tacit understandings and lived experience, building a bank of explicit, shared organisational or professional knowledge (Wenger, 1999; Wenger et al., 2002). Professional learning communities can be instrumental in linking different disciplinary and subject areas around common themes or concerns, with the ability to 'purposely restructure the curriculum to link together courses or course work so that students find greater coherence in what they are learning as well as increased intellectual interaction with faculty and fellow students' (Gabelnick et al., 1990, p. 5).

This suggests a further type of isolation to that of a sole teacher alone with students in a classroom. This intellectual isolation is more in the nature of loyalty to one's discipline or specialisation; this can separate teachers intellectually. Professional learning teams can counter both physical and intellectual isolation through collaboration that promotes integrative approaches to knowledge, rather than the disintegration of isolated disciplines and courses (Gabelnick et al., 1990). Membership of, and accountability to, professional learning communities both within and between schools, however, is supportive of teacher learning that impacts on the quality of teaching (McLaughlin and Talbert, 1993). Building on notions of distributed leadership, where the responsibility for sustaining improvement is shared broadly among school community members (McLaughlin and Talbert, 2001), a case is argued for teachers' positive influence to extend beyond student learning to school culture and the broader community (Crowther et al., 2002).

Teachers' roles will increasingly have to include a greater focus on the formation of strong co-learning relationships with colleagues and parents, shared inquiries into practice rather than hierarchical handing down of wisdom, bringing with this an integrated effort to reculture schools and school systems (Hargreaves and Fullan, 2000). Co-learning can also contribute to personal as well as professional development, with interpersonal relational development resulting in increased self-confidence, self-belief and action orientation (Fletcher, 2000; Hale, 1999; Hargreaves and Fullan, 2000). In the new millennium the role of teacher needs to move from its formerly passive positioning to encompass that of 'a scholar, an intellectual, and a knowledge worker oriented toward the interpretation, communication, and construction of ... knowledge in the interests of student learning' (Shulman, 1999, p. xiii).

2.3.2: Professional Learning for Quality Teaching and Renewed Professionalism

Given that teachers are the most powerful influence on student achievement and that the changed needs of professionalism require a radical transformation of teachers' roles, the current teacher workforce needs to be productively supported in a learning process which assists them to address the challenges thrown up to their literacy teaching practices in the communications environment that continues inexorably to change around them. However, determining the nature of effective professional learning in the rapidly shifting communications environment of the knowledge economy, in order to reflect current literacy teaching and learning needs, requires an ongoing consideration of the knowledge relationships and abilities of quality literacy teachers and how they can be enriched in professional learning contexts. In a knowledge economy that requires students to synthesise, analyse and produce knowledge, a string of logic suggests there must be parallel expectations of teachers calling for 'very deep changes—even a transformation—in teachers' ideas about and understanding of subject matter, teaching, and learning' (Thompson and Zeuli, 1999, p. 350).

This reflects the movements away from the transmission of reproduced, 'declarative knowledge', where literacy teachers who see knowledge as discrete bits of information will base lesson design around teaching these facts by means of students repeating, memorising, and recalling this given information. Instead, teachers who see knowledge as both a personal and social construct, will design classroom practices that involve students in comprehending concepts and use their developed understanding to solve problems (Elmore, 1996). Complex indicators such as deep subject knowledge have a positive influence on teacher quality only up to a certain level of basic competence, after which such benefits decrease (Darling-Hammond, 2000). Categorisations such as teacher IQ (Schalock, 1979; Soar et al., 1983), teacher qualification and teachers' years of experience (Nye et al., 2004) show little relationship with student outcomes. For teacher knowledge of a subject to be effectively used, it needs to be coupled with the knowledge of how to teach the subject to a diverse group of learners. Clearly, pedagogical knowledge is paramount as 'pedagogical skill may interact with subject matter knowledge to bolster or reduce teacher performance' (Darling-Hammond, 2000, p. 5).

Teachers who have specialised knowledge in a subject are more likely to place emphasis on the content of their specialised subject at the expense of content they know less about (Grossman, 1994). However, such solid content knowledge can also allow a teacher to confidently design high quality, interactive learning activities if they have mastered the pedagogical skills to do so. The complexities of quality teaching need acknowledging and the notion of multiple types of knowledge, which interplay in various ways to contribute to quality teaching, is a useful lens to do this. Effective teachers have also developed 'pedagogical learner knowledge' (Grimmet and MacKinnon, 1992), the ability to interpret students' words and actions and design learning experiences which account for learner differences. This involves an understanding of child development and ways to support growth in the cognitive, emotional, physical and social domains; the ability to make connections with learners from diverse social and cultural backgrounds and with different preferred learning styles; and attentive communication with students and engagement and reflection on student work (Darling-Hammond, 1998).

Expert teachers attend to such affective attributes in their task of influencing student outcomes (Hattie, 2003). Such pedagogical learner knowledge has been found to demonstrate a strong correlation with the development of student belonging and transformation through teacher engagement with and development of knowledge of students' diverse lifeworlds (Kalantzis and Cope, 2005; New London Group, 2000). Effective teachers also recognise the subject-specific nature of 'pedagogical content knowledge' (Shulman, 1987) which involves:

... rich and profound understanding of the subject matter one is teaching... as well as understanding of the principles of learning, development, motivation and instruction (Shulman, 2005, p. 20)

Pedagogical content knowledge involves understanding subject matter deeply and flexibly; the ability to help students build cognitive maps; to cross different disciplinary traditions; and to connect disciplinary knowledge to everyday life (Darling-Hammond, 1998). This is the ability to identify essential representations of the subject being taught (Hattie, 2003). In relation to multiliteracies content knowledge, this would involve teacher knowledge, use and development of a metalanguage to give due attention to multiple and intersecting modes of designed meaning, giving consideration to dimensions of meaning (representational, social, organisational, contextual, and ideological) across modes of meaning (linguistic, visual, gestural, spatial, audio and multimodal).

Through a complex coupling of pedagogical learner knowledge and pedagogical content knowledge, effective teachers can combine support for each learner's emotional and identity development with a cognisance of knowledge 'encoded' in different subject matter and reflect on their teaching practice and act reflexively on the basis of professional judgment (Darling-Hammond, 1998). For this reason, professional development approaches need to shift from the older models of teacher training, inservicing and 'train-the-trainer'. To meet the challenges of the new millennium, teachers are now called upon to undertake transformed roles as reflective, inquiry-oriented members of collegiate, knowledge-producing communities; communities which openly engage in researching their practices and beliefs and share their findings not only with colleagues but also with the wider community. This requires a new kind of professionalism: one that directly challenges the lingering isolationist norms which have long denied the voice, the expectation, the scrutiny and the channels for such production and sharing of knowledge.

In designing or reviewing approaches to professional learning, three orientations to knowledge may be used to consider the learner/knowledge positioning or type of knowledge development being undertaken: knowledge-for-practice, knowledge-in-practice and knowledge-of-practice (Cochran-Smith and Lytle, 1999). Knowledge-for-practice positions teachers in the roles of knowledge user, assuming that academics or bureaucrats generate content and pedagogical knowledge for teacher use. Knowledge-in-practice positions teachers in the roles of practical workers, their knowledge emerging through experience in the profession. Teachers are positioned as generating knowledge in their own contexts of practice, mediating ideas, constructing meaning, and taking action based on that knowledge. Knowledge-of-practice, however, positions teachers as generators of knowledge of practice by 'making their classrooms and schools sites for inquiry, connecting their work in schools to larger issues, and taking a critical perspective on the theory and research of others' (Cochran-Smith and Lytle, 1999, p. 273).

An orientation that assumes the goal of knowledge-of-practice shifts the positioning of teachers from that type of technician inherent in knowledge-for-practice and knowledge-in-practice to the teacher as knowledge creator and sharer, in which:

> [t]he teachers' relationship to knowledge is different from the previous conceptions in that they become researchers, theorisers, activists, and school leaders who generate knowledge for the profession and they also become critical users of research (Southwest Educational Development Laboratory, 2002, p. 1)

Effective professional learning positions teachers as agentive, confronting research and theory; regularly engaged in evaluating their practice; and developing the experience and knowledge of colleagues for mutual assistance. Effective professional learning is experiential in nature, with teachers engaged in concrete tasks that give insight into the processes of learning and development; that address teachers' questions through experimentation while considering profession-wide research interests; that are collaborative, involving teachers sharing knowledge; that are contextualised in teachers' work with students, including examinations of subject matter and teaching methods; that are sustained and intensive, supported by modelling, coaching, and problem-solving; and that are intrinsically connected to other aspects of school change (Darling-Hammond and McLaughlin, 1995; Furhman, 2001; Garet et al., 2001; Meiers and Ingvarson, 2005).

In conclusion, the research literature reviewed indicates trends in expanded affordances of multimodal design and related social changes enabled by developments in networked, digitised information and communications technologies which have implications for renewal of literacy pedagogy. Schemas emanating from multiliteracies theory hold potential for engaging teachers in contemporary literacy-focused professional learning and as analytical frameworks. Agentive teacher professional learning can be deployed as means of leveraging changes in literacy education.

Chapter 3
Methodology and Procedures

Chapter Three concerns the conception and design of the research project in the context of the researcher's work as an Early Years Literacy Policy and Project Officer in the Department of Education, Victoria. The chapter is presented in two sections.

Section one is a discussion of the early years literacy policy and professional learning models prevailing in Victorian schools at the time the project was conceived and the data collected. It outlines how the project developed out of a work-based multiliteracies-focused professional learning project, putting this in the context of literacy curriculum policy released subsequent to data collection.

Section two discusses the evolution of the final research design, a case study of participatory action research which accounts for teachers' collaborative engagement with theory and knowledge generation. The research procedure is then explained: the selection of participants and decisions about the processes for structuring for data collection and analysis; the unfolding of the research process and its organisation into phases, as well as the iterative cycle of data collection and professional learning interventions are also detailed.

3.1: Research Paradigm: Victorian Early Literacy Policy

This research project, an investigation into the professional learning of teachers of early years (Prep–Year 4) students, was conducted in the Victorian government school sector during 2003. This was a period characterised by calls for a reform of major aspects of schooling to meet the needs of rapidly changing social, economic and technological conditions. At the time the existing curriculum and approaches to teacher learning had already been shaped by earlier reforms, including a devolved model of school administration through the system-wide introduction of the self-managing, government, 'Schools of the Future' (Caldwell and Haywood, 1998).

Within this devolved context teachers in Victorian schools could personally select what they considered to be appropriate curriculum foci and outcomes from eight key learning areas to meet the needs of their student community in the first eleven years of schooling (Prep–Year 10). The eight learning areas were The Arts, English, Health and Physical Education, Languages Other Than English, Mathematics, Science, Studies of Society and Environment, and Technology (Board of Studies Victoria, 1995, 2000) and course advice (Directorate of School Education, 1995) offered government school teachers exemplars of course outlines, with implementation supported by teacher briefings and workshops conducted by government funded and directed central and regional offices.

Investigating within this broader curriculum context, the work of the researcher related to the Early Years Literacy Strategy, which had been developed to support the literacy teaching and learning of students in the early years of schooling (ages approximately 5–10 years). This strategy included the Early Literacy Research Project (Hill and Crèvola, 1998a, 1998b, 1999a), the Early Years Literacy Program (Education Victoria, 1997f 1998b, 1999b) and accompanying training, conferences, parent initiatives, and annual assessment of reading data collection.

3.1.1: The Early Literacy Research Project

The statewide Early Years policies and programs were based on advice from the Early Literacy Research Project, a joint research project between the Department of Education, Victoria and The University of Melbourne. This section will describe this joint research project, which informed literacy policy and programs at the time of this research project.

Initiated at the end of 1995, the Early Literacy Research Project involved 27 trial schools from low socio-economic areas and 25 reference schools (Hill and Crèvola, 1998a, 1998b, 1999a). The design of this joint research project was informed by those characteristics considered to constitute effective teaching (Scheerens and Bosker, 1997), including time on task; closeness of content covered to the assessment instrument; the structure of the approach, embodying specific objectives, frequent assessment and corrective feedback; and the various types of adaptive instruction that can be managed by teachers. Three factors were named as foundational in informing a whole school design (Hill and Crèvola, 1999a): high expectations of student achievement, engaged learning time, and focused teaching that maximises learning within each student's zone of proximal development (Vygotsky, 1978).

The researchers identified nine design elements for facilitating effective teaching and the way in which these elements operated as an effective and cohesive whole school design: beliefs and understandings; leadership and coordination; standards and targets; monitoring and assessment; classroom teaching programs; professional learning teams; school and class organisation; intervention and special assistance; and home, school and community partnerships (Hill and Crèvola, 1999a). In the knowledge that significant variability in student progress can be found in students in different classes in the same school (Hill and Rowe, 1996; Monk, 1992; Scheerens et al., 1989), the research sought to develop a whole school design approach aimed at minimising these differences and enabling all students to progress at the level of the students in the most effective teachers' classes (Hill and Crèvola, 1999a).

The Early Literacy Research Project involved trial school teachers in a systematic organisation of teaching practices and assessment. The professional development conducted by researchers from The University of Melbourne supported teachers in combining the following teaching approaches within a daily two-hour literacy block: oral language, reading to children, language experience, shared reading, guided reading, independent reading, modelled writing, shared writing, interactive writing, guided writing, independent writing. Many of the classroom teaching practices were already known to teachers through their involvement in programs such as the 'Early Literacy In-Service Course' (Curriculum Development Centre, 1987), which drew on practices widespread in New Zealand classrooms (Clay, 1991; Department of Education, NZ, 1985; Holdaway, 1979). Key foci for the professional development were also drawn from the assessment strategies developed in New Zealand (Clay, 1993a, 1993b; Clay et al., 1983).

Data was collected at the end of each of the three years of the project, using three of the subtests of the *Woodcock Language Proficiency Battery* (Woodcock, 1987), the *Record of Oral Language* (Clay et al., 1983), and the six measures of *An Observation Survey of Early Literacy Achievement* (Clay, 1993a). Pre- and post-test measures, composite scores obtained from fitting a one-factor model to ten separate measures of student literacy, found an effect size estimated at 0.648 with results described as 'large, positive and statistically significant' (Hill and Crèvola, 1999a, p. 10). Discovered to be most significant features in promoting change were those organisational features which schools had been found to implement differentially and the challenge was for schools to become effective in implementing them all. These included:

- a two-hour, uninterrupted daily literacy block for all students
- the setting of rigorous performance standards and targets that seek to have all students performing at a high standard by the end of their second year of schooling;
- a focus on data-driven instruction with assessment of all students at the beginning and end of each year a full range of measures, plus ongoing monitoring on a regular basis throughout the year
- the use of Reading Recovery as a one-to-one tutoring program for all students in Year 1 who are not making adequate progress
- the appointment and training of an early years literacy coordinator with at least a 0.5 time release in each school
- ongoing, externally provided structured professional learning for teaching teams to develop their beliefs and understandings, and promote understanding of use of a range of teaching strategies
- on-site professional development through observation, team teaching, weekly teams meetings and visits, mentoring and coaching
- professional development sessions for principals focusing on the principal as an instructional leader (Hill and Crèvola, 1999a, p. 10–11).

The research measured the extent of improvement in the proportions of students meeting the State-wide Minimum Acceptable Standard of 80% of students (deemed as capable) reading unseen texts with 90% accuracy at or above Reading Recovery level one by the end of their first year of schooling; and 100% of students (deemed as capable) reading unseen texts with 90% accuracy at or above Reading Recovery level five by the end of their second year of schooling. Analysis of both cohorts demonstrated a substantial improvement, with the number of students in their first year of schooling changing from less than half of students underway (level one) to almost three quarters of students underway, with improvement also reflected in the proportions of students performing at higher levels, particularly the proportion reaching level five (Hill and Crèvola, 1999a).

There were high expectations of student achievement as defined by these standards, with professional learning teams taking responsibility for all children's literacy success, with regular discussion focused on student achievement at the school level. On- and offsite support was given by an outside 'expert' and offsite involvement was furthered by a broader community of practice. There were also additional dedicated resources and the principal and a coordinator were positioned as educational leaders whose roles involved attention to the nine design elements. All of these factors contributed to the improvement of student progress in terms of the measures used (Hill and Crèvola, 1997b).

3.1.2: The Early Years Literacy Strategy

The Early Years Literacy Strategy, developed concurrently with the Early Literacy Research Project, was designed to support a statewide focus on raising literacy levels in the Victorian government primary school sector (approximately 1200 schools). The Early Years Literacy Strategy involved teachers in professional learning supported statewide, through a multilayered professional development and conferences network aided by teacher and parent advice materials. Statewide minimum standards for literacy were identified and accountability processes were established for government primary schools (Department of Education and Training, 2003a). In this way a community of practice of early years literacy practitioners from around Victoria was supported by statewide and regional conferences. Attracting as many as 2000 delegates, these enabled teachers to present their own contextualised experiences, not only promoting professional dialogue but also allowing opportunities to discuss implementation issues.

The Early Years Literacy Strategy involved the development of the Early Years Literacy Program, set up to provide practical advice for teachers and teacher leaders. Consisting of a series of books, videos, and other materials that were progressively released in stages, the Early Years Literacy Program's resources included *Teaching Readers in the Early Years* (Education Victoria, 1997h) in Stage 1; *Teaching Writers in the Classroom* (Education Victoria, 1998b) in Stage 2; and *Teaching Speakers and Listeners in the Classroom* (Education Victoria, 1999b) in Stage 3. Professional development modules included *Professional Development for Teachers, Readers* (Education Victoria, 1997f); *Professional Development for Teachers, Stage 2: Writing* (Education Victoria, 1998a); and *Professional Development for Teachers, Stage 3: Speaking and Listening* (Education Victoria, 1999a). In addition to these there were parent programs, including *Classroom Helpers, A Course for Parents, Helpers and Aides* (Education Victoria, 1997a) and *Developing Literacy Partnerships* (Education Victoria, 1997b).

The Early Years Literacy Program recommended the deployment of teaching approaches within an organisational structure for a daily two-hour literacy block. These included whole class, small group and independent teaching approaches during the 'reading' hour; and whole class, small group and independent teaching approaches during the 'writing' hour. The teaching approaches recommended for the reading hour included whole class reading to and shared reading; small group shared reading, language experience, guided reading and reciprocal teaching; and whole class reading share time. Students also worked independently at learning centres. The teaching approaches recommended for the writing hour included whole class modelled and shared writing, small group interactive writing, guided writing, independent writing and roving conferences and whole group writing share time. The program recommended the use of a task management board indicating daily student groupings and deployment of teaching approaches (Education Victoria, 1999b, 1997f, 1998b). The program was initially developed for students in Prep–Year Two and gradually extended to cater for students in Years Three and Four.

3.1.2.1: Schools Television and the Early Years Literacy Strategy

From 1997, the Early Years Literacy Team worked in a collaborative way with Schools Television production team members to produce programs which could be available to teachers and trainers both through the satellite television narrowcast facility and on video for use in training programs and school-based, professional learning teams. Examples of these included *Guided Reading: A Companion Video to Professional Development for Teachers* (Education Victoria, 1997c); and *Learning Centres: A Companion Video to Professional Development for Teachers* (Education Victoria, 1997d). Established in 1994 by the former Liberal state government, Schools Television was the Department of Education's narrowcast satellite television network. Victorian government schools and many Catholic and non-government school were connected to the technology via satellite reception infrastructure, including a satellite dish and decoder technology. The service ceased at the end of 2005, two years after the data collection period of this research project, the rationale behind the closure being both low level usage and the medium's lack of support for the sorts of 'on demand' delivery, interactivity and collaboration afforded by the more recent technologies such as video conferencing, web-casting and pod-casting (Department of Education and Training, 2005).

In the development of films to support teacher learning, a division of roles between the Schools Television team members and the Early Years Branch members had been negotiated but this increasingly went unquestioned. In essence the staff from the Early Years Branch, having a background in education, were responsible for the identification of issues and for finding the 'talent' to be filmed, including 'expert talking heads' and teachers. These issues were generally suggested by the statewide regional training representatives and included topics such as meeting the needs of students who speak English as a Second Language (Department of Education and Training, 2002d) and the teaching of handwriting in the early years (Department of Education and Training, 2002e).

The programs were highly structured and formulaic in nature, with innovation generally only in the area of special effects. The films presented 'talking head experts' and 'expert' practising teachers discussing the theory and practices around an issue but the interview questions and suggested responses had been prepared by the education officers and sent to the teachers before filming. Experts received the questions but not any suggested responses. Generally the experts were interviewed in the in-house studio while the teachers were interviewed in their classrooms. The act of interviewing was performed by a member of the production team with a technical, rather than an educational background.

During film editing, the selection of shots was a collaborative effort between the education officers and the film editor, a specialist rather than an educationalist. However, due to the time consuming nature of this task, work intensity of the education officers, and the usually short timelines before scheduled screenings, the editor was often left to make final shot selections and sequencing decisions.

These films were designed for teachers to watch in school- or region-based professional learning teams. Suggested discussion points when viewing the videos were developed and published on the Department of Education's webpage. Video copies were made of the films and multiple copies of these were distributed to members of the statewide regional training team and were available to schools to purchase.

3.1.2.2: The Work of the Statewide Early Years Literacy Team

A statewide early literacy training team was made up of representatives from the (then) nine metropolitan and regional state education offices. These representatives, all with expertise and experience in the area of early years literacy teaching, worked with the literacy officers from the central office of the Department of Education (including the researcher) to develop and conduct training in early years literacy. A train-the-trainer model was deployed to carry out the centrally designed early years literacy training and regionally implemented professional development program. Regionally-nominated early years literacy trainers were responsible for regionally-conducted training for school-based early years literacy coordinators. Early years teachers participated in initial training and ongoing development facilitated by the early years literacy coordinator at their school. The central office and regional literacy staff met regularly to discuss issues arising from this training; to report on policy developments; and to explore ideas for future resource production. Opportunities for ongoing development were also accessed at a regional level and through statewide and regional conferences.

In line with the national goals set for schooling, statewide minimum standards for reading were developed, with teachers undertaking an annual assessment of reading against Reading Recovery text levels:

- 80% of students reading unseen texts with 90% accuracy at or above text level one by the end of their first year of schooling
- 100% of students reading unseen texts with 90% accuracy at or above text level five by the end of their second year of schooling (Department of Education and Training, 2003a).

The reading ability of students improved for each of the seven years of data collection, from 1999 to 2005 for Prep. In 2005, the statewide minimum standard for Prep students was met, and for Year 1 students was almost met. However, results for Year 2 students levelled out in 2003, and year-on-year reading improvement of students in Prep and Year 1 suggested that a ceiling was being approached, as had happened in Year 2 (Department of Education and Training, 2002a). These trends were becoming apparent at the time of the research.

While the systemic nature of the literacy strategy was applauded as relatively unique in Australia (Luke, 2003a, p. 66), the rigidity of the view taken of literacy, with an emphasis on reading and writing, was unfortunately narrow for a post-typographical age (Comber and Kamler, 2004). The classroom teaching element of the strategy focused on the teaching and learning of reading and writing, or print literacy, and as neither the literature related to the Early Literacy Research Project nor the Early Years Literacy Program attempted to offer a definition of literacy, references to reading and writing still dominated. Within the statewide strategy, however, attempts were increasingly made to incorporate advice on technology into the Early Years Literacy Program (Department of Education and Training, 2002c), and to work with a broader view of literacy more commensurate with the changing times, but this remained somewhat peripheral to the high stakes focus and assessments located in traditional print contexts.

A founding assumption of the Early Literacy Research Project, that there was a close link between learning content and assessment instrument, locked the teaching and assessment of reading/writing-focused literacy into a closed cycle which did not account for teaching and assessment practices that were reflective of a broader view of literacy addressing the prevalent designs of the post-typographical era (Comber and Kamler, 2004). This was exacerbated by the requirement that Victorian teachers report on their students' progress in literacy against statewide and national benchmarks using levelled text. While the results showed improvement in students' ability to read levelled text and other indicators of early print literacy ability, this pervasive emphasis on the level rather than the content and features of the text and its connection to student interests and discipline- or issue-relatedness created a level-led student grouping and teaching focus. The close alignment of assessment tools and teaching practice continued to support a narrow view of literacy at odds with the expansion of modes of meaning deployed in contemporary texts described in the literature review.

Similarly the introduction of a dedicated, daily literacy-focused two-hour block was a counterpoint to complaints regarding a crowded curriculum and was based on the positive impact on student progress of time spent on task. When the Early Literacy Research Project began teachers would complain that:

> [f]requent interruptions within the school day, and the over-crowding of the curriculum, restrict the time available for literacy teaching (Crèvola and Hill, 1997, p. 22).

The resultant move to provide for daily dedicated time protected from interruptions has often resulted in a segregation of literacy from disciplinary content (Australian Government, 2000). Writings on the Early Literacy Research Project have been published not in the area of literacy education, but mainly in the areas of whole school change and leadership (Hill and Crèvola, 1997, 1998a, 1998b, 1999b; Hill and Rowe, 1996). Perhaps this is because what was salient about the program concerned not the teaching practices or the pedagogy, but whole school reform, heightened expectations of students, educational leadership, and school and classroom organisation. Nor have subsequent publications engaged with professional discussion on new literacies (Crevola and Hill, 1997; Hill and Crèvola, 1998a) so, while the teaching approaches may be a 'rich resource to the present day' (Hill and Crèvola, 1999a, p. 5), they require review in light of changed texts and literacy practices.

Of course, statewide and regional conferences for teachers allowed for continued dialogue around issues arising through teacher presentations.

While conference papers were also published, many teachers chose not to contribute—most citing time constraints and already intense workloads as their reasons. Photos were taken and some teachers came to the notice of departmental personnel, who invited them to share their knowledge with others via an early years segment on Schools Television. Others gained promotion to regional offices within the Victorian school system and were invited by the researchers from the Early Literacy Research Project to work on similar projects in New York, where the learnings were being replicated. In this way, a cohort of teachers became professional spokespeople, sharing their knowledge of practice.

3.1.2.3: Victorian Early Years Literacy Policy in Transition

At the turn of the new millennium, shifting governmental priorities focused on literacy researching and resourcing of middle years (Years 5-9) initiatives, including *The Middle Years Research and Development Project* (Department of Education Employment and Training, 2001b) and *The Middle Years: A Guide for Strategic Action in Years 5-9* (Department of Education Employment and Training, 1999). In the area of literacy, *Knowledge, Innovation, Skills and Creativity: A Discussion Paper on Achieving the Goals and Targets for the Future in Victoria's Education and Training System* (Department of Education Employment and Training, 2001a), and *Literacy and Learning in the Middle Years: Major Report on the Middle Years Literacy Research Project* (Culican et al., 2001) contributed to insights about changing requirements in literacy education, including the need to address multiliteracies. The Early Years strategy had increasingly prioritorised numeracy education, with the *Early Numeracy Research Project (1999–2001)* (Department of Education and Training, 2002b) initiated following recommendations about the application of the whole school design approach for improving learning outcomes from the Early Literacy Research Project in other curriculum areas (Hill and Crèvola, 1999b).

Following an unexpected change in government in 1999, the new Victorian Minister for Education launched a statewide review of education, inviting discussion about future directions in public schools (Department of Education and Training, 2000b). Professor Allan Luke, a member of the New London Group that had developed multiliteracies theory, participated in the expert panel discussion on the role of public education (Department of Education Employment and Training, 2000a). The subsequent report made recommendations related to funding, accountability, curriculum, assessment and professional development.

Of interest to this research project were the recommendations made in the review for a further exploration of the way that applications of information and communications technologies could enhance the work of teachers and students; and for the development of partnerships with universities geared towards fostering research and developing pilot initiatives that would feed back into the system, enabling sharing of practice and giving primacy to the professionalism and expertise of practising educators (Department of Education Employment and Training, 2000a).

In the area of curriculum provision, the report affirmed the use of a statewide curriculum framework from Prep to Year 12, with local flexibility in curriculum delivery 'to ensure that all students attain agreed standards in literacy and numeracy and that all students have the skills needed, including skills in ICT, to progress successfully' (Department of Education Employment and Training, 2000a, p. 41). Acknowledging changed affordances of digitisation, the report argued:

> [i]f all young people are to benefit from powerful new tools and possibilities for learning, there is now a need for an imaginative, systemic initiative to widen the scale and increase the pace of innovation, exploring the potential of ICT to make possible new ways of thinking and of bringing creativity to bear on a range of increasingly complex problems (Department of Education Employment and Training, 2000a, p. 34).

Of further interest to the research project is the report's framing of teachers as active agents within the changing environment.

> Apart from enabling teachers to respond to the growth of knowledge generally and in their own areas of specialisation, it [ICT] has the potential to equip teachers to contribute to the creation of knowledge and innovation in the practice of their profession (Department of Education Employment and Training, 2000a, p. 44).

Despite these acknowledgements of the transformative changes and opportunities afforded by ICTs, key targets designed to measure the achievement of government educational priorities remained focused on engagement. Targets failed to reflect the changing digitised networked environment, or give an indication of a renewed approach to literacy education characterised by the development of creativity and innovation. The targets developed were that:

- Victorian primary school children will be at or above national benchmark levels for reading, writing and numeracy by 2005.
- 90 per cent of young people in Victoria will successfully complete Year 12 or its equivalent by 2010.
- The percentage of young people 15–19 in rural and regional Victoria engaged in education and training will rise by 6 per cent by 2005.
- The proportion of Victorians learning new skills will increase (Department of Premier and Cabinet, 2001, p. 8).

A further change of Minister for Education in 2002 resulted in another review of curriculum in schools, acknowledging that, internationally, curriculum provision models were being challenged by the need to be more relevant for twenty-first century learning (Kosky, 2003). While the results of this review were not released until the end of 2003 (Department of Education and Training, 2003b), which was after the data collection phase of this research project, the framing and constitution of literacy education in the early years of schooling (Years Prep–4) within emerging policy and program advice is nevertheless relevant to the discussion of the research data—for details see section 3.1.2.5: Victorian Essential Learning Standards.

3.1.2.4: The Emerging Influence of Multiliteracies Theory

The context of an imminent policy renewal to address the Victorian school sector's curriculum provision for students in the digitised knowledge era contributed to creating an exploratory mood in the central office. While the future direction of curriculum had not yet been articulated, there were indications elsewhere of how it might be influenced. School and curriculum reform initiatives being undertaken by Education Queensland (Education Queensland, 2000a, 2000b, 2002, 2003) gained the attention of the Victorian Department of Education. Of special interest to many literacy educators was the theory of multiliteracies, which was already threaded throughout the Queensland policy documents through the influence of the Queensland academic and senior bureaucrat, Professor Allan Luke, a member of the New London Group alongside, amongst others, Queensland academics Professor Mary Kalantzis, Dr Carmel Luke and Dr Bill Cope.

Under this influence Education Queensland had developed a new definition of literacy as:

> ... the flexible and sustainable mastery of a repertoire of practices with the texts of traditional and new communications technologies via spoken language, print, and multiliteracies (Education Queensland, 2000b, p. 9).

In April 2002, Professor Kalantzis, by then the Dean of the Faculty of Education, Language and Community Services at RMIT University in Victoria, was invited by the Department of Education's Western Metropolitan Region to give a presentation to teachers and project officers on multiliteracies. In September, 2002, Dr. Cope, by then Adjunct Professor at RMIT University, conducted a four-day course for teachers, 'Multiliteracies: Expanding Approaches to Teaching and Learning Literacy'.

The researcher attended the presentation, undertook the four-day course and subsequently developed a work-based report for the Early Years Branch in central office, outlining the multiliteracies theory, its development and rationale (Cloonan, 2002). The report also addressed the interface between the Early Years Literacy Program and multiliteracies theory, suggesting complementarities, divergences and opportunities for expanding notions of literacy and professional learning in the Victorian early years of schooling context. Noting that existing literacy policies did not address the meaning-making resources of modes other than the linguistic, the report suggested that a broadened view of literacy was called for.

> [A]s the New London Group argue, the multiplicity of communications channels and increasing cultural and linguistic diversity in the world today call for a broadened view of literacy (Cloonan, 2002, p. 8–9).

The report also contained recommendations for the deployment of existing resources and infrastructure in generating teacher professional dialogue around expanded notions of literacy and pedagogical consequences.

- Through Schools Television and existing training infrastructure, a statewide professional dialogue exploring multiliteracies as a framework for rethinking literacy teaching and learning will be stimulated.
- Action research into the literacy demands of the 21st century and approaches to support students to make and create meaning and become confident and effective communicators in a world influenced by new and evolving information and communication technologies needs to be considered (Cloonan, 2002, p. 9).

By then it had become evident to the researcher that a broadened view of literacy was required to inform policy and practices in Victorian schools—a view which accounted for the new affordances in multimodality and social dynamics presented by new digitised, networked environments. It had also become evident to the researcher that while some of the aspects of teacher professionalism argued for in the literature review were present in the professional learning design of the Victorian early years school-based, regional and statewide communities of learners, the train-the-trainer model fell short of the positioning of teachers as members of reflective, knowledge producing communities openly engaged in researching their practices and beliefs and sharing their findings with colleagues and the wider community.

The development of films incorporating a wider view of literacy would be a contribution to 'a statewide professional dialogue' (Cloonan, 2002, p. 9) introducing school-based teams and statewide regional training forums to expanded notions of literacy education. In addition, the filmic professional learning resources would present a participatory action research model of teacher professional learning. In a break with tradition, these films involved a series of staged explorations rather than a 'one off' showcasing of classroom practice. Also breaking with tradition within the broader policy and programming context was the idea of inviting collaboration between theorists and teachers. In a context where professional teacher learning was seen as 'training' through a diffusion-adoption model (McDonald, 1988), the films would position the teachers as agentive learners and researchers, exploring their struggles in engaging with and enacting theory in their particular contexts.

When the recommendations were given approval, funding was gained for the development of a series of four films exploring multiliteracies in the early years (Department of Education and Training, 2003c). The research dimension of the project required a very different positioning of teachers within the filming project, making them participatory action researchers into classroom applications of multiliteracies theory.

3.1.2.5: Victorian Essential Learning Standards: A Victorian Literacy Policy Addendum

Released following the data collection period of this research project, the *Victorian Essential Learning Standards* (Victorian Curriculum and Assessment Authority, 2004a, 2004b, 2005b) structures curriculum around a triple helix of intertwining strands, *physical, personal and social learning* (including domains of health and physical education, interpersonal development, personal learning and civics and citizenship); *discipline-based learning* (including the domains of the arts, English, the humanities, languages other than English, mathematics and science); and *interdisciplinary learning* (including domains of communication, design, creativity and technology, information, communications technology and thinking processes).

Standards are set at six levels and the expected knowledge and skills of students are described for each level, with the following relationships—in Year Prep: level 1 standards to be achieved; in Years 1 and 2: level 2 standards to be achieved; and in Years 3 and 4: level 3 standards to be achieved (Victorian Curriculum and Assessment Authority, 2005a). The focus of schooling in the early years, that is Years Prep to 4, is on 'laying the foundations', with a particular focus in Levels 1 and 2 on developing that foundational knowledge which, it is suggested, is required for students to be successful learners at school. Students are assessed against standards in the English domains of reading, writing, speaking and listening; mathematics; the arts domain of creating and making; interpersonal development (with an emphasis on socialisation); health and physical education domain of movement and physical activity).

Table 3.1: Example of the Standards Set for English Level 1

Reading	Writing	Speaking and listening
At Level 1, students match print and spoken text in their immediate environment. They recognise how sounds are represented alphabetically and identify some sound–letter relationships. They read aloud simple print and electronic texts that include some frequently used words and predominantly oral language structures. They read from left to right with return sweep, and from top to bottom. They use title, illustrations and knowledge of a text topic to predict meaning. They use context and information about words, letters, combinations of letters and the sounds associated with them to make meaning, and use illustrations to extend meaning.	At Level 1, students write personal recounts and simple texts about familiar topics to convey ideas or messages. In their writing, they use conventional letters, groups of letters, and simple punctuation such as full stops and capital letters. Students are aware of the sound system and the relationships between letters and sounds in words when spelling. They form letters correctly, and use a range of writing implements and software.	At Level 1, students use spoken language appropriately in a variety of classroom contexts. They ask and answer simple questions for information and clarification, contribute relevant ideas during class or group discussion, and follow simple instructions. They listen to and produce brief spoken texts that deal with familiar ideas and information. They sequence main events and ideas coherently in speech, and speak at an appropriate volume and pace for listeners' needs. They self-correct by rephrasing a statement or question when meaning is not clear.

An example of the standards, in this case for the art domain, for level 1 reads:

> At Level 1, students make and share performing and visual arts works that communicate observations, personal ideas, feelings and experiences. They explore and, with guidance, use a variety of arts elements (on their own or in combination), skills, techniques and processes, media, materials, equipment and technologies in a range of arts forms. They talk about aspects of their own arts works, and arts works and events in their community.

At Level 2, students are expected to achieve standards for ICT. This relates to the manipulation of:

> ...text, images and numeric data to create simple information products for specific audiences. [Students] ...make simple changes to improve the appearance of their information products. They retrieve files and save new files using a naming system that is meaningful to them. They compose simple electronic messages to known recipients and send them successfully. With some assistance, students use ICT to locate and retrieve relevant information from a variety of sources (Victorian Curriculum and Assessment Authority, 2005a).

Students at Level 3 are said to 'begin to respond to information, ideas and beliefs from contexts beyond their immediate experience'. Students are expected to achieve standards in addition to those already mentioned: standards in civics and citizenship, design, creativity and technology, the Humanities, personal learning, science, and thinking processes (Victorian Curriculum and Assessment Authority, 2005b, p. 4). In relation to those domains in which students are not required to achieve standards at levels 1, 2 and 3, it is suggested that these are 'nevertheless important areas of learning for children' (Victorian Curriculum and Assessment Authority, 2005b, p. 4).

At the time of this research, but prior to the development of the *Victorian Essential Learning Standards*, existing policies were acknowledged as outdated and inadequate given the changed communications environment, theoretical responses, and changing teaching practices (Department of Education Employment and Training, 2000a). Although present policy advice has moved to close the perceived gaps to better equip students for a rapidly changing communications environment (Victorian Curriculum and Assessment Authority, 2005d), the inter-relatedness of learning around multimodal forms of representation is exemplified in the triple helix. A broad range of texts is now suggested for study in English, including 'literary, everyday, media or workplace based texts' (Victorian Curriculum and Assessment Authority, 2005b. p. 88–9). An emphasis on students achieving standards deemed as essential from Prep onwards includes not only reading and writing, speaking and listening, but also the creating and making domain within the arts. Despite this, literacies continue to refer only to language aspects of subjects with students' literacy learning involving making choices about appropriate language for effective presentation of ideas and information for different purposes and audiences (Victorian Curriculum and Assessment Authority, 2005b, p. 82). This is similar to the situation in the United States where students' ability to read and use information on the internet is not measured (Leu et al., 2002).

Of particular interest to this research project is the use of the term 'metalanguage' which is deployed solely in relation to a language with which to talk about language: 'a language used to discuss language conventions and use, for example, the terms and definitions used in the various grammars to describe the functions of words in sentences and the terms used to describe and categorise structural features of different kinds of texts' (Victorian Curriculum and Assessment Authority, 2005b, p. 84).

The terms 'mode' and 'multimodal' are also used, the former to refer to processes such as reading and writing; and the latter to refer to designs, as indicated in the following quote.

> In English, the modes of language are reading (including viewing), writing (including composing electronic texts), speaking and listening. Multimodal texts are those that combine, for example, print text, visual images and spoken word as in film or computer presentation media (Victorian Curriculum and Assessment Authority, 2005b, p. 84).

This definition differs from that of the New London Group, who use the term 'mode' to describe linguistic, visual, audio, gestural and spatial modes of meaning and the term 'multimodal' to describe combinations of the other modes (New London Group, 1996, 2000). Clearly the advice acknowledges the impact of the changed technologies on textual forms and the importance of teachers and students engaging with these texts of various forms, but the highly articulated essential standards in the areas of reading and writing are accompanied by standards relating to students' functional use of ICT rather than digital meaning-making. Standards which describe general meaning-making around the gestural, audio (music) and the visual are all situated in the arts. Students are to be assessed in their use of 'arts language' in relation to:

> 'symbol systems' developing skills in speaking about arts in terms of content and use of technique, process, elements, principles and/or conventions, media, materials, equipment and technologies' (Victorian Curriculum and Assessment Authority, 2005b, p. 84).

The advice thus leaves modes other than the linguistic isolated in areas outside of language, thus suggesting different languages, acknowledged in different parts of the curriculum documents, for talking about differing aspects of text. The domains which could offer further insight here—communication, design, creativity and technology—are not accompanied by standards. In this way, despite efforts towards curriculum renewal, the fine articulation of learning and assessment of linguistic meaning-making systems within the context of literacy policy and practice is yet to be matched by adequate articulation of learning and assessment in other meaning-making systems prevalent in the digitised communications environment.

> [T]he pervasive power of an assessment that only measures traditional print literacies profoundly determines what is taught during reading instruction, especially within schools that are under the greatest pressure to raise test scores (Coiro et al., 2007, p. 30).

With language still deemed as essential to assessment, it will inevitably attract teaching emphases, leading to the neglect of visual, audio, gestural, spatial and multimodal meaning-making modes. Clearly, while the policy advice shows a partial movement towards acknowledging and incorporating the affordances of the multimodality and changes in social dynamics, the meaning-making potentials of modes other than language have not been adequately addressed as literacy concerns and literacy policy and required assessment remains largely linguistic-based.

3.2: The Evolution of a Research Project

3.2.1: Transition from Policy and Project Officer to Participatory Researcher

The curriculum review in Victorian state education in 2003 created a context for policy directions which acknowledged the changing social and communicative context and, as an Early Years literacy Policy and Project Officer, the researcher's work was to contribute to literacy education policy and program development within this transitional context. Having secured funding for a series of films in which viewers were promised on a poster that they could 'see the theory in practice demonstrated by Victorian teachers' (Department of Education and Training, 2003c), a mechanism for developing teacher capacities for implementation of multiliteracies-influenced classroom practice was sought by the researcher.

As previously explained, habitual filming practices in the researcher's workplace did not require implementation of teacher professional learning. Habitual practices focused on showcasing known theoretical and practical 'talent' who were filmed independently and footage edited to make a coherent program. However, as the film series *Multiliteracies in the Early Years* was to be a staged exploration rather than a 'one off' showcasing of existing policy theory and implementation, an approach involving professional learning was required.

The workplace innovations suggested by the researcher required exploratory approaches to resource filming and professional learning, breaking from habitual practices in developing film resources and the diffusion-adoption (McDonald, 1988) models of training. The mechanism suggested by the researcher for this undertaking was participatory action research (Carr and Kemmis, 1986; Kemmis and McTaggart, 2005), prompting a research project which evolved, on the researcher's enrolment at RMIT University, to a Doctoral study which sought insights into the generation of a multimodal metalanguage, nested within teachers' pedagogical choices and teacher learning.

3.2.2: Emergence of a Research Project

In this way the research which became the subject of this book, the production of the series of films for use in multiliteracies professional learning, grew directly out of the researcher's work as a literacy policy and project officer. By actively engaging teachers as participants, the series of films opened up questions about the form of professional learning best able to develop teacher capabilities to operationalise multiliteracies theory and articulate their practice through a teacher-generated multimodal metalanguage. The research context that resulted was a work-based professional learning project involving a small group of early years teachers and their classroom applications of multiliteracies theory and the research design was specifically developed to identify a teacher-generated multimodal metalanguage enabled by the deployment of a 'multimodal schema' (New London Group, 2000), a 'dimensions of meaning schema' (Cope and Kalantzis, 2000a) and a 'pedagogical knowledge processes schema' (Kalantzis and Cope, 2004; Kalantzis et al., 2005).

Classroom enactments and teacher descriptions of practice filmed and shared with the Victorian early years professional community through narrowcast satellite and teacher learning networks were the focus of the researcher's workplace requirements. Added to this the teacher professional learning project, prompted by the planning of a series of films focused on teacher operationalising of multiliteracies theory, presented a unique opportunity to learn (Stake, 2005) about professional learning, about renewed literacy pedagogy, and about the emergent and under-theorised area of teacher-generated multimodal metalanguage.

This question of identifying effective features of professional learning for the teachers who participated in the films, therefore, presented an opportunity for case study research, a methodology which allows an intense scrutiny in order to shed light on networks of implications (Campbell, 2003). The case study aimed to shed light on the networks of implications of teacher participation in a set of professional learning interventions and impact of involvement on practitioner literacy knowledge, skills and sensibilities with a particular interest in deployment of multimodal metalanguage. The researcher sought to understand the complex social phenomena presented by this situation and observe the practitioners' responses to theoretical schemas. Case study research offered opportunities for investigation which retained the holistic and meaningful characteristics of these real-life events (Yin, 2003).

Analysis of practitioner learning, enactments, reflections and documentation over the life of the work-based professional learning project presented an unprecedented opportunity to learn about teacher-generated multimodal metalanguage in the Victorian early years context, making the case revelatory (Yin, 2003). Enactments in early years contexts were without precedent, bar one briefly documented example from Bamaga, Queensland (Kalantzis and Cope, 2004; Kalantzis et al., 2005) and one developed by the researcher in the year prior to this research project (Cloonan, 2005; Kalantzis and Cope, 2004). A desire for a richly contextualised 'thick description' (Geertz, 1973; Stake, 2005) contributed to the design of an exploratory case study (Yin, 2003) with an interest in four practitioners' engagement with multiliteracies-influenced schemas through designed professional learning interventions. Exploratory case study is appropriate since the object of the research project, professional learning which led to teacher-generated multimodal metalanguage through deployment of a 'multimodal schema' and a 'pedagogical knowledge processes schema', is 'a contemporary phenomenon, within its real-life context... [and] 'the boundaries between the phenomenon and context are not clearly evident' (Yin, 2003, p. 13).

Specifically, the 'contemporary phenomenon' involved the engagement of four teachers from two Victorian primary schools in interventions designed to enhance their professional learning through the deployment of multiliteracies schemas in order to expand their multimodal teaching and collect evidence of a teacher-generated multimodal metalanguage.

3.3: The Research Design

The research project took the form of an exploratory, group, multiple-case study with revelatory purposes (Miles and Huberman, 1994; Yin, 2003). Within the broader context of the case, the units of analysis are teacher learning and teacher-generated multimodal metalanguage. Due to the deep embedding of teacher language within pedagogical contexts involving designs of meaning, as well as contextualisation within broader curriculum goals, this case is approached as 'a phenomenon...occurring in a bounded context' (Miles and Huberman, 1994, p. 25).

This case study was 'bounded' by the number of participants with their contextualisation within the Victorian government school sector; their involvement in a particular series of professional learning interventions; professional learning and classroom enactments in response to multiliteracies schemas; and a specific data collection period. In countering possible weaknesses in case study research design, the conditions which relate to research quality—construct validity, external validity and reliability—have been maximized (Miles and Huberman, 1994; Yin, 2003). Construct validity has been addressed through the incorporation of multiple sources of evidence, the establishment of a chain of evidence and the involvement of key informants in the review of the data and report.

A case study protocol and database were developed to maximise reliability. However, the emergent nature of the research project led to numerous revisions of the protocol and database, with the final version depicting research questions; names of sites to be visited; data collection plan; data categories and codes (reproduced below); chain of evidence linking research questions asked to the data collected displayed and discussed; data accounting sheet; and displays. Semi-structured interview questions attended to the analytical categories and were emergent in nature as well as strongly contextualised in teachers' classroom issues and practices.

THE RESEARCH DESIGN

Data categories and codes

Teachers	Rachel	TA
	Kim and Meredith	TBC
	Pip	TD
Date	day/month	e.g. 1302
Modes of meaning	Linguistic	L
	Visual	V
	Audio	A
	Gestural	G
	Spatial	Sp
	Multimodal	MM
Learning by Design knowledge processes	Experiencing (E) the known	EK
	Experiencing the new	EN
	Conceptualising (C) by naming	CN
	Conceptualising by theorising	CT
	Analysing (An) functionality	AF
	Analysing critically	AnC
	Applying (A) appropriately	AA
	Applying creatively	AC
Dimensions of Meaning	Representational	R/♀ BLUE
	Social	S/☺ GREEN
	Organisational	O/☼ PURPLE
	Contextual	C/ BROWN
	Ideological	I/♦PINK
Data Sources		
1	Teacher Interview transcripts (semi-structured audio)	TI
2	Artefacts of Staged Filmed Teacher Interviews	SFTI
3	Artefacts of Staged Filmed Classroom Applications	SFC
4	Learning Element: reflective planning for classroom application	LE
5	Researcher reflective journal	RJ

The complexity of designing and undertaking a research project investigating a work-based professional learning project that broke with the tradition existing within the context of the educational bureaucracy in Victoria is acknowledged. The research design process was reflective of the view

57

that 'methods are always more or less unruly assemblages' (Law, 2003, p. 11), as was the context in which the research was designed and conducted. The situation called for a method which acknowledged and dealt with the politics and inherent mess of these complexities; and that acknowledged the role of method in not only describing realities but also in creating them (Law, 2004).

3.3.1: Participatory Research and the Researcher's Role

Grounded in this way, this research project sought to investigate two questions:

1. How was the professional learning of teachers enhanced through interventions designed to operationalise multiliteracies theory?
2. What elements of a metalanguage can be gleaned to inform emergent theories of multimodal meaning?

The research design needed to account for its co-dependent relationship with a work-based teacher professional learning project which engaged teachers with schemas emanating from multiliteracies theory. Characteristics of effective professional learning were considered when designing the work-based teacher professional learning project and teachers were engaged as participatory action researchers. The twin aims of participatory action research were accounted for: as a method investigating reality in order to change it (Fals Borda, 1979) and of changing reality in order to investigate it (Kemmis and McTaggart, 2005).

The Victorian early years literacy education context in which this research project was conducted has been described in the previous section of this chapter. The Victorian devolution of aspects of financial, administrative and curriculum design decisions to government schools and regions is indicative of broader shifts across Australian states (Blackmore, 1993) and has occurred in combination with increased governmental emphasis on standards and accountability (Luke et al., 1999). Together these shifts have contributed to teacher professional learning experiences, emphasising 'risk management and managerialism' (Combe, et al., 2004, p. 82–3). The model of the early years literacy 'train-the-trainer' program described in the earlier section shows some aspects of a diffusion–adoption model (McDonald, 1988), reflecting the historical positioning of teachers as technicians, or policy implementers in hierarchical relationships with policy makers, researchers and principals (Carr and Kemmis, 1986; Cochran-Smith and Lytle, 1993).

Teacher learning practices such as 'train-the-trainer' models exemplify modernist structures and relationships, critiqued as having a positivist orientation, which position teachers as research subjects rather than as participants in effecting change (Carr and Kemmis, 1986). Such critique has led to a re-emergence of action research as an influential research approach (Greenwood and Levin 2000, 2001). However, some contemporary applications of participatory action research have been criticised by supporters of the methodology due to its realisation as change management (Grundy,

2006); and much contemporary action research deployed by the school improvement movement has technical rather than emancipatory aims in relation to teacher performance (Kemmis, 2005).

Avoidance of positioning teachers as implementers or technicians of this project, thereby reducing the aspirations of both the research project and the work-based professional learning project, required consideration of questions beyond those related to methodology or 'questions about how we know the world or gain knowledge of it' (Denzin and Lincoln, 2000, p. 19). Issues of 'ontology (questions about the nature of reality), and epistemology (questions about the relationship between the inquirer and the known)' (Denzin and Lincoln, 2000, p. 19) needed to be transparently addressed, particularly given the risks of action research masquerading as a research model which positions teachers as more than technicians and research subjects (Grundy, 2006; Kemmis and McTaggart, 2005).

The professional learning interventions and data collection procedures deployed in this research project positioned teachers as participatory and critical; were recursive—involving practical, collaborative and reflexive dialogue; and aimed to transform both theory and practice (Kemmis and McTaggart, 2005; Carr and Kemmis, 1986). Critical participatory action research is an appropriate methodology in this instance since 'action research as an expression of a critical approach can, in its turn, inform and develop a critical theory of education' (Carr and Kemmis, 1986, p. 45). The research design involved a small purpose-driven educational community of learners (Wenger, 1999) expanding practices through a spiral of recursive cycles of critical planning, acting, observing and reflecting (Kemmis and McTaggart, 2005; Carr and Kemmis, 1986).

In this research project, teachers were positioned as knowledge generators through engagement with multiliteracies schemas with the view to practical application, reflection and collegiate sharing. Participation was framed by interventions featuring:

>...a lack of hierarchy in mentoring relationships; an emphasis on knowledge production rather than knowledge transmission; the importance of working within the teachers' specific local contexts in order to produce change... grappling with theoretical work... having agency to read these critically and imaginatively (Comber et al., 2004, p. 86)

In this research project, deployment of participatory action research methodology was exploratory, seeking insights into the generation of a multimodal metalanguage, nested within teachers' pedagogical choices and teacher learning.

Resonating with the pedagogical affordances of the communications environment, this research project sought to explore professional learning opportunities for teachers, 'to create as well as consume professional knowledge through self-directed inquiry and research into their own practice' (Grisham, 2000) and avoid a 'devolution drain' experienced by teachers as a result of change management approaches to professional learning (Comber et al., 2004).

Egalitarian outcomes and application of democratic principles present strong reasons for adopting changes in traditional hierarchical flows of knowledge in teacher professional learning and research contexts. However others reasons prevail as well. There is emerging agreement that in an environment where teachers are faced daily with teaching 'digital natives' or insiders, students with lifeworld experiences in the digitised, networked environment are in the strongest position to inform and articulate challenges in teaching digitised learners. In an environment of rapidly changing textual and social practices:

> ...teachers themselves, exploring in their own classrooms hunches and intuitions about the implications for their teaching can provide the strongest lead as to how the future research agenda should be formulated (Unsworth, 2006b, p. 156) after Locke and Andrews (2004) and Leu (2000).

In a context where educational policy responses have been seen to capitalise inadequately on the affordances of changed communications environment, policy makers are seen collectively as:

> ...beginning to understand a bit of the challenge; they are not yet on their way to understanding the solutions. Ironically, most public policy responses to the Internet have typically been framed in terms of older, more traditional notions of print literacy, not from within an understanding of the Internet itself. This may be due to the fact that policy makers are sometimes the last ones to 'get' the Internet or to engage systematically and intensively in its use. One obvious case involves public policies related to literacy education (Coiro et al., 2007, p. 29–30).

This research project seeks to avoid generalisations such as those that set up simple dichotomies of students as digital insiders and teachers as outsiders reticent to adopt technological practices. Rather it seeks to be mindful of trends and inattentions.

In a context of literacy education renewal characterised by emergent theoretical understandings and practice-based responses, collaborative effort to inform the work of teachers, theorists and the two projects of the researcher (as a researcher and as policy and program officer) through a reflective spiral of recursive cycles (Carr and Kemmis, 1986) was deployed. The spiral of cycles involved planning, acting, observing and reflecting (Carr and Kemmis, 1986). The relationship between recursive aspects of the action research cycles and professional learning interventions informed by multiliteracies theory is shown in the following figure.

THE RESEARCH DESIGN

Table 3.2: Action Research Cycle and Professional Learning Interventions

Stages in participatory action research cycle (Carr and Kemmis, 1986)	Professional learning interventions
Planning	Expert input Project-focused workshopping through distributed collegiate mentoring Reflective action planning for classroom applications
Acting	Staged filming of classroom applications Staged filming of teacher interviews including descriptive reflection on classroom applications and professional knowledge
Observing	Collaborative viewing of film artefacts (classroom applications; teacher descriptive reflection on classroom applications)
Reflecting	Collaborative reflection on observed film artefacts

The research project draws on multiple data sources collected as a result of the teacher practitioners' participation in the work-based professional learning project. Eight professional learning interventions were deployed recursively, in differing combinations to support both teacher professional learning and collection of data. These interventions are described below.

1. Expert input during which academic theorists presented multiliteracies theory for collaboration with teachers (Labbo, 2000). This engagement with theory sought to develop 'pedagogical content knowledge' (Shulman, 1987) which involves 'rich and profound understanding of the subject matter one is teaching' (Shulman, 2005, p. 20). Positioning teachers and others with expertise required consideration of whether there is 'an expert telling you what to do' or alternatively 'enough direction to enable me to find my way...without being prescriptive' (Comber et al., 2004, p. 82–3). Theoretical input was directed to teacher development as, 'a scholar, an intellectual, and a knowledge worker oriented toward the interpretation, communication, and construction of such knowledge in the interests of student learning' (Shulman, 1999, p. xiii). The project officer/researcher's awareness that 'teachers may see research as unresponsive to the realities of the classroom or as couched in "user-unfriendly" terms that are difficult to apply to practice' (Grisham, 2000), led to theory being presented, where appropriate, in the form of schemas or frameworks which had immediate application to classroom contexts.

2. Project-focused workshopping through distributed collegiate mentoring involved the teachers, theorists and the policy and project officer/researcher as a community of learners (Wenger, 1999) engaging in '[f]eed-

back, debriefs, [and] professional conversations' (Comber et al., 2004, p. 85), promoting accountability to the team for the quality of teaching (McLaughlin and Talbert, 1993), and enabling problem-solving of curriculum, organisation and learner-related issues. These clarifying workshopping opportunities positioned teachers as researchers of their own practice (Darling-Hammond and Sykes, 1999), considering the theoretical input in relation to specific classroom contextual concerns. It also juxtaposed the theoretical input with 'pedagogical learner knowledge' (Grimmet and MacKinnon, 1992), as teachers considered theoretical offerings in connection with the backgrounds, needs, styles and capacities of diverse learners (Darling-Hammond, 1998).

3. Reflective action planning for classroom applications also sought to foreground teacher's contexts for operationalising multiliteracies theory, acknowledging 'the importance of working within the teachers' specific local contexts in order to produce change' (Comber et al., 2004, p. 86) and involving group problem-solving. Foregrounding classroom applications, teachers planned for enactments which synthesised pedagogical subject knowledge of multiliteracies and pedagogical learner knowledge. As the project developed, the Learning by Design template (Kalantzis and Cope, 2004; Kalantzis et al. 2005) was deployed as both a planning and publishing tool, allowing the writing of classroom practice for public sharing, incorporating principles of teacher as knowledge producer or generator (Cochran-Smith and Lytle, 1999). This allowed the desired transparency of pedagogical practices (Elmore, 2002; Luke, 2003a), opening these practices to scrutiny by placement of planning documentation in the public realm (Kemmis, 2000; Kemmis and McTaggart, 2005).

4. Staged filming of classroom applications for public sharing also incorporated principles of teachers as knowledge producers or generators (Cochran-Smith and Lytle, 1999), transparency of pedagogical practices (Elmore, 2002; Luke, 2003a); opening practices to scrutiny (Elmore, 2002) by placement of filmed artefacts of classroom applications in the public realm (Kemmis, 2000; Kemmis and McTaggart, 2005). Rather than written representations of teachers' work, filming broadened understanding of transparency and sharing (Elmore, 2002) to include filmed segments of teachers' actual practice, an example of educational reform which takes into account 'teachers as embodied subjects with personal histories and dynamic professional identities' (Comber et al., 2004, p. 3).

5. Staged filming of teacher interviews including descriptive reflection on classroom applications and professional knowledge similarly positioned teachers as professional spokespeople and experts, commenting on their classroom practice for the film audience. Agentive positioning of teachers shifted their role from an historically hierarchical positioning with knowledge and research to that of 'researchers, theorizers, activists, and school leaders who generate knowledge for the profession and they also

THE RESEARCH DESIGN

become critical users of research' (Southwest Educational Development Laboratory, 2002, p. 1). This intervention sought to extend teachers' influence beyond student learning to school culture and the broader community (Crowther et al., 2002), creating a public discursive space for teacher description and reflection of their classroom operationalising of the multiliteracies-influenced 'multimodal schema' and 'pedagogical knowledge processes schema'.

6. Collaborative viewing of film artefacts (classroom applications; teacher descriptive reflection on classroom applications) positioned teachers as researchers of their own practice (Darling-Hammond and Sykes, 1999), participating in observation and analysis of a shared bank of data of their classroom practice, the product of a knowledge producing community (Kalantzis et al., 2005). Collaborative viewing and reflection on film artefacts provided a stimulus for the learning community's reflective comment and examination of data, which in turn prompted further planning for implementation through recursive cycles.

7. Collaborative reflection on observed film artefacts during which the community of learners would view and provide feedback on the 'fine cut' of each film, engaged teachers in ongoing reflective examination of their practice. The film artefacts provided a reference point for collaborative viewing, debriefing and ongoing planning, acting and reflection involving a retrospective exploration of events, practices and thought patterns (Schön, 1983). Double loop learning (Argyris and Schön, 1978) undertaken as collaborative reflection within the staged filming process assisted differentiation of unexamined and examined practices, positioning teachers as inquirers into their own practices through examination of personally generated data (Carr and Kemmis, 1986).

8. Collaborative reflection on data and findings during which the teachers engaged with sources data, provided feedback on film artefacts (classroom applications and teacher descriptive reflection on classroom applications), 'Learning Elements' and progressive drafts of tentative findings. Beginning early in the work-based professional learning project, this continued through data collection and analysis. The sharing of data and findings contributed to professional learning and the trustworthiness and authenticity of interpretations of events (Stake, 1995) through this process of 'member checks' (Guba, 1981).

3.3.2: Deployment of Research Interventions

In this section I discuss the production of data through the interventions designed to engage teachers with multiliteracies theory and to enable the application of multiliteracies-influenced practices; and the additional data that was collected through procedures undertaken to further illuminate teacher growth through professional learning and teacher deployment of 'multimodal schema' and 'pedagogical knowledge processes schema'.

In designing interventions to support teacher professional learning and contribute to data collection, the research design was mindful of the limitations and criticisms levelled at participatory action research. Potential limitations include the reduction of the approach to a method concentrating on the use of the action research, self-reflective spiral without consideration of the underpinning epistemological and ontological assumptions (Kemmis and McTaggart, 2005).

To address the potential limitations of participatory action research, design of this research project has given consideration to the positioning of teachers in terms of the knowledge-constituted interests served (Carr and Kemmis, 1986; Kemmis and McTaggart, 2000).

> Different types of research serve different types of knowledge-constitutive interests (the reasons that frame and justify the search for knowledge through research), and they are based in different kinds of reasoning, sometimes described as 'instrumental' or 'technical' reason, 'practical' reason, and 'critical' or 'emancipatory' reason (Kemmis and McTaggart, 2005.

Technical, practical and critical/emancipatory knowledge-constitutive interests represent 'third-person, second-person and first-person standpoints on the social relationships of the setting [which] manifest themselves in quite different attitudes toward the process of change' (Southwest Educational Development Laboratory, 2002).

This research project has aligned the knowledge-constitutive interests with assumptions of knowledge flow and production influencing teacher professional learning endeavours, knowledge-for-practice, knowledge-in-practice and knowledge-of-practice (Cochran-Smith and Lytle, 1999). The interconnection of these views of research and professional learning are represented in the following figure.

Table 3.3: Alignment of Research Interests and Assumptions Underpinning Professional Learning

	Kemmis and McTaggart (2005)	Cochran-Smith and Lytle(1999)
Instrumental/ technical	Third person: the system-focused, disembodied, abstract 'they'	Knowledge for
Practical	Second person: the wise, prudent 'you'	Knowledge in
Critical Emancipatory	First person plural: collaborative, reflective, action of 'we'	Knowledge of

Technical research positioning and diffusion-adoption models of teacher learning are at odds with agentive teacher roles which encompass 'a scholar, an intellectual, and a knowledge worker oriented toward the interpretation, communication, and construction of such knowledge in the interests of student learning' (Shulman, 1999, p. xiii). In line with broader changes in social dynamics, the researcher wished to avoid a design characterised by a diffusion-adoption model (McDonald, 1988), which can result in alienation, exhaustion or cynicism (Darling-Hammond, 2003).

Such assumptions would be made explicit through analysis of interventions in terms of their impact on knowledge flow and production in the teacher professional learning project, knowledge-for-practice, knowledge-in-practice and knowledge-of-practice (Cochran-Smith and Lytle, 1999); and the knowledge-constitutive interests of the research, as having 'instrumental' or 'technical' reason; 'practical' reason; or 'critical' or 'emancipatory' reason (Kemmis and McTaggart, 2005, p. 582).

The design of this research project sought to develop and analyse the development of all three relationships with knowledge but ultimately to position teachers as generators of knowledge–of-practice by 'making their classrooms and schools sites for inquiry, connecting their work in schools to larger issues, and taking a critical perspective on the theory and research of others' (Cochran-Smith and Lytle, 1999, p. 273).

This research project sought to include critical-emancipatory reasoning, which 'manifests itself in attitudes of collaborative reflection, theorizing, and political action' (Kemmis and McTaggart, 2005, p. 585). By positioning teachers as professional spokespeople, as collaborative researchers and contributors to theory, the research questions were to be addressed 'with teachers, rather than on or about teachers' in the belief that 'moving forward on education's major challenges cannot be done for teachers, in spite of teachers or around teachers' (Comber et al., 2004, p. 3).

Nested within the purposes of the research design and the work-based professional learning project, the interventions and research data collection techniques provided a way to promote and track teacher engagement with multiliteracies theory through classroom applications of the 'multimodal schema' and 'pedagogical knowledge processes schema'. The interventions were underpinned by principles which acknowledged the influence of multimodal and social dynamics-related affordances which led to calls for renewal of literacy education, and posing of the research questions. These affordances also required renewed ways of working with teachers in professional learning and research contexts. The approaches to working with the teachers in this research project are discussed in the following sections.

3.3.3: Participant Selection

The sample for the case study consisted of four teachers of students in Years Prep–4, aged approximately 5–10 years of age. They came from three classrooms, as two of the teachers team taught, and were all from two Victorian government primary schools. Teachers with certain attributes had been sought for dual participation in both this work-based professional learning project and the research project, with a number of sampling strategies being deployed, including a type of stratified purposive sampling (Miles and Huberman, 1994). Since there was an expectation that the practitioners would facilitate the expansion of theory, and act as professional spokespeople during filming, the invitation to participate in the research project reflected criterion-based selection (Kuzel, 1992; Miles and Huberman, 1994; Patton, 1990) with selection mindful of:

- balance and variety in that the four teachers invited and selected had between them taught students in the five early years of schooling (Prep–Year 4);
- purposeful selection from schools with student populations characterised by low socio-economic disadvantage;
- strong professional reputations as teachers, preferably with responsibility for regional or school-based training responsibilities;
- sound knowledge of the Early Years Literacy Program;
- teachers' acknowledged predisposition to participate in curriculum initiatives;
- self-assurance to be authentic learners in terms of reflecting on their developing beliefs and understandings and the ability to engage in complexity and paradoxical contradictions and to expose their vulnerabilities as learners;
- voluntary participation in exploring curriculum renewal with few supportive materials; teachers needed accept that they were 'ahead' of the documented curriculum;
- apparent access as evidenced through their flexibility and accommodation of suggested interviewing schedules and school and classroom visits;
- supportive leadership as shown by forthcoming support of the principals and school councils.

Following consultation with regional and central Early Years project officers, Rachel, Kim and Meredith from Westpark Primary School in inner-urban Melbourne; and Pip from Rosegardens Primary School in a small town in regional Victoria agreed to participate in the work-based professional learning project and the research project. Both schools had a high proportion of students from low socio-economic backgrounds. The teachers collectively had teaching responsibilities for students in Years Prep to 4 (aged approximately 5–10 years). Agreement was also gained from Professor Mary Kalantzis and Dr Bill Cope, two theorists from the New London Group, to collaborate in the project, sharing expertise in professional learning situations and in filmed interviews.

Financial support was gained for each of the four teachers from the Department of Education, Victoria to cover teacher replacement in acknowledgement of the time demanded of the teachers by project participation. Travel and accommodation costs were also provided for Pip to travel from regional Victoria to the capital city, Melbourne.

The sample of four teachers, to be described in Chapter Four, participated in both the work-based professional learning project and the research project.

3.3.4: Ethical Procedures

Consent was sought to authorise participation in the production of School Televisions video and television programs from Rachel, Kim, Meredith and Pip; from the parents of the students in their classes; from the principals and the school councils of Rosegardens Primary School and Westpark

Primary School; from the respective Department of Education regional offices with which the two schools were affiliated as well as the Department of Education central office and the university.

Ethical principles included ensuring that Rachel, Kim, Meredith, Pip:

- received a plain language statement;
- were informed of withdrawal options;
- were informed of the availability of the researcher and the researcher's supervisor regarding clarification of potential issues of concern;
- were informed that all data could be checked by participating teachers for accuracy and that any data that potentially disadvantaged or made vulnerable the participant would be discarded.

To avoid undue pressure to participate, intermediaries approached the teachers. Before all interventions, participants were reminded of their right to refuse to answer any question and that they could interrupt, seek clarification or cease participation at any stage.

Parents of the students in their classes also received a Plain Language Statement and consent forms and were alerted that, although the focus of the research project was teacher learning, transcripts of classroom interaction between teachers and students were of interest to the project.

These measures sufficiently addressed issues of informed consent, voluntary participation, withdrawal options, vulnerability, confidentiality, and anonymity (Burns, 2000).

3.3.5: Data Collection Methods

Procedures were established for use in interactions with case study teachers to ensure that processes for data collection were as consistent as possible. Data collection was achieved via methods which are expanded below:

3.3.5.1: Interviews

Semi-structured interviews, filmed and audio-taped, were conducted between the researcher and individual teachers (Burns, 2000; Taylor and Bogdan, 1998). Filmed interviews were conducted three or four times with each of the case study teachers and occurred in the teachers' classrooms. These interviews focused on the teachers' staged implementation of the 'multimodal schema' and 'pedagogical knowledge processes schema' and included general reflections on developing teacher understandings of multiliteracies theory; outlines of classroom applications at strategic points within the participatory action research cycle; and descriptions of student responses to these implementations. The interview questions were structured around the analytical categories; however, they were emergent in nature and strongly contextualised in teachers' classroom issues and practices. The limitations of filming, including the potential for self-consciousness by participants and their subsequent altered behaviour (Taylor and Bogdan, 1998), were countered by assuring participants prior to filming that they could stop at any time and that any film material they did not want utilised would be discarded. A conversational approach was used to enhance natural responses (Minichiello et al., 1995) and a semi-structured interview technique added to the conversational quality (Taylor and Bogdan, 1998).

Semi-structured audio-taped interviews were also conducted with each of the teachers to gain information relating to their professional backgrounds; interests and strengths; school community and teaching contexts and roles; approaches to literacy teaching and learning; knowledge of multiliteracies; motivations for joining the work-based professional learning and research projects; and reflections on developing understandings. Awareness that alterations in interviewee behaviour can result from the use of audio recording devices (Taylor and Bogdan, 1984) was, therefore, counterbalanced by the use of specific techniques deployed during filmed interviews.

3.3.5.2: Participant Observations

Film footage of the teachers' deployment of the 'multimodal schema' and 'pedagogical knowledge processes schema' was gathered. Staged classroom filming was utilised at strategic points in the participatory action research cycle to gain evidence of classroom enactment of theory, with each classroom filmed on three or four occasions over one or two days. Filmed footage enables detailed descriptions since it preserves classroom practice and can be viewed repeatedly, providing a source of data for focused practitioner reflection and analysis of teacher enactments and student responses (Bodgen and Bilken, 1992; Stigler and Hiebert, 1997).

Observations were recorded in a Researcher Reflective Journal (Bodgen and Bilken, 1992; Lincoln and Guba, 1985), including participant observations and reflections (LeCompte and Schensul, 1999) relating to teacher learning within the context of the group team meetings (expert input; project-focused workshopping through distributed collegiate mentoring; reflective action planning for classroom applications classroom; staged filming of classroom applications; collaborative reflection on observed film artefacts) and school-based collaborations (reflective action planning for classroom applications; staged filming of classroom applications).

3.3.5.3: Artefacts

The film artefacts, resulting from the filming of both classroom applications and semi-structured teacher interviews reflecting on classroom applications and teacher professional learning, fell into two categories: published filmed artefacts which appeared in the Schools Television series of programs— *Multiliteracies in the Early Years*, which included *Considering Multiliteracies*, *Exploring Multiliteracies*, *Moving into Multiliteracies* and *Multiliteracies in Action*—as well as unpublished footage which was, metaphorically speaking, left on the cutting room floor.

Teacher planning artefacts were also collected in the form of the teacher-created Learning Elements using the Learning by Design Learning Element template (Kalantzis and Cope, 2004; Kalantzis et al., 2005). Teachers used the Learning Element template as a reflective and prospective documentation and planning tool to consider teaching already enacted and to plan further enactments.

The interventions designed to support and observe professional learning used in combination with data collection techniques for observation were used to capture a range of data over the time span of the research project, resulting in multiple data sets from various sources. The case study design deployed triangulation as a measure of trustworthiness of the research data (Elliot, 1991; Erickson, 1986; Lather, 1986), since through triangulation of multiple sources of data converging on the same issue, insights gained from different sources can be checked and tested, enabling a deeper and clearer understanding of the case and verifying the repeatability of observations and interpretations (Flick, 1992; Yin, 1994, 2003).

Analysis of the data in this research project began during data collection, as is typical for qualitative research, the analysis process including data reduction, including collating, summarising, coding and sorting into themes and categories; data display, including assembling data into a visual form to allow conclusion drawing, interpreting meaning through searching for themes, patterns and regularities (Miles and Huberman, 1994).

Initial viewing and editing processes to select snapshots of classroom footage and interview vignettes for the films to be screened facilitated an inductive kind of familiarity with the data. A paper edit was undertaken prior to each film edit using the researcher's notes and timecodes. Betacam film stock had been used, enabling the timecoding of shots to appear on the filmed data. All footage was viewed, and descriptive notes, categories, and codes were noted with the corresponding timecode for easy retrieval. Interviews, both audio and filmed, were transcribed, thus allowing transcripts of interviews to be coded and patterns assigned. Researcher notes and 'Learning Elements' were similarly coded.

Through an inductive examination of interviews, filmed segments, teacher documentation and researcher notes, data which appeared interesting and related to the themes in the research questions were highlighted and flagged. Descriptive narratives of the three case classroom narratives were developed summarising the teachers' growing understandings around multiliteracies theory and their classroom implementations during the course of the research project. Display formats drawing directly on the research questions drove displays and analysis (Miles and Huberman, 1994). Analytical frameworks related to aspects of multiliteracies theory included the 'multimodal schema' (New London Group, 1996, 2000); 'dimensions of meaning schema' (Cope and Kalantzis, 2000a) and 'pedagogical knowledge processes schema' (Kalantzis and Cope, 2004; Kalantzis et al., 2005). Analytical frameworks relating to the positioning of teachers in professional learning (Cochran-Smith and Lytle, 1999); and as research subjects (Kemmis and McTaggart, 2005) were also deployed.

Collaborative reflection on data and findings was undertaken progressively throughout the work-based professional learning project during which the teachers engaged with data sources through playback of film artefacts (classroom applications and teacher descriptive reflection on classroom applications); analysis of the 'Learning Elements'; and progressive drafts of tentative findings beginning early in the data collection process and continuing after the completion of the data collection process.

Clarification emerged through the exploration and adaptation of matrices for reduction and analysis of various forms of data (Miles and Huberman, 1994) ascertaining threads and contrasts and modified data shells, coding schemes and categories to develop a chain of evidence. This chain of evidence links the questions asked to the data collected and conclusions drawn. Thus, the multiple sources of data were collected within the context of the work-based professional learning project and brought together to converge on the issues that underpin this research project.

3.3.5.4: Professional Learning Interventions within the participatory Action Research Spiral of Cycles

The demands of the screening dates of the work-based professional learning project were such that four films were to be developed and screened via Schools Television network. For advertising purposes, the film titles were accompanied by brief descriptive foci, allowing for emergent content:

- *Considering Multiliteracies*. Explore the term multiliteracies, what it means and why it is an important consideration for teaching and learning;
- *Exploring Multiliteracies*. Explore the increasingly 'multimodal' nature of texts that students encounter;
- *Moving into Multiliteracies*. Explore opportunities for student to experience and use a range of communication forms;
- *Multiliteracies in Action*. See how a multiliteracies approach supports students to understand, explain, analyse and use diverse texts.

The data collection procedures, professional learning interventions, research protocols and proposed timelines for 'Group learning meetings' and 'school-based collaborations' were shared with teachers. Feedback was sought from teachers to enable participation. Within a participatory action research-based spiral of cycles (Carr and Kemmis, 1986; Kemmis and McTaggart, 2005), 'group learning meetings' and 'school-based collaborations' were held to provide opportunities for staged reflective learning and engagement with local contexts.

'Group learning meetings' involving the team of case study teachers, two theorists from the New London Group and the researcher, were held away from the daily work of the participating teachers, generally off-site. Group learning meetings included expert input by Professor Mary Kalantzis and Dr Bill Cope contextualising the 'multimodal schema' and the 'pedagogical knowledge processes schema' with the assistance of overhead transparencies, as outlined below.

Expert input session one: 'Multiliteracies Group Introduction'. An overview and rationale for expanding notions of literacy; the 'why', 'what' and 'how' of multiliteracies. Emphasis in this session was the rationale for a need for expansion in perceptions of literacy, or the 'why' of multiliteracies (RJ/1203).

Overhead transparency slides from Expert Session One

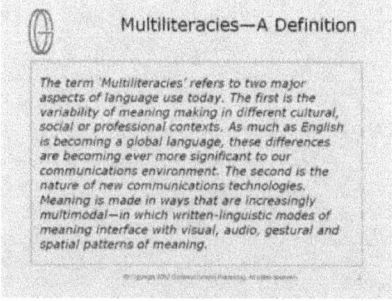

1.

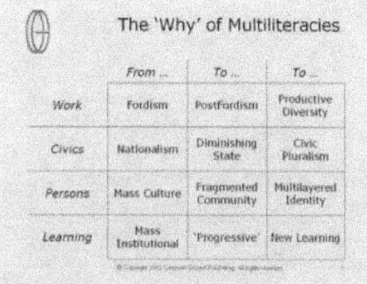

2.

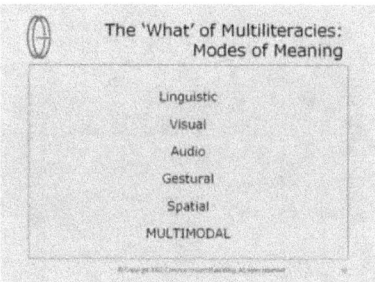

3.

4.

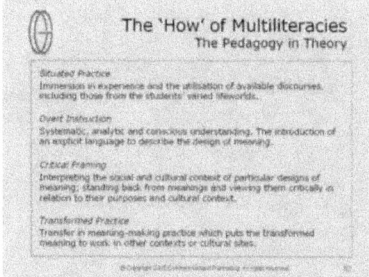

5.

6.

Expert input session two: 'Multiliteracies Group Intensive'. This focused on the 'what' of multiliteracies, that is the 'multimodal schema' and the notion of 'design' (New London Group, 1996, 2000) (RJ/2807).

Overhead transparency slides from Expert Session Two

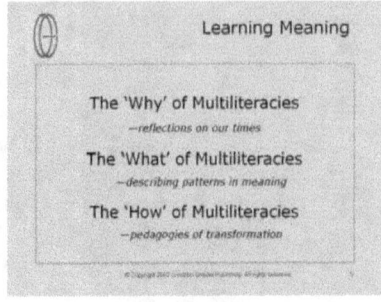

1.

2.

3.

4.

5.

6.

Expert input session three: 'Multiliteracies Group Intensive'. Expert input session three focused on the 'how' of multiliteracies, with an emphasis on the multiliteracies four-part pedagogical schema (New London Group, 1996, 2000), Learning by Design, 'pedagogical knowledge processes schema' and Learning Element template Kalantzis and Cope, 2004; Kalantzis et al., 2005) (RJ/28-2907). Details of the 'pedagogical knowledge processes schema' can be found at http://newlearningonline.com/learning-by-design/the-learning-element.

Overhead transparency slides from Expert Session Three

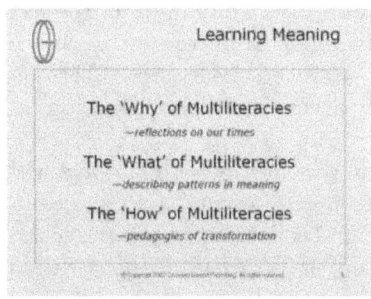

1. 2.

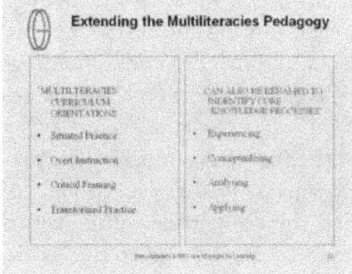

3. 4.

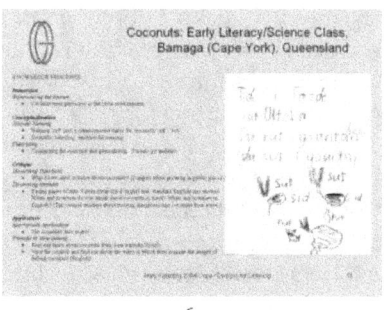

5. 6.

Expert input session four: 'Multiliteracies Group Reflection. The focus was on a review of multiliteracies theory (New London Group, 1996, 2000) and Learning by Design (Kalantzis and Cope, 2004; Kalantzis et al., 2005), with an emphasis on engagement and transformation of diverse learners engaged and transformed (RJ/1809).

Each expert input session was followed by 'planning' (Carr and Kemmis, 1986; Kemmis and McTaggart, 2005), through 'project-focused workshopping' and 'action planning for classroom applications' in which possible enactments of theory were considered by the team in the light of the distinctive contexts of individual practitioners and their pedagogical learner knowledge (Darling-Hammond, 1998). The action planning for classroom applications was refracted through the use of the Learning by Design 'pedagogical knowledge processes schema' and the Learning Element template (Kalantzis and Cope, 2004; Kalantzis et al., 2005) which were introduced during the 'Multiliteracies Group Intensive'. Collaborative viewing and reflection on filmed artefacts involved self and peer 'observation' (Carr and Kemmis, 1986; Kemmis and McTaggart, 2005) of classroom application and of developing teacher knowledge.

'School-based collaborations' involved the researcher engaging with teachers individually and in planning meetings, 'observing' (Carr and Kemmis, 1986; Kemmis and McTaggart, 2005) and collecting data in the school and classrooms contexts. Planning meetings at Westpark Primary School involved Rachel, Kim and Meredith. Principals and regional early years literacy project officers attended at times, and the two multiliteracies theorists on one occasion. 'Reflective action planning' was undertaken through development of 'Learning Elements', and staged filming and researcher observations captured classroom application 'acts' and teacher understandings (Carr and Kemmis, 1986; Kemmis and McTaggart, 2005) as a result of engagement with multiliteracies theory.

In conclusion, this chapter has described the research context—the prevailing government literacy policy and programs as well as the models of professional teacher learning. It has outlined the contextual influences of governmental policy and the program review which gave rise to the work-based professional learning project that became the subject of this research project. It has also described the more recent literacy policy advice in which the meaning-making potentials of modes other than language remain unaddressed as meaning-making resources. The design of the research project, implemented through a case study of participatory action research methodology, accounting for the researcher's role as a practitioner in developing a series of professional learning interventions, collaboratively reflecting on their impact and acknowledging the inter-relationship between data collection, research design and teacher professional learning. The context, parameters and processes of data collection and analysis for insights in addressing the research questions, within a work-based professional learning project have been detailed.

Chapter 4
The Research Project's Case Study Narratives

Chapter Four describes the participating teachers—their school and classroom contexts; their motivations for project participation; their knowledge at the onset of the research; and their starting points for classroom applications.

4.1: Participating Teachers' School and Classroom Contexts

Case study teachers were drawn from two Victorian primary schools: 'Westpark Primary School', an inner-city school of approximately 320 students in the western metropolitan region of Melbourne, where Rachel, Kim and Meredith taught; and 'Rosegardens Primary School' in a small regional town in eastern Victoria, where Pip taught. To protect the anonymity of the participants, the names Westpark Primary School and Rosegardens Primary School have been used as pseudonyms for the two schools.

Westpark Primary School is approximately four kilometres from the centre of Melbourne and situated in the midst of commercial, industrial and residential development. The school buildings have been constructed over the course of the last century, and consist of an original double-storey brick building, which in the 1970s was supplemented by a number of single-storey brick wings housing classrooms, a library, a hall and a large community room. There is also a collection of re-locatable classrooms, some built in the 1980s, and four contemporary re-locatable classrooms. The school grounds are extensive, with play equipment, garden areas for quiet activities and grassed playing grounds.

Traditionally a working class area appealing to migrants who gained employment in the nearby industrial zone, residential property in Westpark Primary School's catchment area is increasingly sought after by more middle class 'inner city gentry' attracted to the area's close proximity to the city centre. The school population in 2003, the time of data collection, was largely drawn from first, second and third generation migrant families from southern European countries and the south-east Asian region. In recent years a number of students from families from the African Horn had enrolled their children. The school population represented 52 different nationalities.

Rosegardens Primary School, a semi-rural school approximately 200 kilometres east of Melbourne, had a population of approximately 240 students at the time of the data collection, many from families experiencing socio-economic disadvantage. Rosegardens Primary School served a small country town and surrounding area. The main forms of industry were agricultural or agriculture-related (sales, agistment, haulage), with a well-represented 'trucking community' (TD/RJ/2803). There was also a nearby smelter where many parents worked, some itinerant. The 'new' school, built to replace a school on the highway considered too old to renovate, was on the outskirts of town near the sporting facilities, off the main highway. A dilapidated caravan park, home to some families, was situated at the end of the school road where the bitumen road turned to dirt.

The school consisted of two brick, single-storey buildings, housing the junior wing (Prep–Year 2), administrative areas and library, supplemented by a number of relocatable classrooms which formed a rectangle around a central meeting area. At one end of this rectangular area were playground equipment, basketball and netball courts and a football oval. At the other was the town's brick basketball gymnasium and preschool, and across the road was the town's football ground. The school was impeccably kept and had won a regional award for its presentation.

All teachers taught year levels in the early years of schooling (Years Prep–4). Students from both communities were required to attend school from 9.00am to 3.30pm Monday to Friday.

4.2: Rachel: Profile, Project Interests, Knowledge of Multiliteracies and Starting Points

Rachel is a primary educator with over 25 years teaching experience in Victorian government metropolitan schools. Holding a Masters in Education from The University of Melbourne, Rachel professed an interest in 'all things educational' (TA/RJ/2103), and presented as professionally capable, curious and responsive.

Rachel has a long standing professional relationship with the researcher of approximately 15 years, pre-dating the researcher's shift into the central educational bureaucracy. When working in the same educational region they had participated in regional professional learning opportunities, including common curriculum days, developing literacy and numeracy teaching, and assessment and strategies for meeting the needs of ESL (English as a Second Language) learners. At the time of the research, Rachel was known to the researcher as an early years literacy and numeracy trainer, having participated in training conducted by the researcher, and had attended conferences conducted by the researcher's workplace.

Rachel is well known throughout the region for possessing expertise in literacy, both as an author of teacher materials to support literacy teaching and learning and for conducting literacy and numeracy professional development for primary teachers from across the region (TA/RJ/2202).

During the period of data collection, Rachel was acting Assistant Principal at Westpark Primary School, a role involving a range of school based responsibilities including student welfare, parent liaison and teacher professional learning. Rachel was coordinator of English in Years Prep–6, which included overseeing all literacy programs including Reading Recovery, intervention programs for students at risk, and programs for students for whom English was their second language. Within various, overlapping roles, Rachel's role as literacy support/English leader involved working with class teachers to support their professional learning, and working with small groups to support students' development. The role included teaching of a Prep class during the daily two-hour literacy block and one hour numeracy block. Rachel worked in the Prep classroom three mornings a week from 9am to 12noon.

> [I am] Rachel, Westpark Primary School, I'm the Early Years coordinator there, AP [assistant principal] and teacher of a Prep grade. The group that I am working on with the video I work with three times a week. I work with them during the literacy block and also during the numeracy block ... supporting the Prep teacher. While I'm working with that group on literacy, the Prep teacher who is usually in that room is taking a group... out of that grade and [a group] out of the other Prep grade and doing computer literacy. My role in this school and in the region [includes] working with teachers in their professional development (TA/TI/2803).

The Prep classroom was one of a pair of two connected, contemporary relocatable classrooms. The two rooms were divided by a walled withdrawal area and a 'wet' area with sinks and storage space. The students from the other class could not be seen or heard. Student bags hung on hooks along the back wall of the classroom, separated from the main teaching space by trolleys holding tubs of student work on which stood the children's water bottles (TA/RJ/2103).

The main teaching space had tables and chairs arranged for seating of groups of four and six students. There was a large 'mat' space, a carpeted area where students sat for whole class activities such as listening to stories. An adult chair was at the front of this space, next to a small low portable whiteboard with a ledge on the front and storage for 'big books' at the back. There were three computers along one wall and a book space with cushions along another. A television and video player stood on a trolley next to the book space. Books were everywhere. Picture story books lined shelves, were positioned along ledges, and stood upright and partly open on trolleys, their covers fully displayed. Children's work was on display covering windows, walls and hanging from the ceiling (TA/RJ/2103).

The Prep class that Rachel worked with consisted of 24 five- and six-year-old students who were in their first year of school attendance. During the researcher's first visit to the school, Rachel explained the collaborative nature of teaching relationships at the school. During Rachel's time allocation to this class, the class teacher would sometimes also work in the classroom with this group of students; at other times the class teacher would withdraw students for assessment, individual support and to develop computer literacy; at still other times, the class teacher would use this time for planning or working with students from another class. During researcher visits to the classroom, the class teacher worked elsewhere in the school with students from other classes (TA/RJ/2103).

During the initial phone call, when the researcher issued an invitation to Rachel to participate in the research, Rachel expressed concern that due to the dispersed responsibilities and teaching roles of the Assistant Principal position, work with the Prep students would not be extensive and so urged additional inclusion of full-time classroom teachers from Westpark Primary School, Kim and Meredith. The researcher agreed (TA/RJ/2402).

Of the 24 students in the Prep class whom Rachel taught for three mornings per week, some students were having their first interactions in the language of English. One child had arrived in Australia from South America just a few months earlier. Approximately half the students had attended kindergarten in the year prior to school. One student had an undiagnosed disability (later found to be an autism spectrum disorder). The students were an equal mix of boys and girls (TA/RJ/21/03).

Rachel had an abiding interest in educational initiatives, particularly those relating to literacy. Rachel was involved in early years literacy and numeracy statewide trainer training and had regional responsibilities for training school based coordinators. These responsibilities also involved Rachel in ongoing professional learning in both statewide and regional networks. Through membership of national literacy associations, Rachel engaged with contemporary professional readings which were pursued regularly (TA/RJ/2103).

Rachel's interest in multiliteracies had been stimulated through attendance at a briefing by Professor Mary Kalantzis that the Department of Education's Western Metropolitan Region had facilitated the previous year—a briefing that had also been attended by the researcher. When asked to elaborate on motivations for participation in the work-based professional learning and research projects, Rachel responded:

> I have been working with Allan Luke's critical literacy approaches for eight to ten years and have been dabbling in visual literacies. I have been impressed by how much you empower learners if you open up those gates of learning and ... [consider] different ways of learning and who the learning is for. I'm interested in finding out how it [multiliteracies] fits into what we are doing (TA/SFTI/0704).

In relation to Rachel's knowledge of multiliteracies, baseline data shows a mixed understanding:

> When I first heard about multiliteracies I was quite confident with some parts, like visual literacy and critical literacy... I'd done a little bit of work on them, but I had to find out about the other aspects or literacies. So it's a steep learning curve as to how everything is fitted in, in making meaning of the different designs of meaning that can be made, and I wasn't sure where it fitted in the classroom in an integrated way, the multicultural aspects and things like that (TA/SFTI/0704).

Rachel claims confident knowledge of critical literacies and visual literacies, having worked with these concepts for nearly a decade. Critical literacies are one element, the critical framing element, of the four-part pedagogy of multiliteracies (New London Group, 1996, 2000); or the 'pedagogical knowledge process' of 'analysing functions and interests' (Kalantzis and Cope, 2004; Kalantzis et al., 2005).

Visual literacies relate to learning of one of the modes of meaning from the multiliteracies 'multimodal schema' which can combine with linguistic, audio, gestural and spatial resources to make multimodal meaning (New London Group, 1996, 2000). Rachel's motivation, because of prior knowledge at entry to the project, was to develop teacher learning and capacities in classroom application of multiliteracies theory, accounting for and extending teacher knowledge and practices in related pedagogy (critical literacies) and in relation to modes of meaning (visual design).

Rachel acknowledged a lack of technological expertise, and anticipated developing technological knowledge and skills and deploying these in classroom situations. Rachel worked with the Prep students during the two-hour literacy block, incorporating the recommended organisational structure, teaching and textual approaches. Rachel's concern in relation to participation in the work-based professional learning and research projects was a perception of limited opportunities for classroom application of teacher multiliteracies learning, since involvement with literacy teaching of the Prep class was restricted to three two-hour literacy sessions per week. This was counterpointed by an intense interest and growing sense of unease at the narrow print-based focus underpinning the Early Years Literacy Program.

> I only have the children for that block for literacy and so much of this can be carried into the other areas ...there's that early years structure ... in the guided reading aspect of the early years one of the biggest things I am really focusing on... is that at this level the text is very basic, 'I like the farm', or 'I like the cat' but in the actual picture there is a whole lot of other information that the children are learning about a farm. There's a barn and there's this and that. So we talk through those (TA/SFTI/0704).

Rachel's connection with statewide Early Years networks, depth of professional knowledge and sensibilities of professional inquiry, equipped Rachel to work productively, testing multiliteracies schemas and informing early years literacy practices more broadly.

Rachel's interest in the project was at several levels, aligning with the multiple roles held in working with students, teachers at Westpark Primary School and with teachers across the region in professional learning capacities. However Rachel was committed to teacher professional learning which was grounded in personal professional teaching experience.

> My role in this school and in the region is in working with the teachers in their professional development. First [before one proposes working with an initiative such as multiliteracies] you have to find out where it sits with you and experience it (TA/SFTI/0704).

At the start of the project, Rachel formed a school-based Multiliteracies Committee with representation from teachers from all areas of the school. Rachel was keen to 'spread the learning' from the project and include other teachers in ongoing professional dialogue, paralleling the project.

> ... every three weeks a group of teachers gets together for about 2 hours and we are actually exploring multiliteracies; we've got two people from Prep and a couple from the 1/2 area, one from 3/4 and one from 5/6 and the ESL teacher, so we're looking at it right across the school (TA/TI/2807).

Rachel initially experienced a struggle in deciding on a starting point for working with the school entrants.

> It was worrying me... what can you do? I imagined what you can do in a grade 3/4 or a 5/6, the depth...but then I thought no, I think the Prep year is quite an exciting time for laying all that groundwork. To begin with the Preps, I thought 'what's the main point they knew about making meaning?' When Preps come to school they come from a variety of different entry points and they've all got to learn a new language at school and a new way to make meaning. The thing they know most about is themselves, so we worked on themselves and their own facial expressions and we played lots of games using facial expressions and getting to know the language of feelings and things like that. So that was our beginning point (TA/SFTI/0704).

Rachel was concerned at the students' ability to make meaning, given their age and lack of experience in schooling. The comment shows that Rachel initially considered Prep students as less sophisticated meaning-makers than students in latter grades, imagining teaching possibilities and then dismissing these possibilities due to the students' lack of experience. Rachel's struggle is in finding a mode of meaning-making which all students can work with, a struggle presumably due to the Prep students' inexperience with the dominant meaning-making mode of print. The gestural mode, presented in expert input session one as a mode of meaning, was selected as a starting point. In considering working with the gestural mode, Rachel described the initial classroom designs to engage the diverse group of students in the following way.

> I have all the kids from different backgrounds, different stages, different entry points. So the first thing I wanted to make sure was that we were all talking

the same language, so that they knew what I was saying when we were talking about gesture, expression, feelings. So the first part was really just setting up. We looked in mirrors, we pulled faces and we looked through magazine pictures and we did a whole lot of pre-language so that when I was saying, 'how do you know that this person is feeling sad?' they could start to talk about their mouth was turned down, or 'how do you know what this person is thinking?' and they said, 'Oh they had their hand on their cheek'. So they started to verbalise actions and things like that (TA/SFTI/0704).

Observations of Rachel in the initial school collaborations show Rachel as a warm and energetic teacher with finely honed classroom management skills. Rachel's approach to the conduct of classroom activities could be described as democratic, based on a genuine interest in the young learners and the experiences they brought to classroom learning situations. An engaged flow of student-based learning was evident; teacher input was succinct and purposeful. Rachel's interest in individual students' learning was in constant evidence. Whether walking around the classroom, crossing the playground, or in the Assistant Principal's office, Rachel engaged with students and parents in conversations about student learning (TA/RJ/2003/0703).

Deep and generous professional engagement, a valuing of ongoing professional learning drawing on a range of sources and ongoing teaching commitments positioned Rachel as a committed, professional learner, intellectually curious and critical in relation to educational initiatives.

4.3: Kim and Meredith: Profile, Project Interests, Knowledge of Multiliteracies and Starting Points

Kim and Meredith are primary educators who met at university a decade before the research and, following dispersed metropolitan Melbourne teaching appointments, had been reunited professionally in their current school. Both had approximately eight years of teaching experience, about half at Westpark Primary School. In relation to other teachers on staff, Kim and Meredith were relative novices in their time spent in teaching. Kim, had entered teaching as a mature-age student, and presented as the more confident of the pair, reflected in broader responsibilities. Their roles were school-based, with their primary responsibility being that of classroom teachers of Years 1 and 2 students (aged 6–8 years). Other school-based roles included committee membership—Kim headed the Welfare Committee and Meredith was a member of the newly-formed Multiliteracies Committee.

> We have a Grade 1/2 class, that's a double unit, and in the double unit there are 43 children in our grade and they come from a variety of backgrounds. In our room we did a survey and we had something like 24 different nationalities in our room alone ... 80 or 90% who, English is their second language (TBC/TI/2807).

Kim and Meredith were urged to participate by Rachel, the Assistant Principal at Westpark Primary School. Rachel had also facilitated their participation in regional early years literacy school-based coordinator training. Kim had undertaken early years literacy school-based coordinator training two years previously and Meredith was in the process of undertaking Early Years school-based coordinator training at the time of the research.

There was a sense of Rachel acting as mentor to these two less experienced teachers. In the first collegiate visit to Westpark Primary, Rachel explained to the researcher the importance of capacity-building of younger teachers given that many of the staff members at Westpark Primary were nearing retirement age. Prior to participation in the research project, Kim and Meredith were unknown to the researcher and the researcher was unknown to Kim and Meredith except as an Early Years policy and project officer with the central branch of the Department of Education (TBC/RJ/2403).

Kim and Meredith had taught in the Years 1 and 2 teaching unit at the school for the past two years. In 2003, the year of data collection, they had been successful in gaining approval and funding to set up a team-teaching situation, sharing responsibility for 43 students in a combined class. Funding had facilitated the removal of a wall between two classrooms to create a large shared space for a double grade of students. This space was in one of the single-storey wings abutting the two-storey brick building. The double room was a long rectangle shape with an indented walled storage area on one side and an indented glassed computer lab on the other. The computer lab, with ten computers, was in what had formerly been a corridor, and was shared with a double class on the other side of the building. Their carpeted classroom had three cleared teaching spaces where students could gather in front of adult chairs and the same portable whiteboard/big book holders as seen in Rachel's room. Students' tables and chairs were grouped for seating of groups of four, six or eight (TBC/RJ/2103).

Kim and Meredith undertook joint planning, teaching and assessing responsibilities for the combined class of students to such an extent they were unsure as to which students were actually on each of the two attendance registers. They had weekly support from Rachel, who worked with small groups and released Kim and Meredith from classroom teaching responsibilities to undertake assessment and small group teaching.

Kim and Meredith shared a strong professional relationship and had set out to share innovative teaching and classroom management philosophies, including team-teaching of the combined Years 1 and 2 class.

> Sometimes we have to think about which [students] are in grade 1 and grade 2, because we don't view them as grade 1 or grade 2 children, we actually work with them at their ability. And there are times when we have to do something in separate grade groups, for other rooms, say, if there is a survey. Meredith might say, 'would everyone in my grade stand up' or 'Kim's grade stand up', and we have to stand there and go 'Jasmine, you are actually on Meredith's roll', 'cause they don't know. And that's the only time when we actually refer to them as separate grades because they really are one grade (TBC/TI/28 03).

Researcher observations during visits to the classroom include reflection on the large management task involved in designing learning for 42 students. Sessions generally began with all students sitting together on the floor, with a teacher-led session followed by teacher direction of individuals and groups to various activities. Much time was spent ensuring that all students were clear about teacher expectations and classroom organisation. Incorporating individual students' voices into whole class discussions was attempted, but sometimes the volume required for all students to hear one another was an obstacle for some students (TBC/RJ/2103/0205).

Kim and Meredith often spoke concurrently, constantly clarifying one another's comments. They were aware of this, pleased about their likeness of mind and professional engagement. Work with students was strongly scaffolded, with teachers modelling work before asking students to attempt it. Students generally worked in groups, sharing responsibility for the outcomes. Social learning and group processes were strongly emphasised. Kim and Meredith requested that due to their shared educational philosophies and practices, they would prefer to be treated as one research 'subject'. Perhaps this request also provided a sense of collegiate support, given their relative inexperience (TBC/RJ/2103).

Their confidence, however, did not extend to being interviewed to camera. While Kim and Meredith agreed to have their classroom practices filmed, initially they refused to participate in filmed interviews. They agreed to audio interviews and to filming of classroom practices. At the start of the project they suggested that Rachel, their Assistant Principal, describe their practices as an accompaniment to the footage. Data sources relating to Kim and Meredith included audio interviews, researcher observatory notes and staged filming in their classroom. On their request to participate in filmed interviews, these became a further source of data.

Passionate, vocal, and proud of their practices, Kim and Meredith's decision to participate in the project was partly due to its contemporary quality, their enthusiasm regarding educational initiatives and Rachel's influence in recommending that they participate.

> We were asked by Rachel if we would be interested, and we had no idea what it involved, or even to a point what multiliteracies really was... we had heard the term, but ... we weren't forced into it or anything...we did it because we wanted to, and I suppose it was an interest then... and its good to explore something that we hadn't been exposed to, or that we didn't really know a lot about, and we were quite happy to try it. And I always trust Rachel's judgement! [laughs] It was a matter of taking that chance and saying 'ok, we are open to new ideas' (TBC/TI/2803).

They acknowledged that their understandings of multiliteracies at the commencement of the project were thin. When asked to describe what they knew of the theory they replied:

> Well I suppose really I didn't have a really big idea of what multiliteracies were. I'd heard the word and you conjure up things like, computers and all those sorts of things, but really I didn't have my head around what it really did mean (TBC/SFTI/0108).

Kim and Meredith were critical of the rigid implementation of the Early Years Literacy Program as experienced in their present and prior teaching contexts. During the Multiliteracies Group Introduction, Meredith described to the researcher experiences at another school where the Early

Years coordinator had rung a bell, at which time all teachers had to begin a particular teaching approach. Kim and Meredith argued that literacy needed to sit within authentic learning contexts (TBC/RJ/1203).

To this end, Kim and C's starting point for classroom enactments within the research project was their integrated social education focus, 'Multicultural Festivals and Celebrations'. When asked how they chose to begin classroom-based applications of their multiliteracies learning, they replied:

> I suppose how we started it was probably how we would always start any new topic, just sort of tuning the kids in and looking at what they know, and even though we have a broad overview of where we want to start, we really let that 'tuning in' part direct us as to where we are going to start... Because it is no use planning three weeks ahead if we don't really know where our kids are. So the first thing was to just get the kids to write everything they know about celebrations (TBC/TI/2803).

Kim and Meredith used an integrated approach to social science, framing their class investigations into the topic with a set of broad questions they worked with students to answer over the course of the unit. Critical to Kim and Meredith was that enactments of multiliteracies be undertaken within this framework of learning.

4.4: Pip: Profile, Project Interests, Knowledge of Multiliteracies and Starting Points

Pip is a preschool and primary educator of over 20 years experience, who at the time of the research had recently returned to the semi-rural school setting of Rosegardens Primary School after a three-year secondment to a non-metropolitan regionally-based ICT/literacy consultancy position.

At the end of 2002, the educational regional office in which Pip had worked had made the majority of their out-of-school-based consultants redundant, Pip amongst them. Pip's ICT/literacy expertise had been deployed by the region in the conduct of initiatives to encourage the use of ICT across the curriculum. Pip was also a regional early years literacy trainer responsible for training school-based coordinators across the region. Unknown personally to the researcher, Pip had been recommended by a former regional colleague, now based in central office, for inclusion in the research project due to combined literacy and ICT expertise (TD/RJ/2003).

Pip's school-based responsibilities included teaching a Years 3 and 4 class (students aged 8–10 although there were a few eleven year old students); early years literacy and numeracy coordination; and integration and technology aide coordination. The early years literacy and numeracy co-ordinator role involved Pip in working with other teachers in their classrooms all day on Wednesdays and for one hour on Monday sand Tuesdays.

Pip's interest in the project was based on a desire to stay connected to wider educational issues, particularly issues relating to technology and literacy, while undergoing the transition from regional office to small school.

Pip continued to be called upon to support regional literacy and numeracy training programs (TD/RJ/2403).

Pip had a long history at Rosegardens Primary School, having worked in association with the school over a decade prior to 2003, the year of data collection. Over this time Pip's role had initially been that of preschool teacher in the adjoining preschool, then as a primary teacher on staff, before taking up the secondment to the regional office. Pip was succinctly spoken, efficient, organised, accommodating and tech-savvy. A strong knowledge of school and regional issues was apparent, due to having lived a lifetime in the area 200 kilometres from Melbourne, apart from three years of teacher education based in Melbourne.

Pip's Years 3 and 4 classroom was one of a pair of relocatable buildings. Separated from the adjoining room by teacher work/storage and withdrawal areas, the room was square with a large blackboard/whiteboard along one end and a linoleum 'wet' area with sink at the other. Four computers were positioned under the windows that ran along one wall and overlooked grazing land. Tables with drawers underneath for student work were placed in groups seating groups of six and eight students. A small area of floor in front of the whiteboard was left clear for students to gather for whole class discussions. Pip offers specific detail of the role and of the students, many of whom had been known since preschool.

> Pip, Rosegardens Primary School, and I'm the Early Years Literacy and Numeracy Coordinator and I'm also an Early Years Literacy Trainer for the region. I work with Grades 3 and 4. Rosegardens is a fairly low socio- economic status area. Very few ESL, in fact no ESL children. A grade of 26 children of which I think 18 or 19 of them are boys, so nearly all boys. Also a huge range of learning needs and also learning experiences. I've got four children who are D & I [Disability and Impairment] funded, all boys, three with severe language disorders, one who is extremely low to the extent where he is a Grade 3 child and still not reading or writing terribly well and also a blind child. Even though it is a Grade 3/4 we've got one child who has just turned eight and we have two children turning eleven so we've got about a four-year age range (TD/SFTI/ I004).

Pip's role involved coordination of two 'integration aides' who were funded to support the students with disabilities and impairments within the context of the classroom programs, one of whom worked full-time with the blind child.

Researcher observations during visits to the classroom saw a group of engaged students, working in apparent harmony. The 'tough school with tough kids' (TD/TI/ 2903) described by the Pip was not apparent, perhaps due to Pip's superior classroom management skills. A task management board which showed the tasks that students were working on was a constant reference point for students and Pip transferred responsibility for classroom management to students via this tool (TD/RJ/2003/1004).

Pip admitted to a superficial understanding of multiliteracies, despite expertise and access to professional learning in the regional position. Early in the project, Pip described perceptions of multiliteracies as:

> ... a term that's been around a long time and I guess I'd heard about it. I didn't know much about it at all. My initial understanding, I think, was probably the changing nature of literacy, particularly now with email, mobile phones and SMS messages, how that's changed. So I really didn't know anything about, or hadn't considered, the multimodal nature of the learning involved with multiliteracies (TD/SFTI/I004).

While Pip was aware of the connection between multiliteracies and technology, these connections did not extend to the 'multimodal schema' and 'pedagogical knowledge processes schema'. When asked about the motivating purposes for joining the work-based professional learning and research projects, Pip's response showed a convergence of professional interests in meeting the needs of students and furthering professional interests in teaching using technology.

> I guess it's in terms of meeting their [students'] needs because I have got such a huge, diverse group, meeting their literacy needs and because I am attracted to technology ...it's my passion. I just felt it [technology] was a way of engaging particularly all those boys and it just hooked in so well with the multiliteracies and the multimodal. The nature of it all is expanding. And through the technology ... I've felt it's a tool that engages children and particularly boys because it's so hands on (TD/SFTI/I004).

Pip's starting point was an amalgam of personal interests and a situating engagement for a diverse group of learners; where nineteen out of twenty-eight students were boys. In Pip's words:

> As a way of connecting to them and making their learning more meaningful to them and engaging them and motivating them, technology and computers was a fantastic link, but linking it to what they already knew (TD/SFTI/I004).

Returning to a school to teach in a combined Years 3 and 4 class after three years as a literacy/ICT consultant, Pip had clarity of purpose and direction, seemingly driven by expertise and enthusiasm for using technologies. Technology was also viewed as a way of engaging a diverse group of learners dominated by boys, many of them struggling with developing traditional print-based literacy knowledge and skills.

In conclusion, the teaching contexts of the two schools from which the teachers were drawn were similar in that they served students from low socio-economic areas, however participants' contexts were diverse in terms of the students' socio-cultural backgrounds, ages, and capacities. Descriptions of the participants show a group conversant with deploying the Early Years Literacy Program, although Rachel and Pip had broader school and regional responsibilities for teacher learning which expanded beyond the classroom contexts. The teachers admitted to superficial knowledge of multiliteracies, despite their combined expertise in literacy, student diversity, ICT and access to professional learning resources and opportunities.

Participants brought varied interests and strengths to the project. Rachel had a strong interest and expertise in literacy teaching. Kim and Meredith had a commitment to integrated learning. And Pip had a passion for incorporating technology and expertise in literacy education. The case study teachers had multiple purposes for project involvement, including personal and professional interest, meeting student and teacher learning needs, building capacity, and the excitement and challenge of an educational innovation. Considerations in establishing starting points for operationalising their learning were many, including the needs of the respective schools, different student stages, experiences and learning needs as well as teacher interests.

Chapter 5
Breakthrough to New Practices

From the Early Years Literacy Program to Multiliteracies Frameworks

5.1: Introduction

Chapter Five, the first of three chapters focusing on discussion of the research data, describes 'breakthrough' classroom practices resulting from teacher deployment of the two multiliteracies schemas. Breakthrough classroom practices resulting from teacher engagement with the 'multimodal schema' are described in terms of teaching which addresses multiple modes of meaning-making. Breakthrough classroom practices resulting from teacher engagement with the 'pedagogical knowledge processes schema' are described in terms of the pedagogical decisions which supported teaching which addressed multiple modes of meaning. The interplay of the teaching approaches and organisational structures in the Early Years Literacy Program, the Victorian literacy policy current at the time of the research, are discussed to highlight and define breakthrough practices.

The discussion in Chapter Five draws on teacher use of a Learning Element template (Kalantzis and Cope, 2004; Kalantzis et al., 2005) to document and plan teaching decisions as a key source of data. Discussion of teacher documentation in the Learning Elements is supported by dated excerpts from semi-structured audio teacher interviews (TI), staged filming teacher interviews (SFTI) and observations noted in the Researcher's Journal (RJ).

Used by the teachers in this research project to both retrospectively document multiliteracies classroom enactments and to plan further enactments, the 'Learning Elements' offer insight into the teacher's Knowledge Objectives; the pedagogical Knowledge Processes deployed to achieve these objectives; and the intended Knowledge Outcomes. Each of the teachers in this case study had agreed to document the first of two Teaching Sequences undertaken during the work-based professional learning project. Interviews with teachers are another data source utilised in the discussion in this chapter, offering each teacher's description of classroom applications and their articulation of influences made on their teaching decisions.

Rachel, Kim and Meredith, and Pip are discussed as three case studies. Involvement in the professional learning interventions produced a kind of sedimentation of teacher learning and teacher practices as breakthroughs in literacy understandings and teaching approaches interplayed with existing understandings from the Early Years Literacy Program.

The data for discussion has been organised in tables for each case study around the following categories:

- lesson title/topic;
- references to multimodal emphases;
- references to the Learning by Design pedagogical knowledge process;
- references to the Learning by Design pedagogical knowledge objective/s
- references to the teaching approaches and organisational structures in the Early Years Literacy Program.

The lesson title and topic; references to Learning by Design pedagogical knowledge process; and references to Learning by Design pedagogical knowledge objective/s are all categories within the Learning Element template. The tables for each case study show data in these categories taken directly from these teacher's Learning Elements. Verbatim data is used in the categories of 'lesson title', 'topic'; references to Learning by Design pedagogical knowledge process; and references to Learning by Design pedagogical knowledge objective/s. This data is supplemented by direct quotes from audio and staged filming teacher interviews, and observations noted in the researcher's reflective journal. Lessons numbers have been assigned to each lesson.

References to 'multimodal emphases' within the data tables have been interpreted by the researcher, since no category or prompts relating to multimodality exist within the Learning Element template. The researcher has drawn on Learning Elements; audio and staged filming teacher interviews and classroom applications; and observations in the Researcher Reflective Journal to develop this data category. References to the Early Years Literacy Program have similarly been interpreted by the researcher, again through drawing on Learning Elements, audio and staged filming teacher interviews, and observations in the Researcher Journal.

Analysis of the impact of multiliteracies schemas on teaching choices has involved weaving a discussion around the influences of policy; influence of the 'multimodal schema' and 'pedagogical knowledge processes schema' as demonstrated in the planning, documenting and in teacher enacted teaching processes.

5.2: Rachel: Meaning-making in Narratives

The lessons or enactments selected for this discussion are the fourteen lessons documented in the Teacher Resource section of Rachel's Learning Element, entitled 'Body Talk: Making and Interpreting Meaning'. The Learning Element template prompted a short description of the sequence of learning planned. Here Rachel wrote:

> This Learning Element guides learning about expression and feelings enabling students to classify and articulate a range of feelings. Children are involved in posing for digital photos and exploring meaning through hands, stance, eyes. Through the use of literature, illustration, movement and sound, students analyse layers of meaning, deconstructing and reconstructing multimodal texts.

Rachel wrote a 'Learning Focus' for the Learning Element which reads:

> All children make and interpret meaning as part of their everyday lives. They have been successfully interpreting facial expressions, tone and gesture in a variety of settings.

Rachel entitled the Learner Resource section of the template, 'Body Talk: I See What You Mean' and described 'What We're Learning', a learning focus directed at students aged 4-6 years thus: 'We can often tell how people are feeling by the look on their face and the way they use their bodies'. During an interview, Rachel elaborated on purposes for planning and developing the particular set of knowledge objectives, knowledge processes and knowledge outcomes described in the 'Learning Element'. Rachel describes consideration of the meaning-making experiences of students on entry to school as well as consideration of students' lifeworld experiences:

> When Preps come to school they come from a variety of different entry points and they've all got to learn a new language at school and a new way to make meaning. The thing they know most about is themselves; so we worked on themselves and their own facial expressions and we played lots of games using facial expressions and getting to know the language of feelings and things like that (TA/SFTI/0205).

The Teacher Resource of the 'pedagogical knowledge processes schema' prompted documentation of Knowledge Objectives under visual 'tags' relating to the four pedagogical knowledge processes: experiential objectives, conceptual objectives, analytical objectives and applied objectives. The Learner Resource prompted documentation of 'Finding Out' under the 'tags' by being, by connecting, by thinking about and by doing. Rachel's knowledge objectives, developed under the pedagogical tags are shown from the Learning Element.

BREAKTHROUGH TO NEW PRACTICES

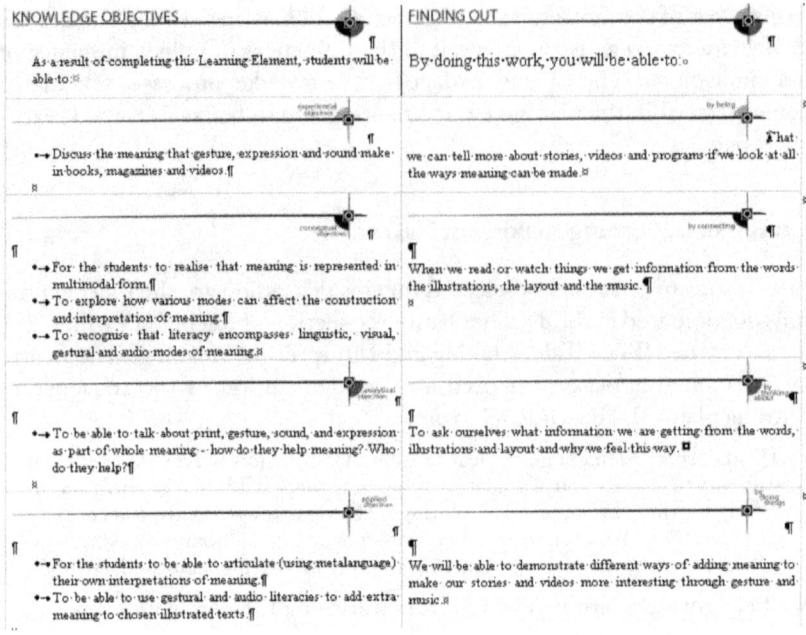

Figure 5.1: Rachel's Knowledge Objectives in Learning Element

Rachel's documentation then shows fourteen lessons described under visual 'tags' of the eight pedagogical 'Knowledge Processes' (Teacher Resource) or 'Knowing Things' (Learner Resource). A sample of Rachel's documentation under tagged knowledge processes follows.

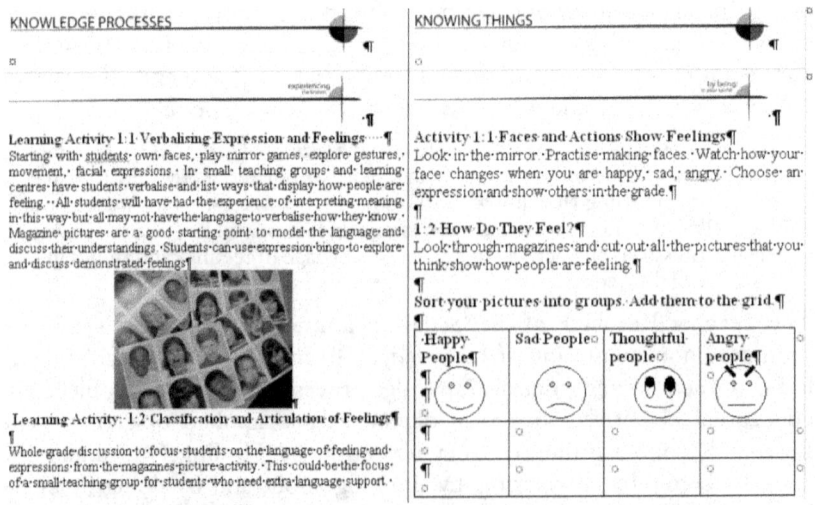

Figure 5.2: Rachel's Knowledge Processes in Learning Element

The left-hand side of this screen grab shows the 'Knowledge Processes' section of the Teacher Resource column of the Learning Element. There is a description of the first two lessons in Rachel's fourteen lesson sequence. The 'tagging' at the top of the descriptions is 'experiencing the known'. This is a piece of artwork which can be inserted by teachers when documenting lessons. There are eight such pieces of artwork, one for each of the eight 'Knowledge Processes'. The right-hand column is from the Learner Resource of the Learning Element. The same lessons are described, but here for a learner audience. There are also eight artwork 'tags', corresponding with the eight detailed pedagogical knowledge processes, for learners. This chapter has chiefly drawn on the Teacher Resource in developing categories of data for discussion.

Data relating to Rachel's movement towards classroom enactments influenced by the 'multimodal schema' and 'pedagogical knowledge processes schema' is given in Table 5.1 and will form the basis for discussion in this section. The following categories are presented: lesson number; lesson title; multimodal emphasis; deployment of Learning by Design pedagogical knowledge processes; deployment of Learning by Design pedagogical knowledge objectives; and reference to the teaching approaches and organisational structures in the Early Years Literacy Program.

These categories are considered in relation to their influence and interplay on teachers' decision-making in planning and documenting classroom enactments.

Table 5.1: Rachel's Data Categories for Discussing Breakthrough Multiliteracies Practices

No	Lesson title	Reference to Multimodal emphasis	Reference to Learning by Design pedagogical knowledge process	Reference to Learning by Design pedagogical knowledge objective/s	Reference to Early Years Literacy Program
1	Verbalising expressions and feelings	Gestural *Peer and personal expressions, gestures, mirrored reflections*	experiencing the known	Discuss the meaning that gesture, expression and sound make in books, magazines and videos.	non-teaching approach specific reference to small teaching groups and learning centres

2	Classification and articulation of feelings	Gestural in visual *Expressions in magazine images; bingo cards*	experiencing the known	As above	non-teaching approach specific reference to whole grade discussion and small teaching group
3	Posing for digital photos	Gestural in visual *Expressions and gestures in peer and personal digital photos Isolated facial features*	experiencing the new	As above	non-teaching approach specific reference to small group work; whole group sharing
4	Exploring how hands, stance, eyes and actions add meaning:	Gestural in visual *Expressions, gestures and stances in peer and personal digital photos Isolated body parts in peer and personal digital photos*	conceptual-ising naming	For the students to realise that meaning is represented in multimodal form. To explore how various modes can affect the construction and interpretation of meaning. To recognise that literacy encompasses linguistic, visual, gestural and audio modes of meaning.	non-teaching approach specific reference to small group work; whole group sharing
5	Exploring literature	Visual including gestural and linguistic *Picture story book characters*	conceptual-ising theorising	As above	whole grade reading to; shared reading

6	Exploring illustration	Visual including gestural and linguistic *Picture story book and enlarged 'story map'; Puppet characters*	analysing functionally	To be able to talk about print, gesture, sound, and expression as part of whole meaning—how do they help meaning? Who do they help?	whole grade and small groups
7	Exploring movement	Gestural in visual *Animation*	analysing functionally	As above	whole class viewing: animation (no audio)
8	Exploring sound	Audio *Speech, music, sound effects in interplay with visual animation*	analysing functionally	As above	whole class viewing: animation (with audio)
9	Making links	Linguistic *Response to audio (speech, music, sound effects), and visual (animation)*	analysing functionally	As above	shared writing
10	Posing for a Body Talk video	Gestural *Expressions, gestures and stances in filming process*	analysing functionally	As above	non-teaching approach specific reference to small group focus
11	Analysing peers' expressions and stances (no audio)	Gestural in visual *Process of viewing film*	analysing functionally	As above	whole class viewing
12	Making meaning explicit	Linguistic and visual *Reflection on gestural representation*	analysing functionally	As above	small teaching groups, language experience, independent writing

| 13 | Music analysis | Audio *Musical resources* | analysing functionally | As above | No reference |
| 14 | Linking music and mood in video | Audio in visual *Musical resources in interplay with visuals on video* | applying appropriately | For the students to be able to articulate (using metalanguage) their own interpretations of meaning. To be able to use gestural and audio literacies to add extra meaning to chosen illustrated texts. | No reference |

Rachel's initial classroom practices focused on 'interpreting' movements and facial expressions through mirror games incorporating peer discussion of possible interpretations of reflected gestural representations. Focus then shifted from student mirrored reflections to represented images of people in magazines, involving students in a search for pictures of people adopting various stances and facial expressions. Students sought, sorted and labelled images according to the feelings expressed—for example, happy people, sad people, thoughtful people, angry people:

> ...we played lots of games using facial expressions and getting to know the language of feelings and things like that... we used the magazines, looking at pictures and going through and cutting out different expressions that people had and different stances, to try and determine how they were feeling, but when we were doing some sorting of them we found that most of those were very happy faces...Then I used the expression bingo game that had children's faces with a range of expressions from really sad and frightened right through to really silly faces ... and then we used those as a prompt with the digital camera for the children to do their own expressions and make their own poster about feelings (TA/SFTI/0704).

Analysis and discussion of the results showed that the range of expressions represented in the magazines was quite limited, so a commercial game, 'Expression Bingo', was used to further build language around a broader range of possible meanings of facial expressions. In the Learning Element Rachel entitled the first two enactments 'Verbalising expressions and feelings' and 'Classification and articulation of feelings', the titles reflecting the heavy emphasis on the development of student language for describing meaning made through gesture. These two enactments were 'tagged' with the pedagogical knowledge process 'experiencing the known'.

Rachel then worked in rehearsal with groups of students exploring various expressions (and stances) before students made selections of expressions for photographic documentation:

> ... the children practised pulling all sorts of faces in front of the mirrors... they had to choose their favourite expression and I took a still [photo] using the digital camera. Then I used the digital video camera ... and got the children to show me the expression again and what movement matched that expression, so that it went that step further because we found the expression and the lan-

guage of that expression is really easy, so it was time to extend them into looking at gestures and what other parts of the body were helping to support that expression or feeling (TA/SFTI/0704).

The third lesson was entitled 'Posing for digital photos' and tagged as 'experiencing the new', since many of the students were unfamiliar with digital photography. The three initial lessons in the sequence drew on the progressivist-influenced pedagogies of connecting with students' lifeworld experiences. This was achieved via a focus on students' own gestural representations and an incorporation of images of other children—peers, in magazines and on cards.

These early enactments show the influence of the Early Years Literacy Program, with documentation referring to small teaching group teaching, learning centres, whole grade discussion and whole group sharing, key structures in the 'whole/small/whole' organisation of the two-hour literacy teaching block of the Early Years Literacy Program. Specific teaching approaches within the organisational structure were not referred to in the documentation of these enactments, rather the organisational aspects of the teaching approaches.

The strong influence of the 'multimodal schema' was evidenced by Rachel's focus on actual gestures and visual representations of gestures during the daily literacy block of the Early Years Literacy Program. A focus on the gestural as a mode of meaning-making was outside the realm of the Early Years Literacy Program. Concepts of gestural meaning-making are traditionally found in drama, dance and physical education curriculum (TA/SFTI/0205).

Lesson four, which Rachel entitled 'Exploring how hands, stance, eyes and actions add meaning', showed a shift in pedagogy with the tagging 'conceptualising by naming' applied. Interpretations of possible feelings shown through expressions were sought and photos were also categorised according to the feelings expressed, e.g. happy people; sad people; thoughtful people; angry people. Individual body parts were cut out from the photographic representations and students prompted to analyse the sections and determine possible gestural meanings to justify their points of view, concluding that gestural meaning can be conveyed in particular through eyes, mouth and hands. A poster with the sentence stem 'We show our feelings with our...' and the words 'mouth', 'eyes' and 'hands' completing three sentences were accompanied by cut out sections of the students' photos. Students also drew representations of a 'feeling' highlighting representations of 'eyes', 'body' and 'mouth'. Pictures were labelled (see below, Figure 5.3: Student artefacts: lesson 4).

As described in the focus statement, Rachel expanded the focus to include children's literature, enabling links with gestural meanings portrayed by characters' expressions and implied actions. In this way Rachel led students into the 'conceptualising by theorising' knowledge processes, exploring meaning-making concepts in different modes: linguistic, visual and gestural (and later audio) modes, making explicit the transferability of concepts. Lesson/s entitled 'Exploring literature' involved readings and discussion of meanings in stories, the words of the stories; the way the print was presented (print size, type); and how the print and pictures made students feel. Students cumulatively documented their reactions to a range of books in a grid under the three headings: 'Print; Picture: How it makes me feel'.

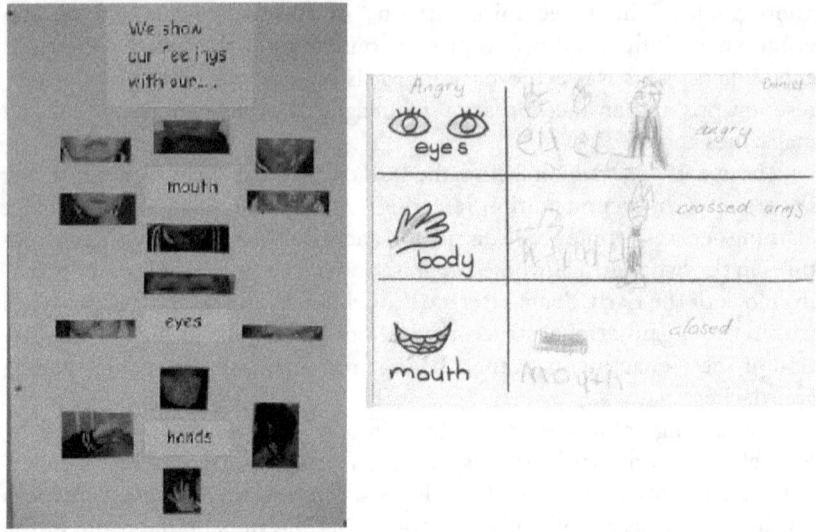

Figure 5.3: Rachel's Student Artefacts, Lesson 4

Rachel's focus on gestural, visual and linguistic meanings reflects the continued influence of the 'multimodal schema', achieved through focusing attention on individual modes of meaning. The Early Years Literacy Program teaching approaches are more specifically described in these lessons which addressed meaning-making in the linguistic mode with 'whole grade reading to' and 'shared reading' strategies evident.

Rachel expressed surprise at the students' ability to use language to describe their learning artefacts:

> I'm seeing how adaptable the children are at using the language to suit the purpose and changing already. When we were doing the drawing of *Rosie's Walk*, one little child, X, came up to me showing me his picture and pointed to a part of his picture saying 'the fox has got a sad mouth because he's feeling unhappy' and just making those connections and using the language that I was using, and we're already going from quite general language about our feelings and the modes to quite specific language. (TA/SFTI/0205)

Rachel's focus receptivity to the children's responses resulted in further focus on isolated modes of meaning from the 'multimodal schema', as described in this interview:

> When we were reading *Rosie's Walk*...children started to say what sound effects, just spontaneously, that might happen, and I thought it would be interesting for them to watch the video [of *Rosie's Walk*] without the sound and see what sort of connections they made (TA/SFTI/0205).

Use of cross-platform affordances (such as picture story book and animation) enabled teaching of a range of modes of meaning from the 'multimodal schema', initially linguistic (through reading the print) and visual (through directing attention to the story in the pictures). When asked to reflect on deployment of multiliteracies theory at this point, Rachel commented:

> [Before this] I kept saying, 'What I'm doing is just natural... I'm a fraud because I am not doing anything new'. Then I actually got the brainwave of bringing in the audio. And then I felt 'yes I have taken my learning and their learning another step' (TA/TI/2807).

Rachel introduced an animated version of *Rosie's Walk*, without audio, ensuring focus on gestures in animated form. Rachel narrated the story, so students had access to the linguistic textual resources, but not audio tracks.

> They saw the pictures [from the book] moving and they got that concept of what was happening; the fox really following and Rosie not watching, but they didn't have any idea of what sounds would be accompanying it (TA/SFTI/0205).

Rachel replayed the animated version of the story this time with the accompanying audio (music, sound effects and the verbalised text read in a male American mid-West accent):

> They were really cued in to what sound effects [were in the animated text]. I noticed that when they heard the sound effect they'd anticipated, or it was something different, they turned to each other and they'd look ... they were really listening for that sort of thing ... and watching them move to the music (TA/SFTI/0205).

In documentation using the Learning Element, Rachel described the explorations of gestural and audio meaning-making in the animation as 'Exploring movement: whole class viewing 1' and 'Exploring sound: whole class viewing 2'. The Early Years Literacy Program does not include viewing or attention to audio (other than listening to speech) as an aspect of literacy, nor does it include animations as textual designs for study. Influenced by the 'multimodal schema', Rachel extended the notion of literacy from reading and writing, the focus of the Early Years Literacy Program, to include visuals, animated gestural meaning, and audio modes of meaning. There is no teaching approach called 'whole class viewing' in the Early Years Literacy Program. Rachel has innovated on the teaching approaches offered by the program to include 'whole class viewing'.

In the 'Learning Element', Rachel tagged the explorations of individual and combined modes of meaning, linguistic, visual (illustration), gestural (animated movement), and audio (music, narration and sound effects) meaning 'analysing functionally'. This analysis draws on traditions of critical pedagogy not explicitly outlined in the Early Years Literacy Program but an area of Rachel's admitted expertise (TA/SFTI/0205).

The heavy emphasis on analytical knowledge processes, specifically analysing functionally, continued with Rachel's further enactments: 'Posing for a Body Talk video', wherein students identified, rehearsed and acted and filmed feelings; 'Analysing peers' expressions and stances (no audio)', wherein students viewed and analysed each others' films and discussed possible interpretations; 'Making Meaning Explicit', wherein students reflected on the experience of acting for camera and watching the footage in terms of 'what I used', 'how I felt when I did it', and 'how I felt when I watched myself'; and 'Music analysis', wherein students considered the mood created by various types of recorded music. Descriptions of lessons which involved students addressing linguistic meaning-making included references to the Early Years Literacy Program, with the description of 'Making meaning explicit' including small teaching groups language experience and independent writing.

> I decided to use language experience with a small group, seeing themselves on video and then talking about what expression they were using and reaffirming what sort of body language they were using. We drew about it and then came back as a group. I modelled writing sentences about the expression they were using and whether they had angry eyes or sad eyes and trying to introduce those sorts of words. Then the group had a go. They're at the very early stages of writing, but just having a go at writing what they saw about their picture and how they felt when they were doing it (TA/SFTI/0205).

Student artefacts from the language experience approach are presented below in Figure 5.4.

Figure 5.4: Rachel's Student Artefacts from Language Experience Approach

Rachel introduced a term not found in the Early Years Literacy Program, 'Whole class viewing', an innovation on whole class reading and writing teaching approaches. Rachel used 'whole class viewing' in describing 'Exploring movement', 'Exploring sound' and 'Analysing peers' expressions and stances (no audio)', reflecting further the impact of the 'multimodal schema'.

The Early Years Literacy Program offers advice on teaching foci which can be addressed within the organisational approaches relating to reading and writing. These are not strongly apparent in Rachel's documentation of the 'Learning Element', nor in interview or classroom observation. The 'Learning Element' documentation addresses more fully the 'newer' areas of meaning-making prompted by the 'multimodal schema', as can be seen in the 'Reference to Multimodal emphasis' column of Table 5.1. This is corroborated by Rachel's description of the meaning-making resources foregrounded in the lessons documented on the Learning Element:

> I focused usually just on the visual literacies, but using the video I was able to think about audio literacy and how much emphasis that adds to meaning and trying to get the children to see that, and that was a really good starting point to move on when we look at our videos of ourselves doing actions, to talk about what sort of sound effects or what sort of music will match that mood and that feeling. So where I want to go is looking at audio literacies and more on gestural literacies. Then much further down the track we'll probably be looking at the spatial effect [sic] too, as we're learning. So once I would only have focused on maybe the visual side and the alphabetical side, but now there's that whole range that I'm aware of (TA/SFTI/0205).

Additional language-based teaching, which was not documented on the Learning Element, was described in the interviews (TA/TI/2807). This suggests that, for the purposes of filming, of documenting in the Learning Element and in response to interview questions, Rachel foregrounded modes other than linguistic.

5.2.1: Rachel Summary

5.2.1.1: Addressing Multimodality

The influence of the 'multimodal schema' can be seen in the data set relating to Rachel's classroom enactments in this teaching sequence, focusing on gestural, visual, linguistic, and audio meaning-making resources. Rachel's focus on meaning-making modes in the fourteen literacy lessons documented on the Learning Element and corroborated by teacher interview and staged filming data are represented in table 5.2 below.

Table 5.2: Rachel's Teaching Focus—Mode

Rachel: Teaching focus: mode	No. of Lessons	%	Lesson No. (from L.E.)
Linguistic including: • Linguistic response to audio and visual (1) • Linguistic reflection on gestural (1)	2	14%	 9 12
Visual including: • Visual including gestural and linguistic (2)	2	14%	 5, 6
Gestural including: • Gestural (2) • Gestural in visual focus (5)	7	50%	 1, 10 2, 3, 4, 7, 11

Audio including:		3	22%	
• Audio (1)				13
• Audio in interplay with visual (2)				8, 14
Spatial		0		

Two of the fourteen lessons focused on print linguistic meaning resources. One was a response to audio and visual in an animation; the other was a reflection on gestural representation in film.

Two of the fourteen lessons focused on visual meaning-making. Both of these lessons addressed different meanings of pictures and print in a range of children's literature and a picture book study involving illustration and print meaning.

Seven of the fourteen lessons focused on gestural meaning-making. Two of these lessons focused on actual student gestures or gestural presentation (Martinec, 1999) including exploration of students' peer and personal expressions and gestures; mirrored reflections and expressions, gestures and stances in the process of being filmed. Five of these lessons addressed gestural meaning-making embedded in visual resources, or gestural representation (Martinec, 1999), expressions in images from magazines and on game cards; and expressions, gestures and stances in photographs of children, including cut-outs of isolated facial features and body parts; and gestural representation of characters in animation; and viewing a film of students for gestural meaning.

Three of the fourteen lessons focused on audio meaning resources. One lesson focused on a range of musical resources. Two lessons explored the interplay of audio with visual meaning including speech, music and sound effects in interplay with visual animation, and the other lessons focused on musical resources in interplay with visuals when constructing a video.

This shows significant foregrounding of meaning-making modes other than the print-based texts recommended in the Early Years Literacy Program.

Where the influence of the Early Years Literacy Program remained apparent, however, was not through the focus of the teaching being planned and enacted but through the organisation structures such as whole and small group focus; whole class reading to; shared reading, language experience and learning centres—i.e. organisational rather than pedagogical. While these references were more strongly evident in the lessons which addressed linguistic meaning-making, it is notable that many teaching approaches from the Early Years Literacy Program are not referred to, including guided reading, shared writing and interactive writing, probably due to their close alignment with print meaning-making. Rachel undertook additional linguistic-focused teaching outside the parameters of the project.

Teaching focus on multimodal design prompted Rachel to re-frame and expand the teaching approaches from the Early Years Literacy Program, such as the use of the term 'whole class shared viewing' to encompass the incorporation of animated texts.

As Rachel drew on the 'multimodal schema', tensions developed between the print-based focus of the organisational structures of the Early Years Literacy Program (a reading hour and a writing hour) and the multiliteracies schemas which could be applied across learning areas.

As Rachel explains:

> When I first thought about multiliteracies it was still probably within the context of an English [two hour] block of teaching. I think the most powerful thing that I found is how it is in all learning and how we've really got to be aware of that and make those links, taking it from just looking at it in one area, one subject area [English], across all subject areas ...I didn't think I'd go that far in my learning, and teaching too I guess (TA/SFTI/0209).

Prior to engagement in the research project, Rachel focused on English teaching and learning, and literacy teaching and learning, on learning language. Teaching engaged with a range of the modes from the 'multimodal schema' challenged placement of literacy and English into a daily block of time.

Some teaching approaches from the Early Years Literacy Program organisational structure were deployed, re-framed and extended within the pedagogical framework, to meet new teaching objectives relating to multimodal texts. Teaching approaches such as 'modelled writing' and 'shared reading' were used as contexts in which pedagogical knowledge processes were deployed.

5.2.1.2: Deployment of Pedagogical Knowledge Processes

The 'pedagogical knowledge processes schema' served Rachel in setting, tracking and evaluating learning goals.

Table 5.3: Rachel's Deployment of Pedagogical Knowledge Processes

Pedagogical knowledge process	No of lessons	%	Lesson no
Experiencing	3/14	22%	1,2,3
Conceptualising	2/14	14%	4,5
Analysing	8/14	57%	6-13
Applying	1/14	7%	14

Of the fourteen documented lessons on the Learning Element, Rachel heavily emphasised the pedagogical knowledge process of analysis, with 57% of Rachel's lessons thus focused. 22% of Rachel's documented lessons attended to the pedagogical knowledge process of experiencing and a further 14% attended to the pedagogical knowledge process of conceptualising. Only 7% of Rachel's documented lessons focused on the pedagogical knowledge process of applying. In terms of the eight detailed pedagogical knowledge processes (Kalantzis and Cope, 2004; Kalantzis et al., 2005), Rachel involved students in analysing functionally in eight out of 14 or 57% of all lessons. Rachel did not deploy analysing critically or applying creatively.

Rachel's strong emphasis on the pedagogical knowledge process of analysis may be accounted for by the 'newness' involved in the consideration of non-linguistic modes as literacy meaning-making resources in their own right. Rachel argues against a curriculum that emphasises linguistic teaching to the neglect of other modes, particularly for school entrants, as evidenced in the following interview excerpt:

> ... young children don't separate meaning into different modes; meaning in their symbols; in their writing...[we need to] continue emphasising all the modes of meaning and teaching explicitly about them. [We] need to continue teaching about all the modes of meaning hand in hand with the alphabetic. At this level [in guided reading] the text is very basic, 'I like the farm', or 'I like the cat' but in the actual picture there is a whole lot of other information that the children are learning about a farm. There's a barn and there's this and that. So we talk through those. And normally we miss that because we are focused on the sentences and miss the richness of what's being communicated visually (TA/TI/2807).

The pedagogical knowledge process of analysis, particularly analysing functionally, involves exploration of what a mode can do. While Rachel suggests 'we talk through those' the teaching foci evident in the documentation is limited, reflecting the lack of obvious or scripted ways of talking with students about modes of meaning in multimodal texts and how they inter-relate. Through the pedagogical knowledge process of 'analysing functionally', exploration of what the meaning-making modes in designs of meaning are contributing would assist students 'to be able to talk about print, gesture, sound, and expression as part of whole meaning' (TA/LE/C).

Rachel's pedagogical learning objectives revolved around understanding meaning presented in various forms. To achieve these objectives, Rachel involved students in experiences which emphasised lifeworld connections with meanings that 'gesture, expression and sound make in books, magazines and videos' (TA/LE/E); and attempted to provide students with conceptual language to 'explore how various modes can affect the construction and interpretation of meaning to describe types of meaning' (TA/LE/C).

Despite the applied objectives, 'for the students to be able to articulate [using metalanguage] their own interpretations of meaning' and 'to be able to use gestural and audio literacies to add extra meaning to chosen illustrated texts', Rachel did not 'tag' any lessons as 'applying creatively' and only one as 'applying appropriately'. It would seem from Rachel's documentation that students had little opportunity to explicitly apply their learning in this unit, although this learning became part of the children's repertoires applied throughout their daily encounters at school, as Rachel described:

> ... [e]ven though we've only been doing this unit for a very short time, I'm seeing how adaptable the children are at using the language to suit the purpose

and changing already... making those connections and using the language that I was using (TA/SFTI/0205).

This quote indicates that Rachel engaged and tracked students in applying their learning in an ongoing way. However, the explicit scaffolding and documenting of attempts to apply new knowledge, to position students as knowing, transformed individuals was not fully available. This was in part due to Rachel's limited time with the students.

> I still think the hard part is that I am narrowed into that block in the timetable, so I can't do as much as if I had those Preps all day...I would have been doing other things at other times so I would have been integrating it more (TA/TI/2807).

Modifications to classroom practices developed as a result of teacher engagement with the 'multimodal schema' and the 'pedagogical knowledge processes schema', but were not sustained by the class teacher, who was not involved in the professional learning project.

5.3: Kim and Meredith: Multicultural Festivals and Celebrations

The lessons or enactments selected for discussion here are the eight lessons documented on the Learning by Design pedagogical Learning Element template (Kalantzis and Cope, 2004; Kalantzis et al., 2005).

Kim and Meredith wrote the following short description of the sequence of learning:

> This Learning Element gives a structure for the exploration and classification of different festivals and celebrations; distinguishing between family and community celebrations. It focuses on the identification of the meanings of graphics and symbols and involves a critical analysis of greeting cards. Students transform their knowledge through creating personalised greeting cards

Kim and Meredith entitled the Teacher Resource section of the Learning Element, 'Analysing Greeting Cards' and wrote the following learning focus:

> Children have had experiences with greeting cards for all different sorts of reasons throughout their lives. Through the different elements of the cards, i.e. the illustrations, text etc., they interpret messages, which enhances meaning. Beginning with students' understanding of the meaning that cards convey we shall develop critical interpretations of the different modes, i.e. text and graphics as they are suited to the recipient.

Kim and Meredith entitled the Learner Resource section of the template: 'Looking at Greeting Cards'. They described the starting point for classroom enactments within the research project as 'Multicultural Festivals and Celebrations', drawing on the Studies of Societies and Environments learning area, approaching the topic in the following way:

The first thing was to just get the kids to write everything they know about celebrations, and we had the main questions that we would like them to answer, and that would form part of our assessment at the end of the term, and that is simply 'What is a celebration?', 'What is a festival?', 'How do people celebrate?'. But it was really a reflection about what are the learning outcomes for the unit (TBC/TI/2807).

Kim and Meredith's teacher resource knowledge objectives and student resource, 'Finding Out' section, are reproduced from the learning element in figure 5.5 on the next page. Data related to Kim and Meredith's growth in developing multiliteracies-influenced classroom practices is presented immediately after in the table 5.4. This, like the data relating to Rachel, will be discussed in relation to influence and impact on teachers' decision-making in planning, documenting, and classroom enactments.

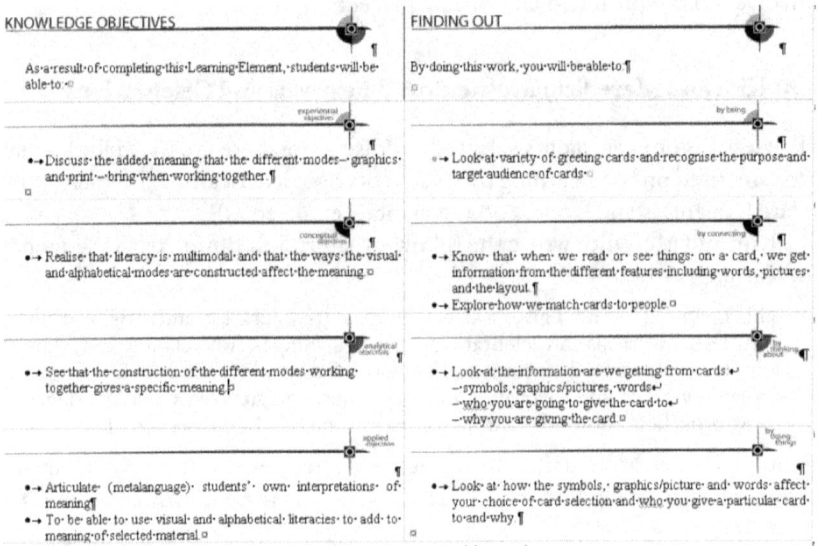

Figure 5.5: Kim and Meredith's Data Categories for Discussion of Breakthrough Multiliteracies Practices

Kim and Meredith's documentation then shows ten lessons described under visual 'tags' of the eight pedagogical knowledge process, a sample of which is inserted below.

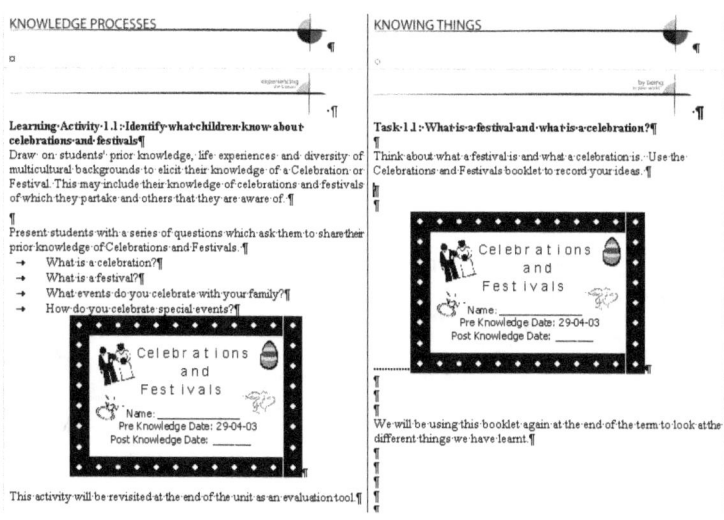

Table 5.4: Kim and Meredith's Data Categories for Discussion of Breakthrough Multiliteracies Practices

No.	Lesson Title	Reference to Multimodal emphasis	Reference to Learning by Design pedagogical knowledge process	Reference to Learning by Design pedagogical knowledge objective/s	Reference to Early Years Literacy Program
1	Identify what children know about celebrations and festivals	Linguistic *Written question and answer*	experiencing the known	Discuss the added meaning that the different modes, graphics and print, bring when working together	No reference
2	Brainstorm shared knowledge and understandings	Linguistic *Oral/ written brainstorm*	experiencing the known	As above	Shared writing whole class focus
3	Family survey of celebrations and festivals	Linguistic *Written survey*	experiencing the new	As above	No reference
4	Define what is a celebration and what is a festival	Linguistic *Oral definition of celebrations*	conceptualising: naming	Realise that literacy is multimodal and that the ways the visual and alphabetical modes are constructed affect the meaning.	Group work

5	Classification: children work in small group	Linguistic *Oral/ written classification of celebrations*	conceptualising: naming	As above	No reference
6	Investigating modes of communicating meaning	Visual and linguistic *Brainstorm of symbols, slogans, jingles*	conceptualising theorising	As above	No reference
7	Investigating cards	Visual and linguistic *Features of greeting cards*	conceptualising theorising	As above	Whole group shared reading
8	Target audience	Visual and linguistic *Features of greeting cards*	analysing critically	See that the construction of the different modes working together gives a specific meaning.	No reference
9	Planning for creating a greeting card	Linguistic and visual *Making cards- written and child illustrated*	applying appropriately	Articulate (metalanguage) students' own interpretations of meaning. To be able to use visual and alphabetical literacies to add to meaning of selected material.	No reference
10	Creating a personalised card	Visual and linguistic *Making cards –ClipArt, Publisher*	applying: creatively	As above	Shared writing Independent writing

Kim and Meredith intention's to address the visual mode from the 'multimodal schema' is evident in Meredith's reflections on early decision-making regarding classroom enactments:

> I remember driving to work …we'd had the discussion [about multiliteracies] and thinking what might we do… and the thing that stuck out was… that literacy is everywhere and everywhere we look there is either a symbol or something to tell us… something that doesn't have to be spoken or written, so when I was driving to work that morning I thought, well, I knew we were going to do celebrations and multicultural festivals as an integrated theme, and I was just trying to think of something that has a lot of symbols, and the first

thing that popped into my head was cards, cards are just filled with symbols or pictures that represent emotion, love (TBC/TI/2807).

The study of the meaning-making affordances in greetings cards was a starting point that resounded with Kim and Meredith, since the learning could be nested within the social science context of a study of multicultural celebrations and festivals. Differentiation of literacy learning from social science-related learning posed challenges for Kim and Meredith in separating out literacy teaching foci from integrated inquiry learning (Wilson and Murdoch, 2004) in which knowledge is seen as integrated, a reflection of the 'real world'; students as inquirers and learning as a process of discovery (TBC/RJ/2803). The purposes of the filming project were to focus specifically on the literacy aspect of learning, and to this end Kim and Meredith were asked by the researcher to focus on discussing and documenting literacy aspects of the integrated unit (TBC/RJ/2803).

However, the first five lessons documented by Kim and Meredith show that, in regard to the 'multimodal schema', linguistic (oral and written) was the only mode addressed. 'Identify what children know about celebrations and festivals' involved a written linguistic question and answer; 'Brainstorm shared knowledge and understanding' involved an oral and written linguistic brainstorm; 'Family survey of celebrations and festivals' involved a written linguistic survey; 'Define what is a celebration and what is a festival' involved oral definitions of celebrations; and 'Classification: children work in small groups' involved oral and written linguistic classification of celebrations.

The documentation of the first three lessons on the Learning Element template, the question and answer, brainstorm and survey, shows 'tagging' as involving students in the pedagogical knowledge process of experiencing, the question and answer involving students in 'the known', and the survey as involving students in 'the new'. However, the knowledge referred to here includes names and dates of celebrations and festivals, more in the area of social science than literacy or design knowledge. This shows an incongruence with the documented Knowledge Objective for these learning experiences which reads: 'Discuss the added meaning that the different modes—graphics and print—bring when working together'. There is a lack of alignment between this objective and the lessons documented.

The 'multimodal schema' had no apparent effect on Kim and Meredith's fourth and fifth lessons which were designed to address the pedagogical knowledge process of conceptualising by naming. The oral definitions of celebrations and the oral/written classification of celebrations into 'family' or 'community' again suggests a lack of prominence of literacy learning, despite the stated Knowledge Objective to 'Realise that literacy is multimodal and that the ways the visual and alphabetical modes are constructed affect the meaning' (TBC/LE/C).

The influence of the 'multimodal schema' became apparent in lessons six and seven, 'Investigating modes of communicating meaning', in which students brainstormed environmental linguistic (slogans, jingles) and visual (symbols) meaning-making resources; and 'Investigating cards', in which students considered greeting card graphics, genres, features, target audience, suitability for different occasions. These and all subsequent lessons in this sequence, addressed both visual and linguistic meaning-making resources. The description of, 'Investigating modes of communicating meaning' refers to audio meaning-making resources:

> This tuning in is to develop an understanding that meaning is gained in various ways—eg from print, pictures and symbols, sounds, and that meaning is gained from a variety of areas. Children work in groups to brainstorm/illustrate as many symbols, slogans, jingles, as they can remember. Discuss the symbols children have depicted. What makes them memorable?—music/ tune, colour, time aired (TBC/LE/1103).

Despite these references, sound and music are not mentioned again in the Learning Element and teaching in this sequence of lessons did not address them.

On the Learning Element template, these two lessons were tagged 'conceptualising by theorising' and aligned with the conceptual Knowledge Objective noted above. The concepts being theorised, those relating to features of greeting cards, were not the concepts being 'named' in the previous lessons, those relating to names and classification of celebrations. The work described as 'conceptualising by theorising' can be more aptly tagged as an amalgam of experiential, conceptual and analytical work relating to environmental symbols, logos, slogans and jingles. Teachers isolated print and visual information and involved students in conceptually naming salient features of greeting cards such as 'greeting', 'photograph', 'image', 'bar code' and 'font' (TBC/RJ/0205).

Kim and Meredith experienced confusion with the different labels used to describe pedagogy in the 'multiliteracies pedagogy schema' and 'pedagogical knowledge processes schema'—for example, 'overt instruction' (New London Group, 1996, 2000) and 'conceptualising: by naming and by theorising' (Kalantzis and Cope, 2004; Kalantzis et al., 2005). Kim at one point used the term 'directed teaching' (TBC/RJ/2803). Kim and Meredith did not teach multimodal design concepts and theory, and showed resistance to the historical connection of 'overt instruction' with didactic teacher-dominated approaches which fail to value student input (TBC/RJ/2803).

There is no reference to 'analysing functionally' in the Learning Element. This pedagogy refers to the function of knowledge, in this case it would refer to function of greeting cards and their multimodal design. While not overtly documented, Kim and Meredith did somewhat address this pedagogy, in the 'amalgam' lesson 'Investigating cards', where students were involved in 'analysing functionally' symbolic connections with particular celebrations (examples included wedding rings and marriages; brand logos and brands; love hearts and caring) as well as the 'purposes' of greeting cards being implied within the broad framing of the sequence within celebrations (TBC/SFC/0205).

Kim and C's Learning Element shows one lesson dedicated to analysing critically, the 'card analysis' in which strategies used by card makers in combining different features to target the emotions, personalities of the audience of the cards are analysed. Reflecting on the students' undertaking of this task the teachers describe the children as:

> ... very picky—critical—about they wanted to choose, really critical...they were thinking about the purpose and then they were thinking how all the elements fitted together for that purpose (TBC/TI/2807).

However, the underlying functions were not explicitly addressed. The social practice of card exchange is not analysed, only the design features and the purposes of card exchange for social cohesion, cultural recognition. The interests of commercialisation were not evident. Teacher emphasis was on consideration of processes involved in making appropriate matches between card giver and celebration and card recipient, so that children understood what's presented to them, what's available to them and had the critical abilities to discern what elements they were selecting and justify these selections (TBC/RJ/0205).

Students then selected a celebration and drew on examples of professionally created greetings and images from examples provided and made cards for their own purposes, see figure 5.6 below.

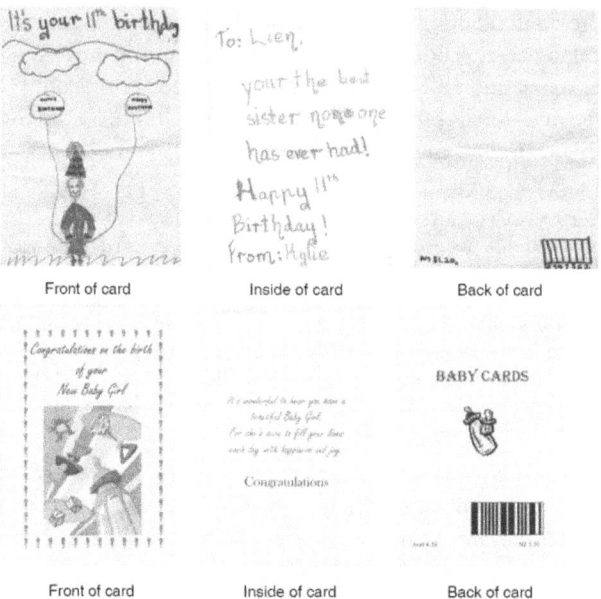

Figure 5.6: Kim and Meredith's Student Artefacts, Student Developed Cards

The Learning Element shows that two lessons were documented addressing the 'pedagogical knowledge process' of applying: 'Planning for creating a greeting card' in which students are applying appropriately; and 'Creating a personalised card' in which they are applying creatively.

The 'applying appropriately' classroom enactment was achieved through creating a shared message for a greeting card to be given to another teacher having a 50th birthday. Consideration was given to the occasion, greeting, images, style of card (e.g. humorous, sentimental) and the personality of the recipient (TBC/SFC/0205). The creative application saw students independently making their own cards, selecting from resources including Clip Art and Publisher, or their own drawings to create all aspects of a card including a border, a written message, images, business aspects including price, bar code, company name and logo (TBC/SFC/0205).

The combining of modes was attended to, in terms of the selection of linguistic and images and symbols, but also other visual elements:

> ... [the meaning is contained] not only [in] the text, it is also [in] the print...we tried to encourage that...because we had so many cards in the classroom, we looked at the font of the cards, and how a birthday card might be bolder and a plainer type text, where a wedding card, the kids will tell you that usually it's in gold and it's fancy, so when they were going through and making their own cards, they were actually selecting appropriate font types (TBC/TI/2807).

The 'pedagogical knowledge process' of applying did not involve students returning to the social discourse of card giving and exchanging. Involvement in the social acts of giving, sending or exchanging greeting cards, the 'authentic purpose' which underpinned the work, does not find a place in the curriculum.

Also, the analytical Knowledge Objectives were for students to 'Articulate [metalanguage] students' own interpretations of meaning' and 'To be able to use visual and alphabetical literacies to add to meaning of selected material'. Kim and Meredith shared a dislike of 'telling' students information, as evident in their description of their teaching foci:

> ... not only are there symbols for specific celebrations, but the audience that it was capturing, so we had symbols that you would have on boys' birthday cards that you would not necessarily have on girls' birthday cards, and we'd discuss that in great detail, the same as if it's a symbol you might find on an older persons' card or a younger persons' card. And again, it went back to finding out what the kids could tell us, it's not us delivering that information, it's talking about 'what makes this a boys' card? what makes this a girls' card? what makes it a juvenile card?, what makes it a card for an older person?' And the kids went off and discussed that and talked about that and came back and gave us those symbols (TBC/TI/2807).

The heavy reliance on progressivist pedagogies to involve students in decision-making and draw on their lifeworld knowledge and experience in offering a flexible, unfolding curriculum, seemed to involve teachers self-censoring the explicit use of metalanguage. While Kim and Meredith made explicit the area of learning and expectations of students, the literacies learning foci were lacking in definition. A specific metalanguage for naming visual and linguistic concepts appropriate to this study was not strongly present in planning documents, although terms did emerge through discussions with students.

5.3.1: Kim and Meredith Summary

5.3.1.1: Addressing Multimodality

Engagement with the 'multimodal schema' in Teaching Sequence 1 resulted in a limited expansion in the approaches to literacy learning. The 'multimodal schema' had no apparent effect in the first five lessons—50% of Kim and Meredith's documented lessons on the Learning Element—a stance corroborated by teacher interview and staged filming data (see table 5.5 below).

Table 5.5: Kim and Meredith's Teaching Focus—Mode

Kim and Meredith: Teaching focus: Mode	No of Lessons	%	Lesson no. (From L.E.)
Linguistic	6	60%	1-5, 9
Visual and linguistic	4	40%	6-8, 10
Gestural	0		
Audio	0		
Spatial	0		

The first five lessons addressed only linguistic meaning-making designs including written questions and answers; an oral and written brainstorm; oral definitions of celebrations and oral and written classification of celebrations.

In lessons six to ten, Kim and Meredith expanded their teaching foci to address the meaning-making resources of the visual and linguistic modes of meaning in greeting cards and the inter-relationships between the visual and the linguistic. Lessons addressing visual and linguistic meaning-making designs included a brainstorm of symbols, slogans and jingles; and exploring and analysing features of greeting cards; and designing greeting cards.

Kim and Meredith entered the project with a strong affiliation with progressivist-influenced inquiry learning. High priority was given to ensuring students could make connections with learning experiences, and while literacy was the particular focus of a daily block of teaching, it was important to Kim and Meredith that literacy linked to inquiry-related topic work, framed by a number of key social science-related questions (TBC/RJ/1203). In comparison to Rachel (and Pip as discussed below), Kim and Meredith showed less affiliation with the Early Years Literacy Program teaching approaches. Where Rachel and Pip were established statewide Early Years Literacy Program trainers, Kim had just completed school coordination training in the year prior to data collection and Meredith was undertaking school coordination training at the time of data collection. The Early Years Literacy Program had little apparent influence on the classroom enactments of Kim and Meredith. References to the 'teaching approaches' from the Early Years Literacy Program were not a dominant feature, with only three references made: 'whole group shared writing', involving a brainstorm of known celebrations and festivals for the purpose of identifying and sharing student knowledge of celebrations; 'whole grade shared reading' in which they read/viewed features of various greeting cards with the learning goal of recognising the purpose and target audience of cards; and 'shared writing/independent writing', in which students created personalised cards to develop knowledge of how target audience and purpose affect design choices. These were not accorded sub-headings in the Learning Element documentation as they were by Rachel and Pip, but rather given passing mention in the description.

5.3.1.2: Deployment of Pedagogical Knowledge Processes

The data shows the mixed impact of the 'pedagogical knowledge process schema' on Kim and Meredith.

Table 5.6: Kim and Meredith's Deployment of Pedagogical Knowledge Processes

Pedagogical knowledge process	No of lessons	%	Lesson no
Experiencing	3/10	30%	1-3
Conceptualising	4/10	40%	4-7
Analysing	1/10	10%	8
Applying	2/10	20%	9,10

Kim and Meredith documented ten lessons on the Learning Element template with 40% of described lessons involved students in the pedagogical knowledge process of conceptualising; 30% of lessons addressed the pedagogical knowledge process of experiencing; and 20% of lessons attended to the pedagogical knowledge process of applying. One lesson, or 10%, involved students in the pedagogical knowledge process of analysis. In terms of the eight articulated pedagogical knowledge processes (Kalantzis and Cope, 2004; Kalantzis et al., 2005), all were addressed except for 'analysing functionality'. The focus of many of the lessons tagged 'experiencing' and 'conceptualising', foregrounded social science content rather than literacy experiences and concepts. Pedagogical documentation and reflection highlighted this foregrounding of social science concepts, with literacy practices used in the pursuit of social education outcomes. The embedding of literacy learning within social science learning, with the social science particulars drawn from and building on the diverse lifeworlds of the students, led to sharing of experiences amongst the students. However, the depth to which students were exposed to the pedagogical knowledge process of conceptualising was limited in general, with conceptualising relating to multimodal designs very limited.

Planning for 'conceptualising' and 'analysing' using the Learning Element template highlighted for Kim and Meredith their preferred deployment for 'experiencing knowledge processes' as they reflected on what they were offering students (TBC/RJ/2907). This realisation influenced Kim and Meredith to shift in focus from foregrounding in their planning the integration of disciplines to consideration of the pedagogies they deployed to support literacy (linguistic and visual) and social science learning. As Kim commented:

> ... we thought we would do a lot different activities and a lot of different things and slowly as we started to get into it we realised that to do the work at the depth we wanted to do it we really needed to be more focused on fewer tasks but do them well... look at the task and peel back the layers and develop the understandings of what we wanted the children to achieve and where we wanted them to go rather than do a whole lot of tasks, just touch on the surface and then go onto the next task (TBC/SFTI/0109).

The influence of the 'pedagogical knowledge processes schema', achieved through involvement in collaborative dialogue when documenting classroom applications on the Learning Element template, prompted teachers to consider a broader range of pedagogies to teach multimodal design.

5.4: Pip: Researching Personal Passions for a Class Website

Of the numerous lessons Pip developed and enacted over the eight months of this research, the lessons which will be discussed are the fourteen lessons documented on the Learning Element template. Pip wrote the following description of the sequence of learning:

> This Learning Element offers ideas for the exploration and critical analysis of the world wide web. It suggests a pathway for the students to build on their learning interests and experiences utilising and enriching a range of information and literacy skills.
>
> It gives opportunities for students to transfer knowledge gained to the creation of their own website as well as the presentation of a research project on a passion of their choice.

Pip entitled the Teacher Resource section of the template 'Web Passion: Developing Passions using the Web' and wrote the following learning focus:

> Using the internet calls for a range of information and literacy skills. We need to provide students with learning experiences to develop a framework for analysing websites and to find information, solve problems, think critically and creatively when using and designing internet resources. This Learning Element will provide a structure for students to explore the world wide web building on their learning interests and experiences.

Pip entitled the Learner Resource section of the template, 'Web Passion: Developing Your Passions using the Web'. The starting point for Pip's classroom enactments, as described in an early interview, was an amalgam of a personal interest in computers, return to teaching from a regional role consulting on the integration of digital technologies across the curriculum, and a situating engagement for the diverse group of learners: a 'tough class in a tough school'. In establishing a starting point, Pip explained:

I've got some really low children but I've got some absolute high-flyers. They're way off the scale. So you really can't teach them how to read because they're independent readers (TD/TI/2907).

Two-thirds of the class of 28 students were boys, and many of them were disengaged, particularly from writing. Another concern was that many of the students, an estimated half of the class, did not have home access to computers (TD/RJ/2103). Pip planned to incorporate a personal interest and expertise in technology to engage the diverse student group with challenging learning needs:

> ... as a way of connecting to them and making their learning more meaningful to them and engaging them and motivating them, technology and computers was a fantastic link, but linking it to what they already knew... I started off looking at technology as a way of hooking them all in, particularly in terms of their writing... writing with an authentic purpose and audience in mind. So we looked at developing our own webpage and initially the focus was really on the content, so they started off doing personal profiles using Microsoft Power-Point (TD/SFTI/1004).

Pip's teacher resource knowledge objectives and student resource 'Finding Out' section are reproduced from the learning element below.

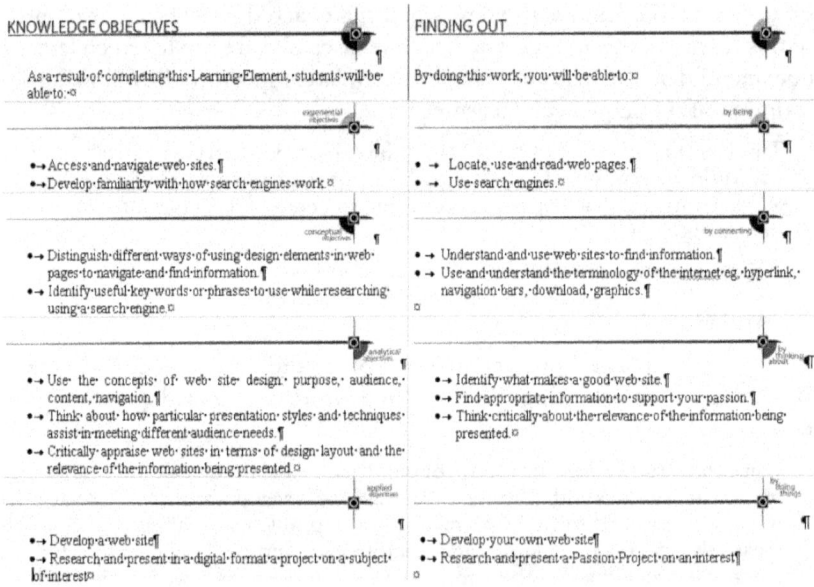

Figure 5.7: Pip's Knowledge Objectives in Learning Element

Pip's documentation then shows fourteen lessons described under visual 'tags' of the eight pedagogical knowledge processes; a sample is inserted below.

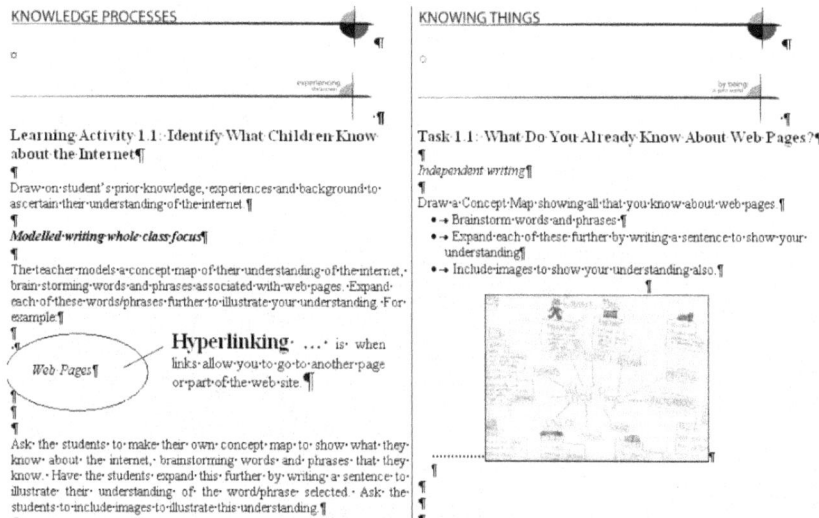

Data related to Pip's work in developing multiliteracies-influenced classroom practices is presented in the following table, which, like the data relating to the other teachers, is discussed in relation to influence and impact on teachers' decision-making in planning, documenting, and classroom enactments.

Table 5.7: Pip's Data Categories for Discussion of Breakthrough Multiliteracies Practices

No.	Lesson title	Reference to multimodal emphasis	Reference to Learning by Design pedagogical knowledge process	Reference to Learning by Design pedagogical knowledge objective/s	Reference to Early Years Literacy Program
1	Identify what children know about the internet	Linguistic and visual *Concept map showing knowledge of websites*	experiencing the known	Access and navigate websites. Develop familiarity with how search engines work.	Modelled writing whole class focus
2	Planning information for Inclusion on a class website	Linguistic *Personal details*	experiencing the known	As above	Modelled writing whole class focus

3	Exploring websites	Linguistic and visual *Listening and responding to stories on website*	experiencing the new	As above.	Learning centre activity reading research tasks
4	Identifying the elements of a website	Linguistic and visual *Navigating websites*	conceptualising by naming	Distinguish different ways of using design elements in webpages to navigate and find information. Identify useful key words or phrases to use while researching using a search engine.	Shared reading whole class focus
5	Representing the elements of a website	Visual. *Website features*	conceptualising: by naming	As above.	Shared writing whole class/ small group focus
6	What makes a website?	Visual *Structure and layout of website*	conceptualising by theorising	As above.	Shared reading whole class/ small group focus
7	Planning research on the internet	Visual and linguistic *Features and use of a search engine*	analysing functionally	Use the concepts of website design: purpose, audience, content, navigation. Think about how particular presentation styles and techniques assist in meeting different audience needs. Critically appraise websites in terms of design layout and the relevance of the information being presented.	Shared reading whole class focus
8	Introducing and planning a passion project	Linguistic *Writing about a 'passion'*	analysing functionally	As above.	Modelled writing whole class focus

9	Investigating on the internet	Linguistic *Researching for information on websites*	analysing functionally	As above.	Learning centre activity: reading research task
10	Considerations for designing webpages	Visual and linguistic *Critiquing features on websites*	analysing critically	As above.	Shared reading whole class focus
11	Analysing the elements of an effective website using PMI	Linguistic and visual *Critiquing features on websites*	analysing: critically	As above.	Shared writing whole class focus
12	Comparing websites and non fiction texts	Linguistic and visual *Comparing websites and books*	applying appropriately	Develop a website. Research and present in a digital format a project on a subject of interest	Shared reading whole class focus
13	Designing webpages (AC)	Visual, linguistic (and audio) *Publishing profiles*	applying creatively	As above.	Independent writing
14	Creating and presenting a digital presentation	Linguistic, visual (and audio) *Publishing and presenting passion projects*	applying creatively	As above	

Before working with Pip, the students' school-related experiences with computers were mainly for 'publishing' handwritten work. Pip wanted to change students' views of computer usage, encouraging them, for example, to compose, research, save and change, download and use a range of programs. Capitalising on the schools' minimal resources, students were encouraged to work on unused computers in other classrooms (TD/RJ/2103).

The literacy learning statement and literacy Knowledge Objectives display teacher knowledge confidence in approaching internet-based literacy learning, including the construction of a class website—a confidence not evident in the sensibilities of Rachel, Kim and Meredith at that time (TD/RJ/2103).

Pip documented three lessons involving students in the pedagogical knowledge process of experiencing with the stated objectives for students to 'Access and navigate websites' and 'Develop familiarity with how search engines work'.

In the first lesson, 'Identify what children know about the internet', Pip modelled a basic concept map of the features of webpages and, following the 'whole class/small group' organisation of the Early Years Literacy Program, students then completed their own detailed concept maps. These records of student capabilities and engagement would be a point of reference for assessment at the end of the learning sequence when students would again undertake the exercise (TD/SFTI/1004).

In a second modelled writing session, 'Planning information for inclusion on a class website', Pip developed a personal profile, outlining basic categories, e.g. name, interests, family, friends, then involved students in developing a handwritten personal profile (TD/SFTI/0105).

In 'Exploring websites', a 'learning centre activity/reading research task'—both references to organisational aspects of the Early Years Literacy Program—students followed directions typing a URL and navigating, browsing, reading and listening to stories on an author's website. Students then wrote an author profile based on the information collected. These experiences involved ongoing discussion of fonts, background colours, graphics and images, although Pip insists that much of the learning was incidental:

> ... picked up along the way... for example, when they're actually using the links. We'd been doing an author study ...and we'd used a website designed as a book so to actually get to the next page... it says, 'turn the page' and there's a picture of a turned over page. So they looked at different examples of linking to other sites, other pages (TD/TI/2907).

In documentation on the Learning Element template, Pip 'tagged' the two 'modelled writing' sessions as 'experiencing the known', the first, known information about the internet and the second, information about themselves appropriate for including on a class website. The experiential work exploring websites was 'tagged' as 'experiencing the new' since the websites were ones students had not visited before. In fact, there were some students who had not surfed the Web prior to this exercise. The documentation shows congruence between stated Knowledge Objectives and the lesson descriptions. There is also cohesion between the students' experiences in what is known and what is new.

The influence of the Early Years Literacy Program is evident in all three of these lessons, and in all subsequent lessons in the sequence, with subheadings referring to the teaching approaches apparent in every lesson. The influence of the 'multimodal schema' is evident insofar as linguistic and visual modes of meaning are both acknowledged and addressed as literacy modes of meaning. Pip's confidence in using new technologies was strongly evident from the beginning of the project. However, like Rachel, Pip's extension of notions of literacy teaching beyond the linguistic (reading and writing) to explicitly include the visual mode was a breakthrough as a consequence of the 'multimodal schema'. This breakthrough saw computer and website explorations merge with literacy learning in the form of exploration of different modes of meaning. This expanded the learning from harnessing computers to engage the students in print literacy concerns, to literacy learning which was inclusive of the visual mode of meaning.

The incidental learning which resulted from the experiential work was formalised through the 'pedagogical knowledge process' of conceptualising. In 'Identifying the elements of a website' Pip led a shared reading of a children's author's website focusing on reading and navigating through text; then in 'Representing the elements of a website' lists of useful words were brainstormed, and fashioned into an enlarged glossary of website words. These lessons, tagged 'conceptualising by naming' in the Learning Element, had the impact of increasing students' familiarity with concept naming:

> ...the children are getting very skilled at using the appropriate language and are able to rattle off "www dot" whatever it happens to be, quite comfortably. [also] words like hyperlink, graphics, fonts, animation (TD/SFTI/0105).

The only lesson which deployed the process of conceptualising by theorising, 'What makes a website?', was a 'shared reading' session in which the class viewed a website for vision impaired children, appropriate for one of the students in Pip's grade. They compared and contrasted structure and layout with the features of the author's website previously viewed. In the Learning Element, Pip 'tagged' work focused on eliciting and documenting the language of websites as 'conceptualising by naming', and the comparative work illustrating the structure and layout of websites as 'conceptualising by theorising'.

Strong congruence is evident between the conceptually-focused enactments and the Knowledge Objectives which were to 'Distinguish different ways of using design elements in webpages to navigate and find information' and 'Identify useful key words or phrases to use while researching using a search engine'.

Pip's most strongly preferred pedagogical knowledge process was 'analysing', which accounted for five of fourteen lessons. Three of the five lessons involved students in processes of 'analysing functionally'. 'Planning research on the internet' involved using a children's search engine including use of key words, formulation of simple questions and appropriate topic choices from pull-down menu selections; 'Introducing and planning a passion project' involving teacher -modelled writing of an area of interest selected from the earlier developed personal profile and student development of an area of passionate interest, to be word processed and later hyperlinked to their web-based personal profiles. 'Investigating on the internet' involved internet research of passionate interests using a search engine designed for children. The foci of these enactments related to function, function of structures and features used in a range of webpages; function of two related web documents (a personal profile and a passion project); and function of a search engine in researching an area of interest.

The other two lessons which deployed the pedagogical knowledge process of analysis were 'tagged' 'analysing critically'; 'Considerations for designing webpages' in which websites designed by peers from local and international schools were explored with consideration given to similarities and differences, and suggested reasons for these, including audience and purpose; and 'Analysing the elements of an effective website using PMI', in which Pip and students considered plus, minus and interesting aspects of each of the Years 3/4 sites read, brainstorming consideration of purpose, audience, content, layout, graphics, background colour and design, animation, font style, size and colour. Design elements of webpages were analysed in terms of the 'interests' of webpage designers. Analysis resulted in additional areas of study, with concepts relating to the world of publishing requiring explanation.

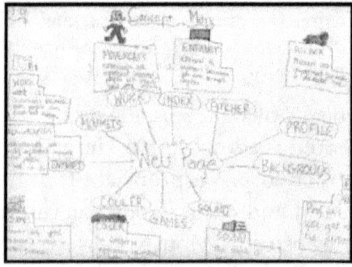

Student artefact: Concept map

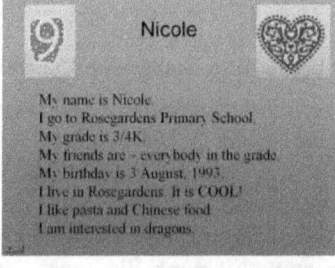

Student artefact: Personal profile (excerpt)

Dancing
Dancing is an act of moving the body in rhythm. Usually it is in time to the music. People seem to have lots of fun to express their feelings through rhythmic movement. For example most children jump up and down when they are excited or sway gently when happy. In dancing people organise the movement of their bodies into rhythm and interesting patterns

Steps
Steps are movements to go with your song. You can use your body to do movements. You always have to practice steps. When you are good you can do it for a song.

Student artefact: Passion project (excerpt)

Student artefact: Passion project (excerpt)

Figure 5.8: Pip's Student Artefacts from Unit of Work on 'Web Passion'

Pip describes the practices of the students in researching their areas of passion:

> ...using search engines, and learning to pick out information that is going to make sense and is meaningful to them; they are also learning to – probably plagiarise! – copy bits of text out into a word document and then reword it or change it, or just use the bits that are relevant to what they need (TD/TI/ 2907).

Plagiarism and related issues of copyright and web etiquette were confronted through the pedagogical knowledge process of analysis, when the students were writing narratives to be published on the webpages, some incorporating peers' names:

> ... not necessarily in unkind ways, but sometimes in an embarrassing way. So we had a big talk about that... we found some adult books that said in the front 'all places and names are fictitious' or whatever it says... if you do write [negatively/untruthfully] about somebody and that person exists you could be sued...the children don't use other peoples' names now unless it is a recount, so it is a factual piece of text (TD/TI/2907).

The 'pedagogical knowledge processes schema' through its prompting of the pedagogical knowledge process of analysis to support functional and critical analysis extended Pip's repertoire, in catering for a range of reading abilities including students who were 'off the scale' in terms of their reading abilities. In regards to these children, Pip explained:

> ... you really can't teach them how to read because they're independent readers so we're doing more of the critical reading type thing but it [use of the pedagogical knowledge process of analysis] has just given them so much scope as to where they're going to go next (TD/TI/2907).

Pip gave students opportunity to apply knowledge through 'applying appropriately' in the lesson, 'Comparing websites and non fiction texts'. Pip had involved students in navigating visual and linguistic structures of print and online designs, particularly contents pages, navigation bars, chapters or sections, glossaries, key words, photographs, captions, diagrams and maps. In 'Designing webpages' and 'Creating and presenting a digital presentation' students applied knowledge creatively, hyperlinking their word processed personal profiles to passion projects developed in 'PowerPoint'.

Hyperlinking was explicitly taught, including selection of appropriate words for transformation into links, and processes for constructing links. Students then worked independently to hyperlink their documents, with an impact on classroom dynamics. As Pip explained:

> We had some children who learnt how to do it very quickly and became very good at it, who then became the experts within the room too, so that if I was working with the teaching group doing something else they could check with one of the experts...[there was quite a lot of] incidental learning...for example, if you change the name of the file after you've hyperlinked it, it won't work, if you get very efficient and file your work in folders inside another folder, again the hyperlink doesn't recognise that (TD/TI/2907).

Enactments of the pedagogical knowledge process of applying creatively involved students making oral presentations of projects, supported by written summaries of key points and incorporation of complementary artefacts. Presentations were videoed and snippets incorporated into digital portfolios While Pip emphasised the characteristics of making effective presentations, the gestural mode was not foregrounded as a teaching focus in the Learning Element. Description of features of oral presentation documented included confidence, eye contact, knowledge of material, use of cue cards and use of artefacts. The gestural here is positioned not so much as a mode of meaning, but as an accompaniment to the oral presentation. Its 'tagging' with the pedagogical knowledge process of 'applying creatively' might indicate that the gestural is seen as a creative or expressive aspect of communication rather than a mode in which meanings are made.

Opportunities also existed for addressing the audio mode of meaning, and Pip has expressed an intention to do so:

> ...we've looked at lots of the linguistic and the visual features of webpages. We're going to explore further mainly the audio, looking at how we can add further audio and video footage as well, it is something we've got the capacity to learn, so we can do that on our [web]pages (TD/SFTI/0105).

However, despite this expressed intention to address the audio, it was not attempted in this sequence and not included in the documentation on the Learning Element.

5.4.1: Pip Summary

5.4.1.1: Addressing Multimodality

The influence of the 'multimodal schema' on Pip's documented classroom practices was limited to the oral and written linguistic and the visual modes of meaning resources. Pip's focus on meaning-making modes in the fourteen literacy lessons documented on the Learning Element and corroborated by teacher interview and staged filming data are represented in table 5.8 below.

Table 5.8: Pip's Teaching Focus—Mode

Pip: Teaching Focus: Mode	No of Lessons	%	Lesson no. (from L.E.)
Linguistic including: • Linguistic (3) • Linguistic and visual (5) • Linguistic, visual and audio (1)	9	64%	 2,8,9 1,3,4,11,12 14
Visual including: • Visual (2) • Visual and linguistic (2) • Visual, linguistic and audio (1)	5	36%	 5,6 7,10 13
Gestural	0	0	
Audio	0	0	
Spatial	0	0	

Nine of the fourteen lessons focused on print linguistic meaning resources. Three of these focused exclusively on the linguistic, including writing personal details, writing about a 'passion', and researching for information on the internet. Five of the lessons focused on the linguistic mode of meaning involved students in the meaning-making resources of the linguistic and the visual, including a concept map showing knowledge of websites; listening and responding to stories on a website; and comparing websites and books.

One of the two lessons focused on linguistic, visual and audio modes, publishing personal profiles and passion projects onto a class webpage and making an oral presentation to the class.

The other five of the fourteen lessons addressed the visual meaning-making mode. Two of these focused on visual resources, including website features; and structure and layout of a website; two visually-focused lessons addressed the interplay of the visual and linguistic, and included navigating websites and features and use of a search engine; and critiquing features of websites. Visual, linguistic audio interplay was addressed in the context of publishing personal profiles in PowerPoint.

Pip entered the project with a blend of expertise in digital technologies and print-based literacy, particularly the teaching and organisational approaches of the Early Years Literacy Program, and was eager to deploy this expertise to engage students in their linguistic literacy learning, with a particular emphasis on writing development. Teacher engagement with the 'multimodal schema' saw computer and website explorations merge within a broadened view of literacy that encompassed the visual as a mode of meaning. Within the documented enactments, the visual and linguistic modes of meaning were given serious attention, and the modal interplay explored in both online and print-based environments. The gestural entered enactments but was not treated as a mode of meaning; an intention to address the audio mode was expressed but not taught as a meaning-making mode in the lessons documented.

Pip's documentation of fourteen lessons all made reference to the Early Years Literacy Program, through the use of these as sub-headings to the pedagogical knowledge processes. However, as the students started to take control of their online research and designing and developing their webpages, literacy work permeated all sessions of the day and students worked at computers located across the school.

In a transferral of teaching approaches from page to screen Pip deployed a range of teaching strategies used successfully in page-based teaching when focusing on screen-based teaching, creating slippage between the two environments. Typical of this is the use of the Plus Minus Interesting thinking tool:

> ...they're used to using PMI, which is the plus, minus and interesting way of looking at things; we've done it with books and with book characters; it was very easy to transfer that to a webpage, so they've been able to pick up things that they think are strengths in design, things that they think perhaps aren't and...interesting things (TD/SFTI/0105).

While passion-based research saw an integration of literacy and various disciplinary areas, Pip was mindful of foregrounding literacy, no so much through a timed allocation of protected time through a literacy block of time, but through controlling teaching emphases across disciplinary content and modes of meaning.

5.4.1.2: Deployment of Pedagogical Knowledge Processes

In relation to deployment of 'pedagogical knowledge processes schema', the lessons in Pip's sequence were relatively balanced.

Table 5.9: Pip's Deployment of Pedagogical Knowledge Processes

Pedagogical knowledge process	No of lessons	%	Lesson no
Experiencing	3/14	21%	1,2,3
Conceptualising	3/14	21%	4,5,6
Analysing	5/14	37%	7-11
Applying	3/14	21%	12-14

'Experiencing knowledge processes' accounted for 21% of the fourteen documented lessons, locating students' initial understandings and engaging students' subjectivities. 'Conceptualising' lessons (21%) took the form of naming visual elements of websites and theorising how organisation and navigational elements inter-relate to make meaning. These concepts were positioned as literacy meaning-making resources, not as technology features in service of print literacy. Relatively heavy emphasis was given to the pedagogical knowledge process of analysis (37%), in which students concurrently considered the function of search engines; and the veracity and usefulness of the information they uncovered in relation to projects. Students analysed the variable currency, truthfulness and relevance of information retrieved from the internet, which led to searching for knowledge from other sources, and understanding strengths and limitations of the internet as a research tool. Students analysed the interests and considerations of web designers and the techniques they deploy in designing websites.

The pedagogical knowledge process of applying underpinned 21% of lessons, with students involved in navigating linguistic and visual information in print and online forms, developing insight into the organisation of information in books and websites, and designing and making oral presentations of website content.

Pip's deployment of the pedagogical knowledge processes represents a balance across experiencing, conceptualising and applying, with preference given to the pedagogical knowledge processes of analysis presenting a teacher strongly in control of pedagogical deployment. The pedagogical knowledge process of experiencing involved students in reflective and embodied experiences of technology use. The pedagogical knowledge processes of conceptualising were deployed in technology-influenced language, specifically the language of websites. The pedagogical knowledge processes of analysis involved students in exploring both functions and interests of websites and print sources. The pedagogical knowledge processes of applying included appropriate use of web creation tools and creative use of these tools in interplay with an oral presentation. The pedagogical knowledge processes were used in comparatively balanced deployment to address teaching of the linguistic and visual modes of meaning, the two modes of meaning from the 'multimodal schema' addressed.

5.5: Generalising from the Data

This chapter has described and analysed three case studies of initial teacher classroom applications resulting from teacher participation in a multiliteracies-focused professional learning project. Discussion has centred on the influence of two schemas emanating from multiliteracies theory: a 'multimodal schema' and a 'pedagogical knowledge processes schema'.

The influence of the 'multimodal schema' on case study teachers during these three teaching sequences, as evidenced by teacher-documented Learning Elements and supported by evidence from staged filming and researcher observations, is shown in table 5.10. Categorisation of the mode of meaning which is the major focus of teaching in each lesson was based on researcher interpretation, drawing on the multiple data sources.

Table 5.10: Rachel-Pip's Teaching Focus—Mode

Teaching focus: Mode	Rachel	Kim and Meredith	Pip
Linguistic	(2/14) 14%	(6/10) 60%	(9/14) 64%
Visual	(2/14) 14%	(4/10) 40%	(5/14) 36%
Gestural	(7/14) 50%	0	0
Audio	(3/14) 22%	0	0
Spatial	0	0	0

The 'multimodal schema' influenced all teachers to expand the modes of meaning addressed in literacy teaching beyond that of the linguistic. Teaching focused on narratives highlighted the gestural and audio modes. Many of the gestural representations were embedded in visual designs. Teaching focused on greeting cards within celebrations and festivals, and teaching focused on researching personal 'passions' and webpage creation, highlighted linguistic and visual meaning-making resources and their interplay. Teaching focused on researching personal 'passions' and webpage creation was addressed mainly to linguistic meaning-making resources in their interplay with the visual in online and print-based environments.

The influence of the 'multimodal schemas' could be seen in teaching that emphasised that modes are meaning-making resources, for example highlighting the meaning-making capacities of a mode such as the visual by isolating visual information from linguistic information in an animation design. The influence was also evident in teaching through mode, such as using the visuals in a greeting card to teach about celebrations; and teaching about mode such as teaching the names and functions of visual components of a webpage. Teachers became more conscious of the variety of meaning-making modes across the curriculum; multimodal meaning-making across the curriculum; teaching multimodality, teaching through multimodality and teaching about multimodality.

Expanded definitions of literacy had implications for teachers in the way they approached the content of the school curriculum. In deploying the 'multimodal schema' the teachers were compelled to draw on other disciplines and content areas for the metalanguage to talk about multimodal designs to teach how different modes, in particular gestural, audio and visual, make meaning.

The 'multimodal schema' also challenged the traditional delineation of subject areas—for example, English was no longer associated only with print-based literacy. The teachers also faced the issue of the relationship between literacies learning and the knowledge of subject areas, be it social science knowledge in a unit focused on celebrations and festivals; a unit on 'body talk', where literacy interfaced with knowledge traditionally found in the Dance and Drama curriculum; or a unit developing website information relating to personal interests bringing ICT, subject areas and literacy knowledge into association. Teacher control over the foregrounding of literacy in integrated studies and of different modes in multimodal studies seems an important teacher ability.

The Early Years Literacy Program influenced teachers differentially. Rachel and Pip, both statewide trainers in the program, showed stronger deployment of the Early Years Literacy Program teaching approaches than did Kim and Meredith. However, both Rachel and Pip re-framed and expanded the teaching approaches suggested in the Early Years Literacy Program in light of the influence of the multiliteracies schemas, including 'whole class shared viewing' to encompass the incorporation of animated texts; 'whole class shared reading' which involved 'reading' symbols which assisted with navigation in the online environment; and 'shared writing' encompassing new teaching foci such as hyperlinking. Some teaching approaches from the Early Years Literacy Program, such as 'guided reading' and 'interactive writing', are not evident in the documentation of classroom enactments, although 'guided reading' teaching foci had been expanded to include greater attention to images in picture story books in the case of Rachel (TA/SFTI/2807); and to visuals such as charts, maps and pie graphs in non-fiction books in the case of Pip (TD/SFTI/2907).

The Early Years Literacy Program classroom organisational structure of 'whole group, small group, whole group' within a daily two-hour literacy block of the Early Years Literacy Program was challenged by classroom practices followed when the knowledge processes were deployed. This resonates with the finding in research on the deployment of the Learning Element template with middle school teachers in Queensland (Neville, 2006) that a 'production house atmosphere' is the most effective context for multimodal teaching and learning.

Teacher deployment of the 'pedagogical knowledge processes schema' in planning and documenting teaching choices showed differential preferences, as shown in table 5.11.

Table 5.11: Rachel-Pip's Deployment of Pedagogical Knowledge Processes by Documented Lessons

	Rachel	Kim and Meredith	Pip
Experiencing	3/14 (22%)	3/10 (30%)	3/14 (21%)
Conceptualising	2/14 (14%)	4/10 (40%)	3/14 (21%)
Analysing	8/14 (57%)	1/10 (10%)	5/14 (37%)
Applying	1/14 (7%)	2/10 (20%)	3/14 (21%)

Rachel placed a heavy emphasis on the pedagogical knowledge process of analysis (57% of lessons) in teaching focused on linguistic, visual, gestural and audio modes of meaning in narrative contexts. Rachel worked with students to analyse the functions of different modes of meaning within a range of designs. Rachel also deployed the pedagogical knowledge process of experiencing, although this was limited to students experiencing the gestural mode and the gestural represented in the visual mode. The pedagogical knowledge processes of conceptualising were deployed less by Rachel, conceptualising being limited to naming body parts that make meaning and theorising about the meaning words and pictures make in picture story books. The pedagogical knowledge process of applying was restricted to matching audio resources with visuals on videos of students.

Kim and Meredith initially placed sole emphasis on linguistic meaning through the pedagogical knowledge processes of experiencing (30%) and conceptualising (20%) in a study of celebrations and festivals. Midway through the sequence of lessons, Kim and Meredith extended the pedagogical knowledge processes of conceptualising to the visual mode (20%) brainstorming symbols, slogans and jingles and exploring features of greeting cards. The pedagogical knowledge processes of analysis were deployed in just one lesson (10%) where the features of greeting cards were explored; and applying processes in two lessons (20%) with students involved in making cards for specific audiences and purposes.

Like Rachel, Pip placed the heaviest emphasis on the pedagogical knowledge processes of analysis (37% of lessons) in teaching focused on linguistic and visual modes of meaning in webpages. Analysis involved the linguistic and visual modes and their interplay in website and search engine features, researching and writing 'passion' projects, and critiquing websites and books. Pedagogical knowledge processes of experiencing, conceptualising and applying were all afforded the same emphasis in lessons (21% each). The pedagogical knowledge processes of conceptualising focused predominantly on the visual mode, specifically navigational and website features and structures. The pedagogical knowledge processes of experiencing foregrounded the linguistic mode (concept maps, personal details and listening and responding to stories on the Web, comparing websites and books; publishing and passion projects; and presenting passion projects), although the linguistic was more in interplay with the visual and audio modes.

The 'multimodal schema' and 'pedagogical knowledge processes schema' allowed for three different teacher responses to meet locally contextualised needs. Notable is the flexibility which teachers demonstrate in designing sequences of lessons to meet the learning needs of their students. While decisions exist within school and state curriculum frameworks, case study teachers displayed freedom in designing teaching sequences, be it narratives told in different forms; a study of greeting cards within a broader topic of celebrations and festivals; or research and development of a personal interest using print and internet sources for a new class webpage.

The pattern of deployment was reflective of teachers' preferences, but the heavy emphasis on the pedagogical knowledge processes of analysis was due to the novelty of positioning modes of meaning other than the linguistic as literacy resources. Within the context of the case study, analysis of the function, aspect and features of modes reflected the teachers' tentative command and knowledge of their affordances. The teachers found themselves in new territory, without obvious or scripted ways of working with students with modes of meaning in multimodal designs, and how they interrelate. In this new context they drew on other disciplines and expertise to extend their capacities.

The sense of being in 'new territory' was also evident in the positioning of teachers as spokespersons in a series of films and as authors planning and documenting classroom enactments on the Learning Element template, working in a collaborative professional learning atmosphere. Articulation of rationalisation, description, and analysis evident in the reflective interview responses represents new challenges resulting from positioning teachers in knowledge creation roles. These issues are explored in the following chapters.

Chapter 6
Towards a Metalanguage for Multimodal Literacies

Drawing on classroom applications, Chapter Six analyses teacher prompts to students and the underlying teacher-intended learning goals that resulted in examples of an emergent lexicon to teach multimodal designs. Analysis attempts to discern emphases, preferences and patterns in teacher planning and teaching of the modes of meaning; to detect influences of pedagogical choices; and to discuss the emergent lexicon in light of theoretical developments of multimodal metalanguage.

In this analysis the 'multimodal schema' has been deployed as an analytical frame relating to the teaching of mode and multimodality and the 'dimensions of meaning schema' has been deployed as a further frame of analysis for interpreting teacher prompts and teacher specified learning objectives within each mode. The 'pedagogical knowledge processes schema' has been deployed as an analytical frame for exploring pedagogical influence on teacher prompts and teacher-specified learning objectives across the five modes of meaning.

6.1: Analysing Teacher Language for a Multimodal Metalanguage

As the case study teachers moved to introduce multimodality teaching into their classroom programs, they documented their intended practices in

Learning Elements; they were filmed and observed in their teaching; and they reflected on their efforts in recorded interviews. These sources of data documenting teachers' efforts have been drawn upon to categorise and analyse actual practices of teachers in the 'new' transitory moment, a moment which is part of a larger epochal shift (Knobel and Lankshear, 2007), a moment in which teachers are moving from literacy teaching focused on print to literacy teaching focused on multiple modes of meaning.

Analysis involved the identification of teacher 'prompts', teacher-generated written and oral questions and directional statements involving students in consideration of multiple modes of meaning in textual designs. Analysis also involved identification of teacher-intended lexicon, terminology deployed by the teachers to describe intended teaching foci related to the design elements or grammars of the linguistic, visual, audio, gestural and spatial meaning-making modes as outlined in the 'multimodal schema' (New London Group, 1996, 2000). Of course, the inherent complexity of classroom environments renders any attempt to capture classroom interactions only partial. This study drew on slices of classroom exchange, and the associated teacher specified goal description and planning, to gain insight into the metalanguage teachers intended to use, and teach about, as they addressed multimodality.

The various sources of data provided evidence of different perspectives and strengths. Teacher-developed Learning Elements offer insight into the prompts and lexicon teachers considered salient and chose to record for sharing with colleagues. Learning Elements also offer an overview of a unit of work spanning several months, including the pedagogical knowledge processes chosen by teachers which form the context of the metalanguage. This positions them as a core resource for analysis of salient teacher prompting and an emerging lexicon. The Learning Elements also offer a link to the teacher 'tagging' of pedagogies through which the lexicon supporting multimodality is being introduced and taught.

Filmed segments offer density rather than salience of practices. Verbatim recording and transcription of a teacher's use of metalanguage is captured within particular lessons. However, the length of time required to undertake data collection which spans a range of pedagogies has prohibited exhaustive filmed observation of teacher prompting. Consequently, the emergent lexicon of the teaching foci intended to support multimodality is not always apparent. Prompts captured in filmed segments support insights gained from analysis of Learning Elements.

Teacher reflective interviews add insights about the emergent lexicon of teaching foci: that is, just what it is that teachers are aiming to address through their prompting. While not exhaustive or necessarily word accurate in terms of what was said in practice, interviews with teachers assist with making links between the other data sources; the overview and pedagogical contextualising of the 'Learning Elements' and the verbatim evidence of the filmed classroom enactments.

These varied sources of data are brought together in an attempt to glean slices of teacher deployment of metalanguage addressing the five modes of meaning as a result of their involvement in the work-based professional learning and research projects. Using a 'dimensions of multimodal meaning analytical framework' (see below), learning within each mode is considered in terms of the 'dimensions of meaning schema'. That is, teacher attention to the representational, social, organisational, contextual and ideological dimensions of meaning within each of the five modes of meaning.

Dimensions of Multimodal Meaning Analytical Framework

	Predominantly linguistic focus	Predominantly audio focus	Predominantly visual focus	Predominantly gestural focus
Predominantly representational meaning				
Predominantly social meaning				
Predominantly organisational meaning				
Predominantly contextual meaning				
Predominantly ideological meaning				

The relationship between the pedagogical knowledge processes being deployed to support the development of multimodal understandings is also analysed using the 'Pedagogical influence on Mode' analytical framework – see below.

Pedagogical Influence on Mode Analytical Framework

	Predominantly linguistic focus	Predominantly audio focus	Predominantly visual focus	Predominantly gestural focus
Experiencing the Known				
Experiencing the New				
Conceptualising by Naming				
Conceptualising by Theorising				
Analysing Functionality				
Analysing Critically				

Applying Appropriately				
Applying Creatively				

Given that this investigation is about how teachers are addressing modes of meaning in literacy teaching, actual use of teacher language from their practice is central. The language they deploy in relation to various modes, the language they use with their students to name design elements, and the language they use in their professional discourse to describe their teaching goals are all of interest.

Categorisation of teaching prompts according to mode (linguistic prompts, visual prompts, audio prompts, gestural prompts and spatial prompts) was undertaken. The relationship of the prompts to their purpose, the teacher lexicon intended to support multimodality or grammar of the linguistic, visual, audio, gestural and spatial modes that the prompts were designed to bring into focus for students, was achieved by identifying teacher specified teaching foci relating to the prompts. Teacher responses to interview questions regarding their classroom practices; teacher responses following the viewing of filmed segments; researcher notes recorded during professional conversations; and teaching foci as recorded by teachers in Learning Elements provided connections between the prompts and the emergent lexicon through which teachers addressed multimodality.

6.1.1: Issues in the Analysis of Prompts and Emerging Teacher-intended Lexicon

The identification and categorisation of prompts and the emerging lexicon intended to support the teaching of multimodality produced a number of issues. Identification of multimodal-focused prompts revealed a large number of teaching prompts devoted to intentions other than forming a recognisable 'grammar' that would support the various modes. These teaching intentions included organisation, student support, classroom management, and so on. Many would be more appropriately classified as classroom organisation-focused prompts, task-related prompts, or socialisation and inclusivity-focused prompts. While the importance of these prompts cannot be overlooked in a classroom teaching situation, if they did not relate to the research question, they have not been included in the data displays.

Tensions became apparent between the analytical need for clarity in classifying teachers' prompts and lexicon, and the reality of overlapping and blurred teacher intentions. For example, prompts which addressed substantive content, such as 'the farm' or 'celebrations', might seemingly have little connection to a focus on mode. However, when they were considered in terms of the five dimensions of meaning, such prompts were intended to draw attention to the contextual dimension of meaning, such as the contexts in which greeting cards are exchanged. In these cases, the substantive content-focused prompts are shown in the displays, since:

... the primary purpose of the metalanguage should be to identify and explain differences between texts, and relate these to the contexts of culture and situation in which they seem to work (New London Group, 2000, p. 24).

Disparities between teacher-specified teaching foci and researcher determination of purpose also became apparent. For example, a series of prompts drawing attention to the illustrations in a picture story book formed part of an imaginative exercise. Prompts included, 'What sound could come there? It doesn't say 'splash', but that would be a good sound. Bump would be a good sound. Crash BOING! Buzz. We can talk about the different sound effects' (TA-6-AF-SFC). The lexicon that intended to teach about a meaning-making mode included 'sound conveys meaning, sound effects, music' (TA-6-8-AF-SFTI). The teacher saw this as addressing the audio mode because the prompts focused student attention on possible audio contributions. However, strictly speaking, the series of prompts was focused on the illustrations as processes (Kress and van Leeuwen, 1996) that were being described as sound effects. This was classified according to the teacher's intent and discussion attempted to reflect the endeavours of the teacher.

The issues of overlap and blurriness in data categorisation were heralded by the New London Group who have suggested:

[we] should be comfortable with fuzzy edged, overlapping concepts. Flexibility is critical because the relationship between descriptive and analytical categories and actual events is, by its nature, shifting, provisional, unsure and relative to the contexts and purposes of analysis (New London Group, 2000, p. 24)

To maintain clarity, the researcher has retained the teacher's original lexicon used to support the teaching of different modes while discussing 'possible emergent metalanguage' in terms of theoretical reflections. Other disparities exist between what the teachers claimed to have done, both in interview and in documentation, and what was filmed and witnessed by the researcher. In some instances the claim was overstated—i.e. teaching did not address what teachers claimed it addressed. In other instances, teaching practices were not referenced to teacher-specified goals in the Learning Element nor mentioned in interview. These instances have been discussed in terms of a teacher-generated lexicon to support the teaching of multimodality and possibilities for teaching in light of established theoretical schemas

In categorising and displaying prompts and teacher-intended lexicon according to the five modes of meaning (linguistic, visual, audio, gestural and spatial) the issue of differentiating grammars or lexicons intended to scaffold multimodal meaning-making, within a series of prompts used in a single lesson, presented many challenges. This issue will be discussed further in section 6.2.

Strategies that were deployed in addressing the issue of categorisation of prompts in lessons which addressed more than one mode led to the creation of a sixth category (column display), 'multimodal prompts and teacher-intended lexicon'. Examples from the data that were placed into this category include instances such as, when the teacher prompts while reading a picture story book, 'What do the pictures tell you? What does the print tell you?' This column of display was abandoned when classification showed that a vast number of prompts could be said to be 'multimodal', and such classification failed to differentiate the lexicon of different modes sufficiently. Although discarded, this method was interesting in demonstrating a pattern of practice and did contribute to the purpose of the research, to glean the elements of a metalanguage for each of the modes under scrutiny.

Another strategy tried was double coding and cross categorisation of a series of prompts which addressed more than one mode. This strategy was also abandoned as replication failed to reveal patterns within mode sets. Similarly, the strategy of decontextualising prompts from the context of their lessons, and classification organised according to the dominant mode of their focus was attempted. The teacher-generated lexicons intended to scaffold and support teaching of mode, associated with decontextualised prompts, were duplicated and displayed in the same row. This process has been undertaken in a very small number of cases, since replication of all such instances seems to detract from clarity in informing a metalanguage for each mode selected.

Ultimately a decision was made to maintain the five modes as major data organisers, with prompts and the lexicon intended to scaffold multimodality teaching, which were 'hybrid' rather than purely associated with the teaching of one mode, integrated into one of the five categories. In such cases, the prompts were classified according to the dominant mode in focus. Such classification allowed a foregrounding of mode, rather than a lesson or a teacher, for analysis. Data was thus arranged according to the chosen linguistic, visual, audio, gestural and spatial modes of meaning-making. The recorded prompts and lexicon intended to scaffold/support each mode, enabled scrutiny of individual modes and their treatment in teaching situations. A secondary classification of the data was by the 'dimensions of meaning schema', with prompts categorised according to the researcher's judgment as predominantly focused on either a representational, social, organisational, contextual or ideological dimension of meaning. The dimensions of meaning were not addressed in detail in the teachers' professional learning, so their use as an analytical frame was confined to researcher judgment, and not teachers' deliberate intention in planning and teaching.

Classification issues arose in the deployment of researcher judgment to determine which of the dimensions of meaning, if any, was the focus of teaching. Many lessons contained prompts which, having a multidimensional focus, addressed more than one dimension of meaning. Attempts were made to decontextualise prompts from the lessons of which they formed a part, and they were classified according to the dominant dimension of meaning of their focus. This again resulted in a replication of teacher-generated lexicon intended to support/scaffold multimodality, associated with decontextualised prompts, which again served to cloud the patterns in the data. Ultimately a colouring and coding system was deployed, wherein prompts addressing a particular mode and teaching goals were colour and symbol coded according to the dimension of meaning. This avoided the cloudiness of replication and enabled the analysis of teacher deployment of prompts so as to further illuminate the dimensions of meaning within each of the five modes of meaning. One axis of classification (vertical) thus became labelled with dimensions of meaning that were used, and again this meant that the classification of the recorded prompts was done according to the predominant dimension of meaning being addressed by the series.

The processes of classification according to the mode of meaning-making and the dimension of meaning were somewhat recursive and complex when deployed in relation to lessons in which teachers addressed multiple modes and multiple dimension of meaning. The emergent nature of a multimodal metalanguage has been established in the literature. Teacher practice is occurring in a transitory moment wherein changes in the textual landscape precede theoretical writings. Teachers incorporating multimodal textual designs are doing so without fully articulated grammars. In an effort to expand the discursive space and to scaffold teacher decision-making of multimodal teaching, case study teachers' efforts are discussed in the context of theories addressed in the literature review. Discussion of the metalanguage deployed by case study teachers also draws on theoretical writing in considering the lexicon deployed to scaffold multimodality, as well as the possible emergent lexicon which might be deployed. The data was assigned multiple codes enabling various classifications described to occur (see Appendices D and G). Coding enabled analysis by teacher, by mode of meaning-making, by dimension of meaning within each mode, and by pedagogy deployed.

6.2: Teaching Multimodality and Mode; Teaching through Multimodality and Mode; and Teaching about Multimodality and Mode

The focus of this investigation is the deliberate, conscious attempts made by Rachel, Kim and Meredith, and Pip to teach in relation to multimodality—that is, teaching about the 'patterns of interconnections among the other modes' (New London Group, 2000, p. 25) or, as Kress elaborates, 'the integration/composition of the various modes...both in production/making and in consumption/reading...[which] presupposes adequate understandings of the semiotic characteristics which are brought together in multimodal compositions' (Kress, 2000a; p. 153). What became evident was that teacher engagement with mode resulted in classroom efforts focused on *teaching* multimodality and mode; *teaching through* multimodality and mode; and *teaching about* multimodality and mode. This resounds with Halliday's triptych, 'learning language, learning through language and learning about language' (Halliday, 1980).

Participation in this professional learning research persuaded case study teachers about the importance of developing student understanding that literacy involved more than linguistic meanings, and that texts are multimodal. This was clearly evident in a number of the teacher documented Knowledge Objectives designed to support student understanding, from the Learning Elements:

- For the students to realise that meaning is represented in multimodal form (Rachel).
- To recognise that literacy encompasses linguistic, visual, gestural and audio modes of meaning (Rachel).
- To realise that literacy is multimodal and that the ways the visual and alphabetical modes are constructed affect the meaning (Kim and Meredith).

Case study teachers also saw the importance of literacy teaching and learning which addressed textual meaning contributed by modes in isolation and in interplay, again, as evidenced in a number of the teacher-documented Knowledge Objectives from the Learning Elements:

- Discuss the meaning that gesture, expression and sound make in books, magazines and videos (Rachel).
- To be able to talk about print, gesture, sound, and expression as part of whole meaning—how do they help meaning? Who do they help? (Rachel).
- Discuss the added meaning that the different modes—graphics and print—bring when working together (Kim and Meredith).

The issues of identification and categorisation which arose in data analysis highlighted the approaches to teaching, teaching through and teaching about mode and multimodality, being undertaken by teachers. Such complexity should not be surprising given the New London Group's description of multimodality:

> One of the key ideas informing the notion of multiliteracies is the increasing complexity and interrelationship of different modes of meaning. We have already identified six major areas in which functional grammars, the metalanguages that describe and explain patterns of meaning, are required—linguistic design, visual design, audio design, gestural design, spatial design, and multimodal design. Multimodal design is of a different order to the others as it represents the patterns of interconnection among the other modes. We are using the word 'grammar' here in a positive sense as a specialised language that describes patterns of representation (New London Group, 2000, p. 25).

Teaching *through* multimodality and mode refers to teaching in which individual modes and multimodality, were deployed not necessarily as the point of teaching, but in the service of another teaching focus. As a result of project participation, teacher incorporation of multimodal textual designs in teaching practice expanded to include a range of modes represented on video, webpages, PowerPoint slideshows, and so on. Teachers consciously expanded the range of modes deployed to address varied subject matter, such as exploration of characters in a narrative, greeting cards exchanged as part of various celebrations and festivals, and searching web-based sources for information related to a topic of interest.

Teaching through multimodality and mode is exemplified by the teachers' efforts to incorporate a range of texts including, but not limited to, print texts, the use of representations including illustrated books, still and moving digital images, animations which included audio, greeting cards, webpages, gestural expression and stances. At times modes within a multimodal text were isolated (for examples the symbols and written message on a greeting card; or the print, images, gestures and audio of a print and animated story book) and the meanings contributed by each mode explored. The focus, when teaching through mode and multimodality, could be related to substantive content, such as the relationship of greetings and symbols to celebrations; or to changes in representation across platforms, such as how a narrative differs when told in words or in images. The focus of an internet search could be the substantive content topic of interest, say 'sharks' or 'dancing'. Teachers' conscious attempts to incorporate texts more reflective of those used in the broader community were often realised by teaching through mode and multimodality.

In many instances, the teachers were learning how to use the technology that allowed engagement with multimodal texts at the same time as they were learning about the actual multimodal texts. For example, Rachel described re-engaging with forgotten school technology and learning how to use unfamiliar technology as part of project involvement.

> I remembered, when I first came here a few years ago, there was this wonderful machine that we had in the library that you could put a book on and it projected the full colour page up. So we rediscovered that together, dug it out, dusted it off and it's been a really powerful asset in the room. Using that was one thing we had to learn. I [also] had to learn how to use the digital video, because I've got no idea of those sort of things. But it wasn't as scary as I thought it would be and I've once again realised what a powerful tool it is to assist in this area (TA/SFTI/0704).

While teacher professional learning around issues of technology is discussed further in Chapter Seven, the issue of technology is raised here in framing analysis of teaching *about* multimodality and mode. Having decided on the value of teaching multimodality and mode as part of literacy programs, teachers often found themselves first needing to learn how to teach through multimodality and mode in order to teach about multimodality and mode. During the analysis of teacher prompts and teacher-specified goals to glean an emergent multimodal lexicon, the researcher continually faced examples of teaching that stopped short of teaching about mode or multimodality, instead focusing on teaching through mode or multimodality.

In seeking to uncover aspects of emerging multimodal metalanguage or intended lexicon used by teachers participating in multiliteracies-focused professional learning, from the sources of data described, 'the primary purpose of the metalanguage should be to identify and explain differences between texts, and relate these to the contexts of culture and situation in which they seem to work' (New London Group, 2000, p. 24). As described above, many teaching prompts and intended goals emphasised the multimodal nature of the expanded selections they incorporated. Perhaps this reflected the teachers' recent appreciation of the multimodal nature of textual designs. Instilling understanding in students that textual designs are multimodal was seen as an important in itself. Similarly, the incorporation of a broader repertoire of modes was an outcome of teacher project involvement.

However, while these observances in part address the first research question, the second question seeks to glean elements of a multimodal metalanguage. Unsworth, in his exploration of e-literature, argues that the development of critical multiliteracies practices requires students:

> ... to understand how the resources of language and image can be deployed independently and interactively to construct different types of meanings. This means developing knowledge about linguistic and visual meaning-making systems and the capacity to use these systems to analyse texts. This entails metalanguage—language for describing language, images and meaning-making intermodal interactions (2006, p. 14).

Teaching about multimodality and mode in the context of the designs of meaning articulated by the New London Group (linguistic, visual, gestural, audio, spatial and multimodal) requires language for describing and comparing how meaning is constructed by isolated and combined modes—a metalanguage, which relates to the functions of various modes of meaning within different contexts. Kress directs us to a broader task, arguing that:

> ... we need to understand how meanings are made as signs in distinct ways in specific modes, as the result of the interest of the maker of the sign, and we have to find ways of understanding and describing the integration of such meaning across modes, into coherent wholes (Kress, 2003, p. 37).

Case study teachers valued literacy teaching and learning about multimodality and mode, teaching which addressed the ability to discuss features and functions of mode and modal interplay, as evidenced in all of the teacher documented Knowledge Objectives from the Learning Elements:

- To be able to talk about print, gesture, sound, and expression as part of whole meaning—how do they help meaning? Who do they help? (Rachel).
- For the students to be able to articulate (using metalanguage) their own interpretations of meaning (Rachel).
- Articulate (metalanguage) students' own interpretations of meaning (Kim and Meredith).
- To explore how various modes can affect the construction and interpretation of meaning (Rachel).
- See that the construction of the different modes working together gives a specific meaning (Kim and Meredith).
- Identify useful key words or phrases to use while researching using a search engine (Pip).
- Critically appraise websites in terms of design layout and the relevance of the information being presented (Pip).

Identifying teaching examples which may be viewed as moving towards development of 'functional grammars, the metalanguages that describe and explain patterns of meaning' (New London Group, 2000, p. 25) involved considering the teaching enactments in pursuit of these objectives, as evidenced through prompts and teacher-specified goals, in light of theoretical examples of metalanguage. A discussion of these considerations follows.

6.3: Teaching Emphasis: Modes and Dimensions of Meaning

The data set, drawn from the first of the two Teaching Sequences undertaken by each of the case study teachers during their participation in this research project, involves a total of 361 prompts addressed to teaching about mode and multimodality. Of these, major emphasis was given to the linguistic mode with nearly half of all prompts (47%) addressing linguistic meaning. A quarter of prompts in the data set (26%) addressed the visual mode; with 20% of prompts addressed the gestural mode; 7% of all prompts addressed audio meaning-making and no prompts addressed the spatial mode. The data set used in this chapter, teaching focus addressing mode based on teacher prompts and teacher-intended lexicon, correlates fairly closely with the data set used in Chapter Five, teaching focus addressing mode based on lesson (see Table 6.1 below).

Table 6.1: Teaching Focus on Mode Based on Prompt/Lesson

Focus on mode	Linguistic	Audio	Visual	Gestural	Total
Number of prompts	170 (47%)	26 (7%)	95 (26%)	70 (20%)	361 (100%)
Number of lessons	17/38 (45%)	3/38 (8%)	11/38 (29%)	7/38 (18%)	38 (100%)

Across all modes, prompts addressing the organisational dimension of meaning account for nearly half of all prompts (45%) in the data set. Prompts addressing the representational (23%) and contextual dimensions of meaning (19%), each accounted for approximately one fifth of all prompts. The social dimension of meaning was the focus of 11% of all prompts, and the ideological dimension of meaning the focus of 3% of all prompts in the data set. This is represented below in Table 6.2.

Table 6.2: Focus of Teaching Prompts: Dimension of Meaning

Dimension of meaning focus of prompts	Total	% of set
Total	361	100%
Representational prompts	83	23%
Social prompts	41	11%
Organisational prompts	159	45%
Contextual prompts	68	19%
Ideological prompts	10	3%

The breakdown of prompts relating to each mode is represented in Table 6.3.

Table 6.3: Focus of Teaching Prompts: Dimension of Mode

Dimension of meaning focus of prompts	Linguistic	Audio	Visual	Gestural	Total
Number	170	26	95	70	361
% of set	47%	7%	26%	20%	100%
Representational	5%	34%	18%	70%	
Social	3%	58%	14%	10%	
Organisational	57%	8%	54%	11%	
Contextual	33%	0	13%	0	
Ideological	2%	0	1%	8%	

An overwhelming number of the prompts addressing gestural meaning-making were directed to the representational dimension of meaning (70%), with the remainder of prompts spread relatively evenly between attention to social (10%), organisational (11%) and ideological (8%) dimensions of meaning in teaching the gestural meaning-making mode. No attention was given to the contextual dimension of meaning in the gestural mode.

The majority of prompts which attended to the visual mode (54%) related to organisational dimensions of meaning with some attention given to representational (18%), social (14%) and contextual (13%) dimensions of meaning. Negligible attention was given to the ideological dimension of meaning of the visual mode (1%). 58% of audio-focused teaching prompts relate to the social dimension of meaning, while 34% of prompts were addressed to representational dimensions of meaning making. Limited attention (8% of prompts) was directed to organisational 'dimensions of meaning' in teaching related to the audio mode of meaning; and no attention directed to contextual and ideological dimensions of meaning in the audio mode. 57% of linguistic-focused prompts concerned the organisational dimension of meaning; 33% of linguistic-focused prompts addressed the contextual dimension of meaning with limited emphasis addressed to the social (3%), representational (8%) and ideological (2%) dimensions of meaning.

A discussion of teacher addressing of each mode, the gestural, visual, audio, linguistic and spatial, follows. This discussion calls on examples from the data and considers these in terms of the dimensions of meaning. Teacher intentions and related theoretical insights are considered as well in this discussion.

6.3.1: The Gestural Mode: Discussion of Dimensions/Pedagogy

In considering teacher addressing of the gestural mode, the data is discussed in terms of teacher attention to the five 'dimensions of meaning schema' (Cope and Kalantzis, 2000a). In this study, analysis and discussion of the gestural mode of meaning relates to the conscious, explicit teaching *about* gestural meaning, elements of the gestural mode which are the focus of teaching; not the gestural processes involved in teaching and learning interactions.

Gestural representations which were the focus of case study teachers included gesturing by people (including students themselves) depicted in mirrored reflections, magazines, and photographs; as well as people and humanised animals illustrated in picture books and videos. Prompts which focused attention on emotive reactions, such as 'How did you feel when you saw yourself on television?' were not included in this discussion, but in discussion of the visual mode, because influences on the viewer's emotive reactions fall within the social dimension of meaning of the visual mode as they display an interpersonal function and relate to the interplay between the viewer and the viewed (in this case with the viewed being a representation of the self).

Overall, there appeared to be moderate emphasis in case study practices on the gestural mode, with 20% of teacher prompts in the data set directed towards teaching about the gestural. However, analysis of prompts from teacher interview, filming, teacher documentation, and the accompanying articulated intended lexicon for student learning showed that this was all attributable to Rachel.

Apparent during the data collection were teaching incidents involving gestural presentation—for example, children make an oral presentation to the class. While the classroom enactment of this example, witnessed by the researcher, attracted many teacher prompts, such as, 'How will you sit? Where will you stand? How will you hold your book?', this teaching was incidental to the major teaching point which related to students' ability to 'transfer their knowledge of website design, gained through reading and discussion into their own website layout and project presentation' (TD-LE). Therefore these prompts were not included in the data set.

The data set did include gesturally-related prompts such as, 'Look in the mirror and make faces. Watch how your face changes. "Pretend" a feeling and make a face. What kind of face is that? What sort of expression? How does your face change when happy, angry, thinking?' (TA-1-EK-TI) These prompts foregrounded the gestural as a meaning-making mode, and attended to a teacher-intended lexicon which attempted to engage students in 'Discuss(ing) meaning that gesture and expression make'; knowing that '[e]motions and 'states' are conveyed through facial expressions'; 'articulating existing knowledge' and through a 'focus on language of feeling and expressions' developing a 'common language [of] expressions; actions, feelings' (TA-EK-TI).

One point to be made in regard to this example, and one that relates to the majority of examples collected through this study, is the difference between the teachers' understanding of 'metalanguage' and the theorists' understanding of 'metalanguage'. The teacher saw development of vocabulary which assisted students to describe 'states' and emotions as 'metalanguage', a language for describing feelings. The theorists would use the term 'metalanguage' (Halliday, 1994; Kress et al., 2001; Kress and van Leeuwen, 1996; New London Group, 2000; Unsworth, 2001, 2006) to refer to language which assisted in describing the patterns and structures of a mode of meaning such as the gestural.

What this teaching example does address explicitly is that meaning can be represented in different forms—for example, that happiness can be expressed as a word or as a facial expression, or that the state of 'thinking' can be represented through speech or a gestural representation of a tilted head resting in a cupped hand (TA-1-EK-SFC). In terms of the contextual dimension of meaning this can be described as a modal 'cross-reference' (Cope and Kalantzis, 2000a) wherein gestural meanings relate to verbal linguistic meaning and gestures indicate expressions or emotive types of meanings. The accompanying teacher-intended lexicon, 'Verbalise and list ways that display how people are feeling; and *how* [students] know', was enacted through verbalisation, writing and drawing of gestural meaning-making and assisted in understanding that 'various modes can affect the construction and interpretation of meaning' (TA–1-EK-LE).

Another example of teaching addressing the contextual dimension of meaning was indicated in the teacher-intended lexicon, 'Focus on different ways to express feelings or 'states' (TA–11-AF-LE) and 'To talk about gesture and expression as part of whole [multimodal] meaning—how do they help meaning? Who do they help?' (TA-AF-LE). A key teaching intention was that expressions and movements can depict and convey different states and feelings and that expressions and movements can give viewers meaning that words do not.

The major focus in this data sample addresses gestural representation (70%), with prompts addressing the use of the face as the 'participant' in showing mental states (sleepy, thinking) or feelings (anger, happiness, sadness), a particular category of processes (Halliday, 1994, p. 28–9; Unsworth, 2006); or conscious processes (Cope and Kalantzis, 2000a).

The data shows further articulation of the representational dimension of meaning (Cope and Kalantzis, 2000;) through focus on eyes, mouth and hands as participants in conveying gestural meaning, expanding gestural participants from the face to include other body parts, and to more finely specify facial features (the eyes and mouth) as gestural participants. Teacher-intended lexicon that 'Eyes, mouth and hands convey a range of meaning' (TA–1-EK-LE) was initially actualised indirectly through an exploration of a broadening range of gestural representational dimension of meaning examples. Prompts such as, 'Identify feelings in magazines and cards. Cut out all the pictures that you think show how people are feeling. Sort your pictures into groups' (TA–2-EK-LE) were followed in subsequent lessons by prompts such as, 'Show me how you would look if you were angry; thoughtful; sad; happy' (TA–2-EN-SFC); and 'Classify photos of classmates using the same grid (happy people, sad people; thoughtful people; angry people)' and 'How were the children in the photos feeling?' These prompts developed understanding that 'Feelings [various] are shown through gestures and expressions' (TA-EK-2-TI), extending understandings that body parts other than facial features can be used to make meaning. These prompts also drew attention to gestural representation in a broadening range of media (mirrored reflection, magazines and cards, digital images of self and others).

The data shows that the role of body parts as representational participants in conveying gestural meaning was highlighted through focus on eyes, hands, mouth, and 'stance' as evidenced in the teacher-intended lexicon, 'Body parts indicate meaning' (TA-4-CN-TI); and 'Various body parts can indicate meaning: hand gesture; stance; mouth; eyes' (TA–4-CN-LE). This learning was actualised through prompts such as 'What body part can you see on cut up faces? How do you know how this person may be feeling? What is telling you that? Look at hands, stance, mouth, eyes. Talk about the different body parts that help us understand what is happening' (TA–4-CN-LE).

The data shows further articulation of gestural representation through focus on movements as gestural participants. Teaching indicated that movements can signify 'states'; such as a yawn signifying sleepiness or stamping feet signifying anger' (TA-9-AF-LE). This teaching was actualised through prompts such as, 'Who's that? [on the video screen] How do you know how he's feeling? Have a look at the actions X is doing. What sort of actions did X do to show she is sleepy? Did she use her hands? How do we know X is angry? His eyebrows are down, aren't they? What's he doing with his feet?' (TA-11-AF-SFC).

The data shows further articulation of gestural representation through focus on the attributes and location of characters through attention to characters' expressions and movements within the context of still and animated illustrated narratives. This further broadened the use of a range of forms to include the expressions and movements of humanised animals in character form. Prompts such as, 'Discuss the characters' movements. Did she look? What is he doing? What's his body doing? Rosie still looks the same. How's the fox looking? What would he do if he caught her? What's his body doing now? Watch the way he's sneaking. Where's she going? He's close again. He's sneaking up again' (TA-7-AF-SFC) are utilised to address identity attributes (Halliday, 1994), including motives, interests and personal characteristics. In this instance these identity attributes are gleaned from tiptoeing movements and a character adopting a crouching position so as to avoid detection by another character. Examples of processes or 'acts' of 'doing' realised by movement; (Martinec, 2000, p. 314) include 'going' and 'sneaking'. Processes of 'state' realised by lack of movement (Martinec, 2000, p. 314), are exemplified through 'looking' and 'waiting'.

The data shows a gap between the richness of the prompts and the non-specific nature of the teacher-intended lexicon relating to these prompts, 'Gestures and expressions show the meaning of feelings. Gestures enhance meaning' (TA-4-6-7-AF-TI). These teacher intentions lack specificity in relation to the functions of the gestural, failing to describe how the meaning of feelings is shown through gestures and expressions and how gestures enhance meaning.

Although absent from the data, gestural participant identity attributes such as attitude and motive can also be explored in terms of speed and rhythm of movement, movement dynamics such as smooth, sharp, direct, meandering, strong or light; space used in movement and combinations of different rhythm patterns (Russell-Bowie, 2006). Just as McNeill (1992) argues that circumstances of time are evident in the 'beat' of hand movements, characters' movements in time can offer insights into meaning. For example, indifference or an oblivious attitude is conveyed through steady tempo, and rhythmic regularity of gait and actions. A covert aggressive character motive is shown contrasting small then large actions (Russell-Bowie, 2006), irregularly timed hiding, sneaking and sudden pouncing.

As McNeill (1992) argues that the circumstances of space are evident in the pointing of a finger to a space in front of the listener to denote 'there', so characters' movements in space, body positioning so as to be unseen by another character, and then attempting to pounce on them, show relative position as a function of gestural meaning.

There is a sense in which the gestural mode has, by its embodied nature, an abiding connection to the social, particularly in the data examples which emphasise feelings and emotions. However, a functional view of gestures as the focus of taught meaning-making resources begs analysis in terms of gesturer/viewer and gesturer/gesturer interpersonal relationships or interactivity; the social dimension. In the data set used in this chapter, the social dimension of meaning in the gestural mode attracted (10%) of the prompts of teaching in the gestural mode.

These included, 'What difference did seeing the characters moving make?' after viewing still and animated images of a cross-platform text. 'Did Rosie know the fox was there? Will he catch her?' (TA-7-AF-SFC) These examples direct attention to gestural participant roles, to the statements made by body part movements and facial expressions. Gestural participant roles are achieved by contrast between two characters' gestures and each gesturer's interactivity with each other and viewer: A steadfast gait undertaken at regular pace showed a goal of simply walking through a farm. Hiding, sneaking and sudden pouncing showed more aggressive intentions. Gaze averted from the viewer showed either unawareness of impending danger, due perhaps to innocence or superior sense of knowing, while a gaze directed at the viewer served to either conspire or suggest guilt (Kress and van Leeuwen, 1996, p. 162). Prompts such as, 'We're going to make a video of a way you sometimes feel. You will be videoed looking and moving in that way. The other children in the group will have to guess what you are feeling' (TA-10-AF-SFC), offered potential for elaboration of the social dimension of meaning of the gestural mode of meaning-making. However the teacher-intended lexicon, 'Focus on different ways to express feelings (TA–10-AF-LE) 'Whole body movement shows feeling/matches expression' (TA-10-11-AF-TI), lacked a specificity in describing possibilities, offering instead more general foci.

As with the other modes, the data showed examples of prompts not accompanied by teacher intentions but which have potential for teaching lexicon. While explicit teaching intentions relating to the ideological dimension of meaning of the gestural mode were absent from the data, prompts such as 'Pretend a feeling and make a face' moved towards the ideological dimension of meaning, for example that gestural meanings of mental states can be 'pretended' or lack 'truth value' (Cope and Kalantzis, 2000a). Ideological dimension of meaning prompts of this kind made up 8.5% of the gestural data set, including, 'the magazines had mostly happy faces' which indicates possibilities for teaching that focused on the ideological dimension of meaning; perhaps that gestural meanings can be over-represented to serve advertising interests. The data also included the prompt, 'What did you do when the camera was on you?' (TA-1-EK-SFC) as a consequence of which ideological teaching addressing the status that a meaning-maker attributes to message—in this case in the context of 'acting' compared to authentic sentiment (Cope and Kalantzis, 2000a). Similarly, the prompts regarding an animal, 'He does look a little bit angry. Does he look happy? I think he looks a bit sad', indicate the depiction of animals as characters through humanised gestural representation. A hen whose gestures show a lack of awareness, naivety or possibly cleverness and a fox whose gestures show aggressive intentions and disappointment due to hapless endeavours at hunting, have been humanised by the meaning-makers rather than represented as animals seeking exercise and food.

Specific teaching of the organisational dimension of meaning of the gestural mode as an independent mode was not strongly evident in the data, with 11% of prompts directed to this purpose. To the extent to which it existed it is shown by prompts such as, 'Think about how your face would be; your eyes, your hands, the way you stand; how you move. How do you walk when sad? How does your face move? What do your hands do? What does your body do?' (TA–10-AF-LE) These prompts draw attention to the teacher-intended lexicon, 'Focus on different ways to express feelings' (TA–10-AF-LE) and 'Whole body movement shows feeling/matches expression' (TA-10-11-AF-TI)'. This example from the data shows organisation of a gestural label, a single emotion displayed in gesture. To a lesser extent the narrative events in the cross-platform text were shown through gestures—for example, plot complications were heralded through gestures; outcomes were also conveyed through gestures—rather than through developing the organisation of these events.

Teaching of the organisational dimension of meaning in general, rather than gestural-specific teaching of the organisational dimension of meaning, could be said to be focused on emphasising a broad view of meaning made in multiple modes, particularly in narrative contexts as reflected in the teacher-intended lexicon, 'To talk about gesture and expression as part of whole meaning—how do they help meaning? Who do they help?' (TA-AF-LE).

Kress et al (2001) draw on the work of Merleau-Ponty and Crowder in describing the gestural meaning-making mode as:

> ... the combined use of the face, arms, and hands in motion and is usually associated with the expression of emotion or symbolic meanings... including those that refer explicitly to objects (usually described as iconic, metaphoric or sym-

bolic), the movement of the body, of body posture and position, and the body and use of space as meaning-making resources (Kress et al., 2001, p. 61).

The data has shown that while one of the case study teachers addressed the gestural, there was a limited dexterity in asking questions about the gestural mode. Concerted focus on the gestural mode was confined to Rachel, whose teaching about the gestural mode addressed emotional expression. And while implicit, teaching did not explicitly address that different expressions might represent different meanings depending on contextual conditions, with no attention given to the contextual dimension of meaning of the gestural mode.

Overall, the predominant focus of teaching about the gestural meaning-making mode was on naming *what* feeling gestures represent and *what* the facial and body parts do in order to express or convey meaning. The focus was on the actual vocabulary, or 'getting to know the language of feelings' (TA-SFTI), or 'what the meaning is', rather than the meta-vocabulary 'how the meaning is made' in gestural mode.

6.3.2: The Visual Mode: Discussion of Dimensions/Pedagogy

In considering teacher addressing of the visual mode, the data is discussed in terms of teacher attention to the dimensions of meaning (Cope and Kalantzis, 2000a), explicit teaching *about* visual meaning, or elements of the visual mode which are the focus of teaching. The data indicates that, in the visual mode, there is concentration of teacher prompts on the organisational dimension of meaning (54%), with a spread of deployment of prompts relating to representational (18%), social (14%), and contextual (13%) dimensions of meaning. Negligible attention was given to the ideological dimension of meaning of the visual mode (1% of prompts). This spread indicates a relatively high degree of teacher confidence and flexibility in teaching related to the visual mode, as does the 26% of all prompts which were directed to teaching about the visual mode. The data suggests that in relation to the representational dimension of meaning, teaching focused both on 'narrative' and on 'conceptual' representations of aspects of things going on in the world (Kress and van Leeuwen, 1996).

Narrative-focused representational dimension of meaning prompts included, 'Look at the book. What's going to happen?' (TA-6-AF-SFC), which drew attention to visual elements such as participants, processes and circumstances in narrative contexts. 'Why is he going to fall down? What's happening in the picture?' (TA-6-AF-SFC), prompted students to articulate examples of visual elements which indicated actional, and mental processes such as vectors achieved through gaze and participant positioning (Kress and van Leeuwen, 1996). Prompting drew attention to contextualised visual elements, the 'what' of the visuals, with discussion addressing the specific participants, processes and circumstances within the context of particular stories, rather than the functioning of the visual in depicting participants, processes and circumstances.

The teacher-intended goals related to these prompts addressed the interdependence of the semiotic resources, 'Print/pictures make meaning' (TA-5-CT-LE-SFC-TI), which was enacted by prompts focused on both organisational and representational dimensions of meaning. The organisational dimension of meaning of a visual narrative was addressed in broad terms through prompts such as 'Words don't tell us? [There are] lots of things words aren't saying' (TA-6-CT-SFC), developing awareness of the visual as a mode contributing to meaning (in a narrative); that print and pictures add different meaning; and that pictures and texts can be interdependent. For example, a particular character or their actions might only be evident through the visual mode, or plot complications may only be evident in the visual mode, making the visual and the linguistic symbiotic in representing meaning. The teacher-intended lexicon was that 'Meaning (narrative) can be made from pictures' (TA-5-CT-LE-SFC-TI). This is reminiscent of descriptions of interdependent relationships of modes, for example, how modes can amplify, extend, counterpoint, illustrate and 'complement, reiterate, anticipate and contradict each other' (Burn and Parker, 2003a, p. 63).

Visual processes are evident in story events, in the same example: a series of unsuccessful ploys by one character or actor to attack another character, who escapes all attempted attacks, seemingly oblivious to them. Prompts deployed to address the gestural in the visual include, 'Did she look? What is he doing? What's his body doing? Rosie still looks the same. How's the fox looking?' (TA-7-AF-SFC). These prompts suggest that there are two main characters, or participants, a hen walking and a fox stalking, and elements such as coop, buildings, lake which denote a walk around a farm as the narrative circumstances. Prompts which draw attention to *how* the visual mode was deployed to depict representations (participants, processes and circumstances) through visual elements such as line, tone, colour, texture, shape, form, space and pattern (Russell-Bowie, 2006, p. 153) were not strongly evident.

The data shows the book and animated versions of a cross-platform text were deployed to draw attention to the contextual dimension of meaning, including intertextual references through prompts such as 'Discuss the characters' movements. What difference did seeing the characters moving make?' (TA-7-AF-SFC); with questioning directed towards characters' understandings, such as 'Did Rosie know the fox was there?' While the data shows the animated version was used in further development of gestural knowledge, this also touches on social relations between two characters and visual elements which infer relational meaning (Kress and van Leeuwen, 1996).

Implied, but not strongly evident in the data was teaching directed to the social dimension of meaning in animated images and images involving lens and camera movement such as pans, zooms and dollys which can result in varying perspectives—low as opposed to high angle, and planes of involvement, oblique as opposed to frontal or the eye contact of a demand and the non-eye contact of an 'offer' (Kress and van Leeuwen, 1996).

While not strongly evident in the data, using cross-platform texts holds potential for developing knowledge of the organisational dimension of meaning. Representations in the visual mode such as still images on pages and 'transitions' in moving images such as cuts, wipes, and dissolves show the organisational dimension of meaning relating to participants' involvement in processes and circumstances, particularly spatiotemporal meanings, or changes in place and time (Burn and Parker, 2003b, p. 59). Organisational and social dimensions of meaning are both evident in the integration of moving image and sound through the organisational processes of filming and editing which frame and assemble representations—what Burn and Parker call the 'kineikonic mode' (2003b, p. 59).

Teaching focused on literature tended to concentrate on narrative, visually-related teaching, echoing the analysis on e-literature undertaken by Unsworth (2006). Greater focus was evident on conceptual representation (Kress and van Leeuwen, 1996) in teaching focused on web design, where conceptual visuals such as Venn diagrams and concept maps were deployed to develop classificational taxonomies. These were realised through prompts such as, 'Draw a concept map showing all you know about webpages. Brainstorm words and phrases. Expand each of these further by writing a sentence to show your understanding Include images to show your understanding also' (TD-1-EK-LE). However, the major focus of these prompts was to develop a piece of writing which described students' knowledge of webpages, and the visual conceptual representation of the concept map was the means for doing so.

The social dimension of meaning was evident in the data through prompts which directed students to consider their responses to images. How did you feel when you watched the animation? (TA-9-AF-LE). How did you feel watching yourself on TV?' Here the teacher-intended lexicon relates to developing understanding of feelings such as, 'Feeling in response to visual meaning' (TA-12-AF-LE). Prompts which directed attention to knowledge of an interpersonal response such as, 'How do we know when reading something that it might be a funny card? It's a funny message? Bubble writing? Fancy writing? The writing can actually look wriggly' (TBC-8-AI-SFC), originated in the context of a discussion of a multimodal text (a greeting card) but the responses took discussion to the social dimensions of meaning of the visual aspects of print. Retrospectively the teacher-intended lexicon was described as 'Visuals (including font) offer meaning' (TBC-8-AI-SF).

Absent from this data set was teaching focused on the social dimension of meaning between the producer and the viewer of visuals, including 'contact', demand or offer depending on gaze; 'social distance', intimate social or impersonal differentiated by the view of depicted participants: close, medium or long shots; and 'attitude', levels of involvement dependent on angle as frontal or oblique; and levels of power dependent on high, eye, or low angle (Kress and van Leeuwen, 1996). The level of realism an image conveys—naturalistic, abstract or scientific/technological—could be addressed with naturalistic images showing high colour saturation, colour diversification and modulation. High modality is also seen in the level of participant features' detail as opposed to schematised detail (Kress and van Leeuwen, 1996). Teaching did not extend to prompting relating to the effect of the use of shot angles in the picture story book, in which shots were predominantly at eye level, except where danger is imminent such as when a fox is about to jump on a hen. In this case the fox is positioned higher on the page as it prepares to jump, lower following failed attempts; and 'contact' is mainly through offers, rather than demands, with character gaze directed within the text, except following the failed attempts at attack, where the fox appeared to look despondently at the viewer.

In addition to the organisational dimensions of meaning described above, teaching related to the organisational dimension of meaning of conceptual participants, addressed through prompts such as, 'What do you notice about the organisation and navigation of the X website? What website terms have you come across? Make an ongoing class glossary of website terms that students have come across' (TD-5-CN-LE). All these were used to support the teacher-intended lexicon, 'Understand and use websites to find information. Use and understand the terminology of the internet, eg, hyperlink, navigation bars, download, graphics' (TD-5-CN-LE). Attention to the organisational dimension of meaning was heavily emphasised in teaching related to website design.

A focus on salience or grounding was implied in the prompt series which focused attention on hyperlinks and navigation icons as salient visual organisational elements, such as, 'Let's look at the rest of the (web)page. It's one of those ones where you have to scroll down. Let's read the bit at the bottom. Who can tell me something they like about this webpage? Thinking about design, what were the good things on the website? What do the underlined bits mean? When I put the cursor over the hyperlink, it turns into a hand; and the text goes bigger. On the top of the page there was something that told you what you would read' (TD-11-AI-SFC).

Not evident were the greater/lesser of centre/margin placement; the left/right placement of given/new information in Western cultures; and the vertical over/under polarisation of ideal/real value (Kress and van Leeuwen, 1996). Cohesive devices, such as the framing of elements by borders, and the location of elements' connection or disconnection from one another (Kress and van Leeuwen, 1996), are focused on implicitly in prompt series which addressed the organisational dimension of meaning of screen-based visual elements. One example is the prompt series, 'Your name is being "lasered" in; it is coming in 1 by 1 [letter]. Can we look at F5 so we can see your PowerPoint presentation? Let's see the first one; let's see a second slide. Can I have a look at how you added animation effects and sounds to your PowerPoint? You went to "slide show": what did you do next? "Custom animation?" What effects did you add? You added sound. Go to "preview" and see if you are happy with your name. I think we have to change the order and timing. Is your passion project hyperlinked to that (profile)?' (TD-13-AI-SF). This series of prompts was concerned with the teacher-intended lexicon 'Develop a website, [Research and] present in a digital format a project on a subject of interest' (TD-12-AA-LE). 'Use the concepts of website design: purpose, audience, content, navigation' (TD-AA/AC-LE). The teacher prompts and intentions touched on borders and framing (such as of individual letters being lasered into a PowerPoint presentation) and held potential for a focus on greater/lesser of centre/margin placement; the left/right placement of given/new information (in Western cultures) and the vertical over/under polarisation of ideal/real value in relation to of website elements (Kress and van Leeuwen, 1996).

The data shows that that emphasis on the contextual dimension of meaning of the visual mode was predominant in prompts and intended teacher lexicon that explored purpose and audience of visuals. Prompts such as, 'We're going to cover the writing and look at cards... What features tell you what celebration it's for? Why would we give this to someone? Would you give an Easter egg card for a birthday?...Think about the features, purposes, who you'd give the card to?...This could be a couple of occasions. What else? What might the roses and love heart mean? Why would it make you think of weddings? Why do you say that? Is there anything that gives you that indication? What features of the card made you think it's for these purposes?' (TBC-7-CT-SFC). These prompts pursue understandings related to the purpose and audience of greeting cards as suggested by the images alone. The teacher-intended lexicon in the Learning Element was very general, 'Realise that literacy is multimodal and that the ways the visual and alphabetical modes are constructed affect the meaning' (TBC-C-LE) However, in interview the teachers discussed developing knowledge of 'Occasion-specific symbols; card purposes and audiences; symbols font types (bold, plain, gold) in relation to celebrations, purpose and audience' (TBC-7-CT-SF-TI). Many of these examples came from responses by the students to the teachers' prompts.

In analysing the visual mode, the data shows scant teaching attention was directed to the ideological dimension of meaning. Application of PMI (Plus/Minus/Interesting) tool in an analysis of webpages, involved teacher prompting, 'What were the plus, minus and interesting aspects you found on this school website?' This was followed by prompts which addressed the organisational dimension of meaning, such as 'Let's look at the rest of the page. It's one of those ones where you have to scroll down. Thinking about design, what were the good things on the website? What else could we have besides that picture/animation?' (TD-11-AI-SF) The further prompt to, 'Brainstorm PMI for each school site' did not lead to comparison and contrast of the webpage designer's affinities, interests and motives (Gee, 1996, 2005) through analysis including the visual mode. Development of teaching addressing the ideological dimension of meaning was not evident in the data.

The data has shown there was broad uptake amongst the case study participants in relation to the visual mode, and some degree of confidence and dexterity in teaching of the visual mode. Teachers addressed representational, social, organisational and contextual dimensions of meaning of the visual, although no attention was given to the ideological dimension of meaning. However, as was the case with the gestural mode, much teaching drew attention to the 'what' of the visuals: the context-specific representations and students' social responses to these representations within the context of particular still and animated visuals and greeting cards. There was a strong emphasis on structure and the organisational dimension of meaning of visual elements in teaching related to website design.

6.3.3: The Audio Mode: Discussion of Dimensions/Pedagogy

In considering teacher addressing of the audio mode, the data is discussed in terms of teacher attention to the five dimensions of meaning (Cope and Kalantzis, 2000a), that is, explicit teaching *about* audio meaning. Overall there was limited emphasis by case study teachers on the audio mode, with only 7% of prompts attending to teaching in this area. All of these examples were drawn from the classroom applications of Rachel.

34% of prompts were addressed to representational dimensions of meaning in the audio mode. Examples from the data of audio mode-related prompts focused on the representational dimension of meaning include, 'What sound could come there? It doesn't say splash, but that would be good sound. Bump would be a good sound. Crash! BOING! Buzz. Sneak. Splash. Boom. We can talk about different sound effects. Do you think we'll hear other things?' (TA-6-AF-SFC). These were deployed while viewing a video with the volume turned off, a predictive exercise addressing the teacher-intended lexicon, 'To recognise that literacy encompasses linguistic, visual, gestural and *audio* modes of meaning. When we read or watch things we get information from the words, the illustrations, the layout and the *music* [emphasis added by the researcher]' (TA-CN-LE) and '[t]hat sound conveys meaning: that noises can include sound effects and music (TA-8-AF-SFTI). Here students are urged to name sounds, some which could be described as onomatopoeic imitations of humanised animal characters engaging in plot events. In analysing which dimension of meaning this teaching addresses, the prompts were categorised as representations of processes. This analysis is supported by van Leeuwen's argument that '[s]ounds are not things, nor can they represent things. Sounds are actions and can only represent the actions of people, places and things; the cries of street vendors, not the vendors themselves, the lapping of water against the shore, not the lake itself. Sound messages only have verbs, so to speak. The nouns are inferred' (van Leeuwen, 1999, p. 92–3).

Further teaching involved students in another viewing of the video with the sound turned up. Prompts included, 'What sort of noises suit this video? What did you hear in the animation? Were you surprised hearing music? Did it add to the meaning of the story? What else did you hear?' (TA–8-AF-SFC). The prompts in this example address a number of dimensions of meaning. 'What sort of noises suit this video?' involves students in considering the contextual and social dimensions of meaning of audio resources, the type of story which the animation tells, the mood or tone of the story and the way it has been depicted by the animators. 'What did you hear in the animation?' asks students to name audio representations the teacher specifically wanted to focus on: narration, music and sound effects. The question, 'Were you surprised hearing music?' involves students in a self-reflection of their own predictions (which had included sound effects but hadn't included music) and invites a focus on the social dimension of meaning through students' responses as listeners.

Overall there was a concentrated emphasis given to the social dimension of meaning of the audio mode, with 58% of audio focused teaching prompts relating to the social dimension of meaning. Prompts including, 'Very softly creeping. Do you think it will be soft or loud noise? (TA-6-AF-SFC) suggested sounds were designed to carry a certain distance through use of the semiotic resources of 'loudness' (van Leeuwen, 1999, p. 23). Teaching focused on a connection between a character's motives and the 'loudness' of the sound effect suggesting 'a set of possible social relations' between sounds and listeners including 'close' (intimate, personal and informal distance) to more 'distant' (formal and public distance) (van Leeuwen, 1999, p. 212).

Also within the social dimension of meaning, students' attention was directed to their own feelings and physical responses in relation to music through prompts such as, 'Does it make you want to move? How? How does it make you feel? Which do you like best? Why?' (TA-13-AA-LE) What music would add extra information to show feeling? How do you feel watching it? Without music? With music? With different music?' (TA-14- AC-LE-TI). The teacher-intended lexicon was to focus on 'Movement and mood in response to music' (TA-13-AA-LE) and 'Sound effects and music add emphasis to match mood' (TA-13-AA-14-AC-LE-TI).

It has been argued that the representational, or ideational, resources of sound 'have to be realized on the back of interpersonal resources' since social relations such as "disharmony" can only be represented by two clashing human or instrumental "voices", just as "tenderness" requires that the listener is addressed in a tender fashion (van Leeuwen, 1999, p. 190–91). This may account for a strong emphasis on the social dimension of meaning and on the students' responses to the mood created by music.

Teaching did not focus on the social dimension indicated in the use of the major key, which invites optimism, despite the underhanded intentions of one of the characters; the quadruple (4/4) beat which denotes a steadfast march and invites an evenly rhythmic foot-tapping or hand-clapping response. Inferred in the data, through the emphasis on 'mood', was an exploration of the social dimension of meaning through the use of perspective which puts into a hierarchy what's being represented, such as in the film soundtrack which at times foregrounded dialogue with music in the background and at other times foregrounded music with an absence of dialogue (van Leeuwen, 1999, p. 14).

The data suggests that, in the audio mode, there was limited teacher attention given to the organisational dimension of meaning, except as discussed above, as a mode of meaning within a multimodal text (8% of audio-focused prompts). Teaching did not focus on the contextual dimension of meaning such as the mid-Western American accent of the narrator and the use of banjo, violin, and string bass to carry the melody or the informality of the social distance created by the foregrounding of laughter by the narrator at the commencement of the film (van Leeuwen, 1999, p. 14).

Teaching did not focus on the organisational dimension of meaning, such as the repetitious cycles of audio journey of the hen and fox indicated in the soundtrack—the informal tuning up of the violin is followed by the narrated introduction of the title; laughter; a violin solo introduction; a verse in which a banjo carries the melody with a string bass accompaniment; and a chorus wherein a violin carries the melody with string bass accompaniment. There is a repetitive structure of verse and chorus which builds to a climax and resolution.

Teaching did not focus on the contextual dimension of meaning such as, in the example from the animation soundtrack, audio elements and their reference to context which include the use of laughter at the beginning of the audio track, which foreshadowed comedy; the deployment of a narrator with a mid-Western American accent and prominent use of string instruments (violin and banjo) and marching beat (string bass) which together denote a hillbilly country and western style reminiscent of 'Turkey in the Straw'.

Also absent in the data was teaching addressing the ideological dimension of meaning. The ideological dimension of meaning was displayed in the animated soundtrack through the use of a constant, prominent bass line and banjo melody to depict a character as steadfast and focused in undertaking a walk around the farmyard, attributing human feelings to an animal. Similarly, the ideological dimension of meaning can be noticed in the intent of the upbeat or optimistic nature of the audio track, created by the interplay of major key, selected instruments and percussive effects.

Sound is a 'relatively unexplored semiotic terrain' (van Leeuwen, 1999, p. 192), and van Leeuwen's attempts to transfer principles from systemic functional linguistics through interrogation of metafunctions of audio resources—as had been done with visual resources—proved problematic. The audio resources were found to be less specialised than language and visuals, and not as clearly structured according to metafunction. Lack of metafunction clarity can be noted in the use of audio perspective, foregrounding and backgrounding of audio elements, mentioned as a resource for achieving the social dimension of meaning in this discussion. Consideration can be given to perspective as having an organisational dimension of meaning function, the grounding of elements positioning them as more or less salient, such as foregrounding an instrument which is used to denote a certain character or backgrounding another.

Perhaps this is an example of a lack of metafunctional clarity around the audio. As van Leeuwen found, 'I always ended up feeling that a given sound resource (say pitch or dynamics) was used ideationally *and* interpersonally, or both ideationally *and* textually and so on' (1999, p. 190-1)'this provides a reason for adopting an analysis based on *material* aspects rather than communicative functions of audio, considering what uses could be made of resources such as *dynamics or pitch* in speech, music and other sound.

6.3.4: The Linguistic Mode: Discussion of Dimensions/Pedagogy

As with the modes already discussed, the data relating to teacher addressing of the linguistic mode is analysed in terms of attention to the five dimensions of meaning (Cope and Kalantzis, 2000a): that is, explicit teaching *about* linguistic meaning. The linguistic mode was heavily emphasised by teachers with 47% of teaching prompts in the data set used in this chapter addressed to teaching about the linguistic mode.

The data does show that, in the linguistic mode, 57% of linguistic focused prompts were directed to organisational dimensions of meaning, and many teaching examples attend to multiple dimensional foci. An example from the data of a series of prompts used to pursue understandings of the teacher-intended lexicon is, 'Ascertain understanding of the internet (TD-1-EK-LE) through focus on elements including 'webpages, Microsoft FrontPage, hyperlinks between/within webpage/s, backgrounds, graphics, words, phrases, sentences' (TD-1-EK-SF-TI-SF). Introductory lesson prompts included, 'We are going to do a concept map for our webpage. What do we use a concept map for?' The teacher wrote the word, 'webpage' on a whiteboard and prompted, 'I'm going to do a modelled writing about what I know about the webpage' which established the context of the lesson. The teacher then drew an arrow from the word 'webpage' and wrote the words, 'Microsoft FrontPage' and prompted, 'I know I can use Microsoft FrontPage to design my webpage'; drew another arrow from the word 'webpage' and wrote the word 'hyperlink' and prompted, 'I know how to do a hyperlink so I can link from one page to another or from the top to the bottom of a page'. The teacher wrote the word, 'graphics' and prompted, 'I'm going to write the word, *graphics*'. The teacher explained that students should...'choose one idea that you know something about and write something that you know about that idea. I'm going to do that for 'hyperlink'. So what do I actually know about hyperlinks? I know they link pages and websites together' (TD-1-EK-SF).

This example from the data displays the use of a concept map as an organiser for a piece of writing in which students will record, in words and images, their knowledge of websites. While the teacher's primary purpose was to ascertain what students know about websites, this is achieved through a scaffolded process of headings, such as 'hyperlink' and 'graphics' which were then elaborated into sentences and explanatory images. Through writing structured by the use of a heading and sub-headings, students were being taught to organise their knowledge of the features of a webpage, making this most appropriately categorised as attending to the organisational dimension of meaning in the linguistic mode. However it obviously has strong connection to the visual mode, particularly conceptual visual, representational and organisational dimensions of meaning with its emphasis on layout with arrows, boxes, and illustrative diagrams showing relationships.

However, these were not emphasised in the teaching as were the organisers of headings, words, phrases and sentences.

The data shows some evidence of teaching addressed to the representational dimension of meaning (eg participants; being and acting; roles of participants in the communication of meaning; and commitment) in the linguistic mode, such as naming 'sentence' and hyperlink' (Cope and Kalantzis, 2000a).

This focus on the organisational dimension of meaning was characteristic of the linguistic data, with other examples including, 'Draw/write to plan writing: what I used; how I felt; how I felt when I watched myself' (TA-12-AF-LE); 'We are going to write a sentence about what you did on the video. What can you tell me about what you are doing? In a sentence, "I was..." What do you want your sentence to say?' (TA-12-AF-SFC). This latter example could have been categorised as attending to the social dimension of meaning, as it required students to call on felt responses, although the overall intent was to develop cohesive text representing students' experiences in words. Again, the word 'sentence' is used but was not supplemented by metalanguage describing the participants, processes and circumstances.

An engagement of the students in literate behaviours and habits, such as author studies and book responses was evident through prompts such as 'We're going to read a book' [Read and pointed to words] (TA-5-CT-SFC) with the teacher emphasising that 'Meaning is made from printed words' (TA-5-CT-SFC) and that stories have a 'beginning, middle and end' and an emphasis on 'comprehension'. The comprehension-focused discussion related to represented characters, their actions and circumstances, but, since the stories were illustrated, discussion was prompted by illustrations and language rather than the contribution of the linguistic data. The negligible attention to the representational dimension of meaning, with just 5% of linguistic-focused prompts addressed to this aspect, indicates that when addressing the multimodal, teachers de-emphasised linguistic representation within the bounds of the project. Teaching approaches from the two-hour literacy block in the Early Years Literacy Program which are recommended for knowledge of language, including 'guided reading' and 'interactive writing' were not present in the data of classroom applications, though it was present in teacher interview (TA/SFTI/0704) This suggests that the teaching of language happened outside the parameters of the research study, at another time of day when the researcher was not present.

In relation to 'meaning being made from printed words' contributions of different modes to meaning in a multimodal design, for example alternative meanings, amplified meaning and extended meanings were not explored. A focus on the narrative structure of 'the beginning, middle and end' suggests teaching attention was given to the organisational dimension of meaning, however this was only evident in teacher interview, not in filmed classroom practice, researcher observed classroom practice or teacher documentation in the Learning Element.

Interestingly, in data collected subsequent to the slices being analysed in this chapter, there was evidence of teacher attention to the organisational dimension of meaning in the linguistic mode and the interplay of print and visuals:

> We look at the one fairytale over the week but we read the different versions and compare, so as well as comparing the story line and the narrative and the fairytale, the beginning, the middle and the end, we are also comparing how the artists look at the pictures and what is selected to support the story (TA/SFTI/0209).

Prompts such as, 'Go to this [children's author] website. Look at and read the [web]pages. Listen to a story read by the author. Find information to write a profile on an author' (TD-3-EN-LE) supported the teacher intention to enable students to, 'Access and navigate websites. Locate, use and read webpages (TD-EN-LE). How to type in a URL and ...navigate, browse, read and listen to stories; write an author profile' (TD-3-EN-LE). This example from the data shows involvement in learning the language of webpages, touching on the representational dimension of meaning, as well as learning about an author through language.

The data shows examples of teaching which attended to the organisational dimension of meaning across modes but foregrounded the linguistic. An example from the data that illustrates this is a teacher-led comparison between a 'big book' and a webpage using a Venn diagram to note similarities and differences. Teacher prompts included, 'Is a hyperlink the same as a contents page? Even though they both have a structure, they are different in how they are set up. How is this different or the same as using a webpage to find information?' (TD-12-AA-LE -SFC) These prompts were deployed to assist the students to, 'Compare and contrast the structure and layout of the big book to a website and how they support readers to find information' (TD-12-AA-LE -TI).

The data shows limited attention directed to teaching about the social dimension of meaning of the linguistic mode (4.5%). What evidence was present was characteristically addressed to felt responses after engagement with the linguistic mode with, 'How do you feel about the story?' (TA-5-CT-LE), typical of these, with the teacher directing attention to the students' responses to the linguistic aspects of multimodal texts. This would require a focus on 'how' the linguistic elicited felt responses, such as how specific linguistic features affected students.

An example from the data which shows opportunity for such teaching involves a teacher-led class writing of a greeting card to another teacher, 'How are we going to start our message? Maybe "Dear Ms X". That might help you think about what's in the middle. Happy Birthday? That greeting could be on the inside and outside. Anything you would put on top or bottom of message?' (TBC-9-AA-SFC) This example predominantly addresses the organisational dimension of meaning through the teacher-intended lexicon, 'Greeting organisation: card manufacturer's greeting and greeting of sender' (TBC-9-AA-SFTI), and through exploration of the compositional elements of greeting cards, the use of 'person' and mood within specific language choices could be incorporated.

Possibilities for teaching that focuses on a number of dimensions of meaning can be illustrated through considering the linguistic information in one of the picture story books evident in the data. The linguistic consists of one sentence, organised over the length of the book (organisational dimension of meaning) recounting a journey. The sentence begins with a nominal group with character and species (representational dimension of meaning) in theme position (organisational dimension of meaning), followed by the process undertaken, elaborated on through a series of three-word prepositional phrases to show circumstances (representational dimension of meaning).

The sentence is a narrative recounted in detached third person, past tense, deploying an economical use of words (social dimension of meaning). The sentence beginning acts as an orientation, each three-word phase 'poetic' in its succinct description of an uneventful narrative with no plot complications (contextual dimension of meaning). The single character is depicted as purposeful and safe and plot complications and resolutions are deliberately omitted from the linguistic information (ideological dimension of meaning).

The contextual dimension of meaning is well represented, with 33% of linguistic-focused prompts addressing contextual aspects, particularly in the teaching relating to greeting cards. The contextual dimension of meaning was approached through consideration of purpose, audience and context, with teaching prompts in this area including, 'What are different celebrations you, or someone else gets cards for? What are some of the days we receive cards?' (TBC-5-CN-SFC) 'During which celebrations do you give or exchange cards?' (TBC-5-CN-LE) The teacher-intended lexicon was to focus on 'Groups who celebrate. How do they celebrate? Where do they celebrate?' (TBC-5-CN-LE). The occasions in which the exchange of greeting cards took place were heavily emphasised, as were the likely audiences of greeting cards and particular sensibilities of possible recipients.

In a similar vein, 'Read a number of Years 3/4 school websites. Who were the sites written for? While reading schools' websites you need to consider good, bad and interesting aspects' (TD-10-AI-LE) involved students in 'think[ing] about how particular presentation styles and techniques assist in meeting different audience needs' (TD-10-AI-LE). In this latter example, the emphasis shifted from contextual considerations of audience and purpose to an assessment of effectiveness of the 'good, bad and interesting'. The PMI (Plus/Minus/Interesting) technique can involve students in a number of dimensions; in this example, the teacher wanted them to concentrate on strengths in design and the exploration veered into the organisational dimension of meaning, with the social and representational dimensions of meaning backgrounded.

The data suggests that, in the linguistic mode, there is a negligible focus by teachers on the ideological dimension of meaning with just 2% of prompts attending to ideological aspects of meaning-making. What evidence there is in this area addresses student consideration of responses to web searches. Prompts include, 'Keep thinking about the information that you find on the websites. Is it relevant to your topic? How up to date is the information? Where could you check that this information is correct?' (TD-9-AF-LE) 'Is it relevant to your purpose? Where else could you find out?' (TD-9-AF-TI). The teacher-intended lexicon was to, 'Critically appraise websites in terms of design layout and the relevance of the information being presented' (TD-An-LE): 'relevancy, currency reliability' (TD-9-AI-TI). A teacher interview gave insight into potential for developing teaching around the ideological dimension of meaning.

> [W]e had one boy doing trucks and one boy doing cars. There is nothing on the internet that gives you information on trucks and cars... they want to sell you a truck or sell you a car. And they (the students) are like 'I don't want to buy a truck—I just want to find out how an engine works (TD/SFTI/0105).

The interests of manufacturers were also touched on in relation to the work on greeting cards, with the prompt, 'Pretend you are a card manufacturer going to write a greeting' (TBC-9-AA-SFC), offering the potential for involving students in considering different interests and motivations, including commercial interests and how they might be served. However, the teacher-intended lexicon doesn't quite articulate an ideological dimension of meaning focus. Instead the intent is to focus on 'Greeting organisation: card manufacturer's greeting and greeting of sender' (TBC-9-AA-SFTI).

Again, the ideological dimension of meaning is somewhat addressed but lacks specificity and clarity and is backgrounded in terms of the teaching foci or purpose.

6.3.5: The Spatial Mode

The data shows no explicit attention given by teachers to the spatial mode. The lack of attention to this mode, evidenced through an absence of deployment of prompts, may be indicative of a lack of teacher knowledge of the meaning-making potentials offered by the spatial mode. This is reflective of the lack of energy given to this under-theorised area (van Leeuwen, 2006) and its lack of presence in literacy-based curriculum documents. Insofar as any attention was given to this area, the data indicates teacher use of an enlarged story map with moveable puppets for re-tracing characters' journeys, deployed as a tool for working on 'comprehension' or to 'retell events by moving characters around the map.' (TA-6-AF-LE) No prompts were addressed specifically to learning about the spatial mode, but at best this example could be considered as learning *through* the spatial mode.

The researcher also witnessed an example of teaching addressed to the spatial mode within the data collection period, but subsequent to the documentation of the Learning Element, and so it is not part of the data set underpinning analysis in this chapter. This example involved the design and construction of 'dioramas' to depict stage designs, an example which shows teaching involving spatial participants such as characters and props (representational dimension of meaning); the influences and consideration of the audience and purpose (contextual dimension of meaning); the possibilities for placement of props (organisational dimension of meaning); and effect of participants manipulated for particular purposes (ideological dimension of meaning).

6.4: Deployment of Pedagogical Knowledge Processes to Address Teaching of Modes

The data set, which underpins the discussion in this chapter, includes 361 teacher prompts that were originally classified according to the mode of meaning which they predominantly addressed. Of these, major emphasis was given to the linguistic mode with nearly half of all prompts (47%) addressing linguistic meaning. A quarter of prompts in the data set (26%) addressed the visual mode; 20% of prompts addressed the gestural mode; 7% of prompts addressed audio meaning-making; and no prompts addressed the spatial mode (see table 6.4 below).

Table 6.4: Teacher Prompts Classified According to the Mode of Meaning

Focus of prompts (mode)	Linguistic	Audio	Visual	Gestural	Spatial	Total prompts
No.	170	26	95	70	0	361
% of set	47%	7%	26%	20%	0%	

In table 6.5 and table 6.6 below, these prompts have been reorganised according to the pedagogical knowledge processes from which they arose: experiencing, conceptualising, analysing or applying. The classification of pedagogy was according to the teacher documentation on the Learning Element and the aim of this organisation of the data was to detect patterns in deployment of pedagogy to address different modes.

Table 6.5: Teacher Prompts Classified According to Pedagogical Effect on Mode

	Predominantly linguistic focus	Predominantly audio focus	Predominantly visual focus	Predominantly gestural focus	Total
Experiencing	39 prompts (23%)	0 prompts (0%)	0 prompts (0)%	21 prompts (30%)	60 prompts (17%)
Conceptualising	21 prompts (12%)	0 prompts (0%)	36 prompts (38%)	0 prompts (0)%	57 prompts (16%)
Analysing	39 prompts (23 %)	15 prompts (58%)	39 prompts (41%)	49 prompts (70%)	142 prompts (39%)

Applying	71 prompts (42%)	11 prompts (42%)	20 prompts (21%)	0 prompts (0%)	102 prompts (28%)
Total	170 prompts (100%)	26 prompts (100%)	95 prompts (100%)	70 prompts (100%)	361 prompts

Table 6.6: Summary of Pedagogical Effect on Mode

	Prompts: linguistic focus	Prompts: audio focus	Prompts: visual focus	Prompts: gestural focus	Total
Experiencing	23%	0%	0%	30%	17%
Conceptualising	12%	0%	38%	0%	18%
Analysing	23%	58%	41%	70%	37%
Applying	42%	42%	21%	0%	28%

The influence of the pedagogical knowledge processes on deployment of modes of meaning was analysed in terms of frequency of teacher prompts within the deployment of each of the pedagogies. As with the analysis relating to teaching related to mode throughout this chapter, this discussion is mindful that not all classroom enactments were documented, and that teachers' categorisation of prompts according to pedagogy may differ to that of theorists.

42% (71 prompts) of linguistic-related prompts were deployed through the use of the 'knowledge process' of applying; 23% of linguistic-related prompts were underpinned by the 'knowledge process' of experiencing (39 prompts); and another 23% through the 'knowledge process' of analysis (39 prompts); the 'knowledge process' of conceptualising underpinned 12% of linguistic-related prompts (21 prompts). This may be partially explained by teachers involving students in applying knowledge in ongoing ways, rather than as a test at the end. For example, students throughout the unit on 'Web Passion' undertook 'applying creatively' in the form of webpage development. In a recursive approach, students worked for many months on this project, which was interspersed with involvement in the 'knowledge processes' of conceptualising and analysing.

The heavy emphasis on the 'knowledge process' of applying (42% of linguistic-related prompts) in teaching the linguistic mode is curious however, when considered in relation to a relative under-emphasis on the 'knowledge process' of conceptualising (12% of linguistic-related prompts). The overall inattention in the data set to the 'knowledge process' of conceptualising suggests that students were not being heavily involved in learning new linguistic-related concepts but were applying existing linguistic-related knowledge in multimodal design environments.

A further explanation for the lack of student involvement in the knowledge process of conceptualising, is that teachers in the case study were attending to teaching of linguistic concepts outside of this project—for example, in guided reading and interactive writing sessions not documented in the Learning Element. As noted in Chapter Five, a relatively heavy emphasis on the knowledge process of analysing (37% of all prompts) is likely to stem from the newness of the approach taken by case study teachers in positioning modes of meaning other than linguistic (the visual, audio and gestural modes) as meaning-making resources. This new framing of modes of meaning as literacy resources prompted teachers to test the modes, to see how they functioned—in short, to work with students in analysing their affordances as meaning resources.

70% of gestural-related prompts were deployed through the use of the knowledge process of analysis (49 prompts) and 30% through the knowledge process of experiencing (21 prompts), with no deployment of the knowledge processes of conceptualising and applying to address the gestural mode.

58% of audio-related prompts were deployed through use of the knowledge process of analysis (15 prompts) and 42% of audio-related prompts were deployed through the knowledge process of applying (11 prompts), with no deployment of the knowledge processes of conceptualising or experiencing to address the audio mode.

Teachers particularly favoured the knowledge process of analysis in teaching the gestural (70% of gestural-related prompts); audio (58% of audio-related prompts); and visual (41% of visual-related prompts) modes. Linguistic-related teaching deployed the knowledge process of analysis in 23% of teacher prompts used in teaching the linguistic mode. Clearly the less well theorised modes have been taught through the intensive use of the knowledge process of analysis.

The knowledge process of applying was deployed most heavily in linguistic-related teaching (as discussed above), and in audio-related teaching (42% of audio-related prompts). As mentioned earlier, all audio and gestural prompts related to the one teacher. In this case the gestural was approached through the knowledge process of experiencing; both gestural and audio were taught through the pedagogical knowledge process of analysis; and the audio through the use of the knowledge process of applying. In this case the audio mode applications were 'new' to the teacher and students, the environment of student 'body talk' videos incorporating audio soundtracks. The gestural, but not the audio, had been foregrounded during the early part of this learning through the knowledge process of experiencing; both audio and gestural had been addressed through the knowledge process of analysis; and the audio had been addressed through the knowledge process of applying. Neither of these modes were taught through the knowledge process of conceptualising.

In teaching the visual mode, 41% of visual-related prompts arose from the knowledge process of analysis, like the gestural and audio mode-related teaching, involving teachers and students heavily in working with the affordances of the mode's resources. 38% of visual-related prompts were deployed through the knowledge process of conceptualising, reflecting the more strongly developed theoretical base of the visual mode (Kress and van Leeuwen, 1996). 21% of visual-related prompts were deployed through the knowledge process of applying. Interestingly, there was no deployment of the knowledge process of experiencing in teaching of the visual mode.

6.5: Generalising from the Data

The analysis of teacher prompts and teaching intentions has provided insight into a number of aspects concerning teacher deployment of multimodal metalanguage with students in the early years of schooling (with students aged 5–10 years). Case study teacher effort was dedicated to addressing meaning-making potentials of modes previously taken for granted or overlooked in 'literacy' programs: modes perhaps once considered to be extra-linguistic, auxiliary or as belonging to another part of the curriculum.

Analysis of 361 teacher prompts and associated teacher-specified goals in an attempt to identify and analyse examples of teaching *about multimodality and mode* was curiously confounding. Teachers were clearly working towards fostering students' abilities to describe the constructedness of texts in terms of mode and multimodal contributions. However, the teaching enactments in pursuit of these objectives, as evidenced through prompts and teacher specified goals, were often found to not actually attend to function, when compared with theoretical examples of metalanguage.

This may in part be due to the clear differences between the meaning attributed to the term 'metalanguage' by the teachers and the theorists. Metalanguage, in the way the New London Group describe, assumes that meaning arises from the designed—i.e. by the way modes are structured. Metalanguage offers a systematic approach of describing meanings produced through the choices implicit in different structures. The teachers' focus seemed to be on the articulation of context-bound meaning-making elements and behaviours, rather than the structural meaning-making functions of the design elements offered by different modes. This can be illustrated as a focus on, 'Do you know what that means?', rather than 'How do you know what that means?'

In a movement reminiscent of earlier expansion of the professional responsibilities of literacy teachers to develop knowledge of 'language across the curriculum', case study teachers were focused on incorporating and heightening student awareness of 'modes across the curriculum'. Patterns identified in the case study's approaches to the teaching of multimodality can be categorised in terms of *teaching* multimodality and mode; *teaching through* multimodality and mode; and *teaching about* multimodality and mode.

The 'newness' of the communication types and the vacuum of metalanguage articulating the various modes and their meaning-making affordances left teaching displaying a lack of balance in deployment across modes of meaning with the heavy emphasis on linguistic meaning (45%) reflective of traditional literacy concerns; with lesser emphasis on the visual (26%) and gestural (20%), audio (7%) and spatial (0%) modes. Modes that have not been well theorised as meaning-making resources attracted less teaching attention.

Teachers' efforts in generating metalanguage with their students were analysed using the five dimensions of meaning to explore teacher prompts and teacher-intended lexicon in teaching each of the modes. This analysis showed further patterns of teacher attention, with prompts addressing the organisational dimension of meaning accounting for nearly half of all prompts (45%) and with less attention given to representational (23%), contextual (19%), social (11%) and ideological (3%) dimensions of meaning.

All audio and gestural-related prompts were gleaned from the practices of one teacher, making the data set quite limited. Other case study teachers taught only the linguistic and visual modes as their primary mode of focus in the Teaching Sequences analysed in this chapter. None of the teachers taught the spatial mode of meaning in this data set. In relation to teaching gestural meaning-making, the data shows clear teacher preference for teaching the representational dimension of meaning (70% of gestural-related prompts); some attention to organisational (11%), social, (10%) and ideological (8%); and no prompts addressing the contextual dimension of meaning.

Teaching focused heavily on naming *what* feeling gestures represent and *what* the facial and body parts do in order to express or convey meaning. Teaching did not explicitly address that different expressions might represent different meanings depending on the context, with no attention given to teaching the contextual dimension of meaning of the gestural mode.

In teaching audio meaning-making, the data shows teacher preference for teaching the social (58% of audio-related prompts) and representational (34% of audio-related prompts) dimensions of meaning, some attention to organisational (8%), and no prompts addressing the contextual and ideological dimensions of meaning. The social dimension was largely addressed through focus on the mood created by music, and the feelings evoked in students in response to music. Teaching addressed to the representational dimension of meaning focused on naming audio elements in soundtracks.

In teaching visual meaning-making, the data shows teacher preference for teaching the organisational dimension of meaning (54% of visual-related prompts), some attention to representational (18%) and social (14%) dimension of meaning, with limited or no prompts addressing the contextual and ideological dimensions of meaning. The emphasis on the organisational dimension of meaning was mainly in the context of multimodal texts and concerned organisation of visual and linguistic resources. Studies of narratives, of greeting cards and of webpages provided the design environments for this focus on organisational dimension of meaning. Representational dimension of meaning concerned the participants in these designs; social related chiefly to student responses to these designs, and contextual addressed the audience and purposes of the designs.

In teaching linguistic meaning-making, the data also shows teacher preference for teaching the organisational (57% of linguistic-related prompts) and contextual (33%) dimensions of meaning, with little attention to representational (5%), social (3%) and ideological (2%) dimension of meaning. The evidence that teachers addressed linguistic teaching outside the parameters of this project (see earlier discussion) clarifies the meaning of this data. Within the parameters of this project, teachers addressed the organisational dimension of meaning in linguistic teaching, chiefly in terms of the organisation of visual and linguistic meanings in multimodal designs (narratives, greeting cards and webpages). As with teaching of the visual, teaching of the contextual dimension of meaning focused on the audience and purpose of these multimodal designs.

Attempts to glean an emergent lexicon for multimodality continually faced the challenge of examples which stopped short of teaching about each mode present in designs. Emphasis was given to teaching that meaning is represented in multiple modes, reflecting the teachers' own developing awareness, and directing attention to the organisational dimension of meaning of multimodality, particularly the organisation of the linguistic and visual modes of meaning in multimodal texts. The organisational dimensions of meaning of the linguistic and visual were heavily emphasised with far less attention given to organisational dimension of meaning of audio, gestural and spatial modes.

The data shows that case study teachers have not moved to a technical way of describing the multimodal, such as those grammars described by Kress and van Leeuwen (1996), Martinec (1999), Unsworth (2006) and van Leeuwen (1999). The data shows that teachers' attempts lacked specialisation of terms and a systematic framework as they grappled with emerging understandings of a range of modes as meaning-making and, in this way, literacy resources. Teacher-intended lexicon reflected a lack of specificity in terms of teaching about multimodality and mode as meaning-making resources. This is not surprising given the relative newness and emergent nature of theoretical schemas which offer such specificity, and the paucity of advice particularly in relation to the gestural (Martinec, 1999; van Leeuwen, 1999) and audio (van Leeuwen, 1999) modes. The visual was the most flexibly and comprehensively taught of the non-linguistic modes, reflecting its more fully developed theoretical base (Kress and van Leeuwen, 1996).

The discussion and analysis in this chapter has involved possibilities for teaching of modes; possibilities suggested by teachers' prompts and teacher-intended lexicon; and possibilities for teaching of modes as described by theorists drawing on textual or design based analysis and schemas. The use of the five 'dimensions of meaning schema' has enabled a systematic discussion of the teaching of different modes evident both in the data from classroom applications and from theoretical offerings, the five 'dimensions of meaning schema'. In this regard the five 'dimensions of meaning schema' proved useful, but further development of the schema would have helped clarify categorisation of teacher prompts and intended lexicon. Clarification was sought from theoretical offerings but these generally illustrated categorisation of design elements, rather than categorisation of teaching prompts and intentions.

Another issue was that prompt series were often found to be 'multi-dimensional', suggesting a division of prompts amongst the dimensions of meaning. However, prompts taken out of the context of a teaching series were often found to lose meaning. The colour coding of prompts within their original prompt series was found useful in this regard.

Analysis of the influence of the pedagogical knowledge processes in teaching linguistic, visual, audio and gestural modes of meaning showed patterns in teacher preferences in addressing different modes of meaning in classroom enactments.

The knowledge process'of analysis (37% of all prompts) was heavily deployed in teaching modes of meaning re-framed as literacy resources (the visual, audio and gestural modes) as a result of teachers' participation in the work-based professional learning project. The knowledge process of analysis prompted teachers to test the modes, to see how they functioned, in short to work with students in analysing their affordances as meaning resources. The less theorised modes (gestural and audio) were addressed most heavily through use of the knowledge process of analysis.

The knowledge process of conceptualising was strongly deployed with the visual mode, the non-linguistic mode with the most strongly developed theoretical base (Kress and van Leeuwen, 1996). In teaching the other less well-theorised modes of the gestural and audio, the knowledge process of conceptualising was not apparent, and limited in teaching relating to the linguistic mode undertaken as part of this research project. This is explained by the finding that teachers undertook additional linguistic teaching outside the parameters of this project. This fragmentation demonstrated a lack of cohesion in case study teachers' breakthrough attempts to operationalise multiliteracies-influenced teaching; a fragmentation between the 'new' practices which were documented by teachers in the Learning Elements and were the object of filming, and teachers' pre-existing linguistic-focused classroom practices.

The knowledge process of experiencing was confined to linguistic and gestural-related teaching, with linguistic resources addressed through experiencing known and new information. Teachers used the knowledge process of experiencing at the commencement of the project to ascertain students 'prior knowledge', with the linguistic a key mode in exploring and recording what students already knew.

The knowledge process of applying was heavily emphasised in teaching the linguistic (42% of linguistic-related prompts) and audio (42% of audio-related prompts) modes, with moderate deployment in the visual (21%) mode and none at all in the gestural mode. In this case the audio mode applications were 'new' to the teacher and students, the environment of student 'body talk' videos incorporating audio soundtracks. The knowledge process of applying was deployed in contexts of multimodal design, with the linguistic mode combined with the audio and visual modes. Since there was a lack of emphasis on the knowledge process of conceptualising in the teaching of the linguistic and audio modes, students appeared to be involved in applying knowledge gained through the knowledge processes of experiencing and analysing (linguistic); and the knowledge process of analysis (audio), without the benefit of conceptual input relating to these modes. Again this points to a lack of available theoretical resources for developing conceptual knowledge which can be then drawn on during the knowledge process of applying.

The analysis undertaken in this chapter has explored the deployment of a 'multimodal schema' and a five 'dimensions of meaning schema' as frameworks for gleaning examples of a teacher-generated multimodal metalanguage from teacher prompts and teacher-intended lexicon used in classroom applications. Discussion has drawn on the theoretical literature to develop further possibilities for teaching within the context of the 'multimodal schema' and the 'dimensions of meaning schema'. Deployment of pedagogical knowledge processes in teaching the modes has also been analysed and teaching patterns discussed.

Chapter 7
Developing Teacher Professionalism

Multiliteracies Theory and Practice

This chapter evaluates the efficacy of interventions to enhance teachers' professionalism in operationalising multiliteracies. It examines the effect of engagement with the multiliteracies schemas ('multimodal schema' and 'pedagogical knowledge processes schema') on teacher professional knowledge, practice and identity. The following discussion addresses the impact of participation on each of the individual case teachers.

7.1: Rachel's Impact Story

Rachel, acting Assistant Principal with management, welfare and local and regional professional learning responsibilities, joined the work-based professional learning project somewhat hesitantly due to limited opportunities for classroom application of multiliteracies-influenced teaching. In comparison to Kim and Meredith and Pip, who had major responsibilities for grades of students, Rachel's teaching responsibility with the Prep grade was limited to three mornings a week during the literacy and numeracy blocks (TA/TI/2803). The data shows that Rachel's awareness of the importance of practical application in supporting professional learning was keen, 'First you have to find out where it sits with you... [and] experience it' (TA/SFTI/0205).

7.1.1: On Multimodality

The data shows that Rachel's initial espoused confidence with the visual literacies and critical literacies aspects of multiliteracies theory (TA/TI/0704) was not adequate for teaching Prep students (TA/RJ/2003). Data collected during interventions designed to support 'planning' (Carr and Kemmis, 1986; Kemmis and McTaggart, 2005) for Teaching Sequence 1, highlights Rachel's concerns related to the degree of sophistication of Prep students' meaning-making abilities based on students' lack of experience with print literacies (TA/SFTI/0704). Further concerns related to a lack of personal professional expertise in using technology, 'I had to learn how to use the digital video, because I've got no idea of those sorts of things' (TA/SFTI/0205).

Rachel showed a collaborative disposition, reflecting on these concerns with colleagues and engaging with collegiate suggestions such as 'trying one mode at a time' with the Prep students (TA/RJ/2003) and employing the skills of a teenage daughter to facilitate learning to function the digital camera by 'playing around at home' (TA/RJ/0704). Expert input on the 'multimodal schema' and consideration of students' learning needs influenced Rachel's decision to address the gestural mode as a starting point for teaching, because 'what they [Prep students] know most about is themselves and their feelings' (TA/RJ/0704).

The data illustrates Rachel's heightened awareness as a result of the expert input related to the 'multimodal schema', of the meaning-making resources of modes other than the linguistic in the midst of practical application, the reading of a picture story book.

Rachel	When we were reading *Rosie's Walk*...children started to say what sound effects, just spontaneously, that might happen, and I thought it would be interesting for them to watch the video [of *Rosie's Walk*] without the sound and see what sort of connections they made.
Researcher	Is that different to the focus you'd usually have, teaching with that book, before the multiliteracies project?
Rachel	It's interesting, thinking of multiliteracies, because with *Rosie's Walk* I focused usually just on the visual literacies, but using the video I was able to think about audio literacy and how much emphasis that adds to meaning and trying to get the children to see that...So where I want to go is looking at audio literacies and gestural literacies. Then much further down the track we'll probably be looking at that spatial effect too, as we're learning. So once I would only have focused on maybe the visual side and the alphabetical side, but now there's that whole range that I'm aware of.
Researcher	How are the students responding?
Rachel	I'm seeing how adaptable the children are at using the language to suit the purpose and changing already... going from quite general language about our feelings and the modes to quite specific language (TA/SFTI/0205).

The influence of the 'multimodal schema' is evident in Rachel's choices of designs of meaning and literacy teaching foci, including the gestural, visual, audio and linguistic. The spatial was addressed in Teaching Sequence 2. Rachel also displayed confidence in using digital and stills visual cameras (TA/SFC/0704). This illustrates the combined power of expert input and filmed artefacts as a stimulus for reflection that allowed Rachel to reflect on how to implement new knowledge.

Filming of teaching acts served to concentrate Rachel's attention on multimodal teaching opportunities arising from the act of teaching itself—an example of practitioner 'reflection-in-action' (Schön, 1983, 1987). Filming also served to foster 'reflection-on-action' in teaching (Schön, 1983, 1987), including Rachel's reflection on student capacities. The incorporation of technology, and teaching addressed to a range of modes (the gestural and visual) beyond the linguistic, was viewed by the teacher as an exciting innovation deployed within the parameters of the Early Years Literacy Program.

> I think it's been really exciting using an extra focus in our teaching and learning and fitting it within the early years block. We're seeing it's part of what we're doing, and yet it's slightly different and a little bit more exciting than some of the things we've been doing too. The kids are getting lots of different ways of meaning and we're going to continue to build on that focus and to see that the alphabetical mode is a really important mode and we're not disregarding that in any way, but we're saying that there's so many other ways to make meaning and giving the kids ways of acknowledging that and valuing all the different ways of meaning and they know they can use them in different situations (TA/SFTI/0205).

Rachel expanded understandings of literacy to include placing importance on teaching the meaning-making affordances of modes other than the linguistic, and modes other than the linguistic or alphabetical mode are emphasised alongside the teaching of the linguistic. Teaching multiple modes is not seen as a distraction to linguistic teaching goals, but as an expansion to them. There is a sense of excitement which, rather than the 'dazzlement' of engagement with new technologies (Kalantzis et al., 2005; Virilio, 1997), is based more on the expanded view of what constitutes literacy teaching.

Collaborative viewing of film artefacts, an intervention designed to facilitate observation (Carr and Kemmis, 1986; Kemmis and McTaggart, 2005), enabled collaborative refection-on-action (Schön, 1983, 1987) with the filmed artefacts acting as a focal point for reflective discussions and feedback from Rachel.

Researcher Let's talk now about the actual experience on the video tape. You start off by saying...that you were familiar with one mode, the visual, and that you are comfortable with that and so you wanted to start there and then added the other modes.

Rachel I actually probably started a bit before that because as I said all the kids I have are from different backgrounds, different stages, different entry points. So the first thing I wanted to make sure was that we were all talking the same language,

	so that they knew what I was saying when we were talking about gesture, expression, feelings. So the first part was really just setting up. We looked in mirrors, we pulled faces and we looked through magazine pictures and we did a whole lot of pre-language so that when I was saying, 'How do you know that this person is feeling sad?' they could start to talk about their mouth was turned down, or 'How do you know this person is thinking?' and they said, 'Oh they had their hand on their cheek'. So they started to verbalise actions and things like that.
Researcher	You think it's important, establishing a common language and understandings?
Rachel	Because otherwise you start assuming that…when you move too fast and they're not building up that knowledge underneath to come with you and go beyond you even, and we often assume children know things because we have said it once. We need to do lots of work on it.
Researcher	And gestures might be different things for different people particularly facial expressions. Do the kids talk about that too?
Rachel	No, they didn't. I think the older kids would have but these ones didn't.
Researcher	Because they are just beginning…?
Rachel	Yes, and that's what I found difficult. I kept saying, 'What I'm doing is just natural. I am not doing anything. I'm a fraud because I am not doing anything new'. Do you know?
Researcher	How did you overcome that feeling, now thinking back?
Rachel	When I actually got the brainwave of bringing in the audio. And then I felt 'Yes I have taken my learning and their learning another step'. They are doing a lot of learning at this stage but you don't want to overwhelm them with too many concepts and I think even taking this one about making meaning through our gestures and our faces. I have a whole year's work looking at characters in books, looking at point of view, perspective, artwork. There is so much you can do (TA/TI/2807).

Rachel recognises the importance of a metalanguage because 'that knowledge underneath' is corroded in classroom teaching of modes other than the linguistic by lack of rigour in the available metalanguage, resulting in the nagging feeling of practice which is 'just natural' and not rigorous. Rachel's desire to take 'learning to another step', however, is undermined by a personal lack of confidence and expertise. In the absence of a metalanguage that marks expertise there is evident difficulty in legitimating modes other than alphabetical literacy. Despite these doubts, Rachel used a version of metalanguage, reflecting upon teacher and student performance in the filmed artefacts. The filmed artefacts also acted as reference points for grounding collaborative dialogue between the participating teachers. The documentation and transparency enabled by the filmed artefacts was enhanced by Rachel's preparedness to articulate, in an audio interview, nagging doubts regarding the authenticity of the 'newness' of her early classroom applications of the multimodality dimension of multiliteracies theory—an example of a teacher inquiring into issues in education through 'making problematic the current arrangements of schooling' (Cochran-Smith and Lytle, 1999, p. 18).

Rachel's admission to partial, developing knowledge, and collegiate sharing of uncertainties in professional learning, show a preparedness to undertake a new kind of professionalism characterised by

> ...new kinds of social relationships that assuage the isolation of teaching... inquiry communities structured to foster deep intellectual discourse about critical issues and thus to become places where uncertainties and questions intrinsic to teaching can be scrutinised [not hidden] and can function as grist for new insights and new ways to theorise practice (Cochran-Smith and Lytle, 1999, p. 22).

This instance of Rachel's learning, stimulated by attempted application of the 'multimodal schema' and supported by documentation, raises the question of a teacher's tacit beliefs about the importance of gradual introduction of conceptual metalanguage to avoid overwhelming students. Collective viewing and debriefing of other case study teachers' classroom applications, particularly Pip's classroom explorations of website-based concepts, served to challenge Rachel's tentative approach to deploying specialised multimodal metalanguage with Prep students (TA/RJ/2907). Rachel's expectations of students, based on age and competence in print literacy, and beliefs about the speed and extent to which metalanguage is introduced to young students shifted during the course of the project, as shown in these two interview excerpts.

Researcher	And have there been any surprises for you, from the kids, or....?
Rachel	My surprises were how quickly they did things, whether it was just that I was more focused on my language, but how quickly they reflected the language, it was amazing how quickly they can, if they are given the opportunity to display their learning back at you all the time.
Researcher	So your expectations of them have changed since you participated in the filming project?
Rachel	Yes, and as I have said, they are a very diverse lot, I mean...there's the layers, and it's peeling off those layers and really understanding those layers. Me understanding them as a teacher first, so really exploring what I want [to teach]. I've read stories a million times and never really thought of using the pictures to predict at that level, like predicting use of colour, predicting expressions, perspective and using that as an entry into the book. So it's the extra layers again that we're looking at... I'd never have thought at this stage of Prep teaching that I'd be talking about 'close-ups' and 'angles' and things like that. They are really quite sophisticated ideas, and these kids have taken them on board (TA/SFTI/0209).
Researcher	What did you expect when you agreed to be in the filming project and how has that played out?
Rachel	Being part of the project, the multiliteracies project has...I've realised that I've made assumptions about the children's learning. I've realised that there are much deeper layers to learning, as I said, being aware before of visual literacies, being aware of critical literacies, I have found that I can look at it at a much

> deeper level, and I'd never have unpacked pictures to that level before, I'd never have dreamt of doing something like that with Prep children and what's really blown me away is that this age group children are more able to take this on board than some of the children I work with in other areas of the school. I've worked with a literacy support group in [Years] 3 and 4 and I've tried to use the same ideas and it's harder for them to take on board. They've got to actually unlearn to focus on the alphabetic literacy and learn that it's fine to use all those other areas that are there to support them in the meaning, so all those other modes.... The Preps' language and understandings is much deeper or they're much more willing to use that or demonstrate that (TA/SFTI/0910).

This exchange corroborates findings on teacher expectation and the impact it has on student performance (Good, 1987). It suggests that learners are much more attuned to multimodality than teachers are aware of (Lankshear et al., 2000; Prensky, 2001). And young students of 5 and 6 years of age, from a school with a diverse population in a low socio-economic area, are well able to take on specialised multimodal metalanguage—language which is essential for knowledge development because it is the process by which experience becomes knowledge (Halliday, 1994). It also suggests that the narrow focus on literacy as exclusively alphabetic or linguistic has to be 'unlearnt' by teachers and learners taking a broader view of literacy as multimodal.

Rachel experienced deepening frustration with limited opportunities available for classroom application in what Grimmett calls the 'crucible of action' (1988, p. 13) due to growing recognition of the potential for application of multiliteracies in areas other than the literacy block.

> I have difficulty myself because I only have the children for that block for literacy and so much of this can be carried into the other areas and ...I'm a numeracy trainer too and we were talking about multiliteracies and maths and all the different ways of making the use of designs and learning in maths... I was thinking about how we get the children to see the ties like recognise that a collection's a collection without counting, like 5 is 5 on a dice and all that sort of thing. And that's a very strong sort of visual thing as well as a cognitive thing. ...I think it [multiliteracies] can be an umbrella and that everything is going to be encompassed within it (TA/TI/2807).

Rachel displayed a broadening repertoire of understanding in this insight of designs in mathematics as multimodal; transferring knowledge gained through expert input, applied in one area of the curriculum in the classroom, reflected on collaboratively in the form of the filmed artefacts, to mathematics and other subject areas. Rachel, who placed great value on finding out 'where it sits with you... [and] experience[ing] it' (TA/SFTI/0205), saw essential knowledge for teaching embedded in practice and approached the classroom as a 'student of teaching and learning' (Grimmett and MacKinnon, 1992, p. 387) with a strong interest in developing professional teacher 'craft knowledge' (Grimmett and MacKinnon, 1992) through classroom applications.

In relation to multimodal teaching emphases, Rachel's focus, within the context of the literacy block, was firmly on narratives. Teaching expanded to include modes of meaning other than linguistic and tended to concentrate on narrative visual representation (Kress and van Leeuwen, 1996), resounding with analysis on e-literature undertaken by Unsworth (2006). As shown in data from Teaching Sequence 1 discussed in Chapter Six, Rachel's prompting drew attention to visual elements such as specific participants, processes and circumstances in narrative contexts, encouraging articulation of examples of visual elements which indicated actional and mental processes such as vectors achieved through gaze and participant positioning (Kress and van Leeuwen, 1996)—the 'what' of the visuals within the context of particular stories, rather the functioning of the visual in depicting participants, processes and circumstances. Rachel shows a strong preference for prompting towards the representational dimension of meaning in prompting associated with the audio, visual and gestural modes, as shown in table 7.1.

Table 7.1: Rachel: Addressing of Dimensions of Meaning in Each Mode of Meaning. Teaching Sequence 1

		Linguistic	Audio	Visual	Gestural	Spatial
Representational	TA		34%	7%	70%	-
	TB&C	5%		6%		
	TD			3%		
Social	TA	2%	58%	2%	10%	-
	TB&C	1%		5%		
	TD			7%		
Organisational	TA	9%	8%	2%	11%	-
	TB&C	14%		1%		
	TD	34%		51%		
Contextual	TA		-		-	-
	TB&C	27%		13%		
	TD	6%				
Ideological	TA		-		8%	-
	TB&C					
	TD	2%		1%		

In the data from Teaching Sequence 1, analysed in Chapter Six, Rachel was responsible for all audio and gestural prompts. In teaching the gestural mode, the representational dimension of meaning was significant, with 70% of prompts addressing the use of the face as the 'participant' in showing mental states (sleepy, thinking) or feelings (anger, happiness, sadness), a particular category of processes (Halliday, 1994). Considering that much of the gestural-related teaching was embedded in visual representations, Rachel is displaying a strong preference for teaching related to the representational dimension of meaning.

7.1.2: On Pedagogy

Rachel articulated the emerging finding of transferability of multiliteracies across subject areas, particularly addressing visual designs in mathematics, during collaborative reflection at the 'Multiliteracies Intensive' (TA/RJ/2807) as shown in the following extract involving exchange with one of the multiliteracies theorists.

Rachel	I'm getting really excited about the way it can be used in a much more broad way such as opening it up to numeracy.
Prof. Kalantzis	And for the numeracy I am suspecting it is not just the multimodal [schema which is relevant] but also the pedagogies.
Rachel	Yes, I really haven't even started to think about that! (TA/RJ/2807)

Grappling with relationships and terminology used to describe the multiliteracies pedagogies in literacy teaching, prompted Rachel to form a cross-school project team to support teacher professional learning of multiliteracies (TA/RJ/0205). Rachel's motivation to gain understanding from the schema, resulted in collaborative dialogue between project team members, with Rachel leading the 'exploring of multiliteracies through round table discussions regarding conceptions and misconceptions of multiliteracies' and aligning multiliteracies terminology with terms generally used amongst colleagues (TA/RJ/2807).

The temporal filming and screening of the series of films, and associated foci, saw the 'how' of multiliteracies, or 'pedagogy' as the focus of film three, 'Moving into Multiliteracies', shot after the 'Multiliteracies Intensive'. Expert input 1 had addressed all aspects of multiliteracies theory (see Chapter Three). Expert input 2 and 3 reviewed all aspects of multiliteracies theory but focused respectively on multimodality, metalanguage and design (see Chapter Three); and on the 'pedagogical knowledge processes schema' and the Learning Element templat as a tool for teacher documentation and sharing. Case study teachers decided to retrospectively and prospectively document Teaching Sequence 1 as Learning Elements. Filming during the second cycle of participatory action research would focus on pedagogy deployed in Teaching Sequence 2. This had the effect of directing the researcher's and the teachers' attention to the 'pedagogical knowledge processes schema'.

As indicated by the interview excerpt above, Rachel's focus had been on addressing multimodality in the literacy block, and the transferability of notions of multimodality to numeracy had not been accompanied by consideration of multiliteracies pedagogies in the context of mathematics teaching and learning.

Rachel sought to connect with pedagogies through collaborative discussion focused on 'the texts of teaching' (McDonald, 1992), mapping various terminology which might be applied to examples and practising using the language of the schemas.

Researcher	How have you engaged with the multiliteracies pedagogies and the pedagogical knowledge processes?
Rachel	Probably first of all was the framework, as in just starting to talk about 'situated practice', when I'm used to 'immersion', and now 'experiencing' so changing the titles, and that took a while to get my head around, but then, that was when I was by myself trying to get my head around it, but then at one of our project team meetings we just sat there and went through a unit of work and went 'what would that be?' 'critical framing', and once we started using the language, it started to make sense to us...
Researcher	So it's mapping really, all those terms...
Rachel	Yes, that's right, it's like 'where does this fit in?', and what is it really talking about? .... like immersion, its sort of doubling up on those now too, making those links anyway, so that it is better.
Researcher	Now you are going to go and try and write it up, do you think it is going to work?
Rachel	Some aspects, because I had already started thinking... but not the way it's mapped it out...
Researcher	What is it about the way it's mapped out?
Rachel	Mmm, it's in that 'in-and-out-of'...nothing is ever sequential, you know, it is that flow in and out isn't it, where you pick up that 'Oh, they are not quite ready for that, I'll take them back and we'll re-do this part...' And I still think the hard part is that I am narrowed into that block in the timetable, so I can't do as much as if I had those Preps all day...I would have been doing other things at other times so I would have been integrating it more.
Researcher	So the multimodal thing...?
Rachel	Yes, you need that sort of time and integration, it really is hard just to keep it, I mean I talk to the Prep teacher and stuff, and we're working together, but I think it is different when you have got two different heads [like Kim and Meredith] working at it in one grade.
Researcher	You need time for that kind of integration?
Rachel	Yes, and also because, my whole reasoning was starting with that too, it was 'What do Preps know most about?'—themselves, and interpreting relationships with other people, so I think starting points are really important, so if you consider for this unit, what entry points do we have to have? (TA/TI/2807)

Retrospective documentation of teaching and learning was challenged by perception of the template as being linear and unable to capture the somewhat recursive and overlapping applications of taught lessons. Rachel sought 'practical illustrations' of what the 'pedagogical knowledge objectives, processes and outcomes might look like' (TA/RJ/2807). Rachel used the examples as guides, to document the sequence of lessons taught (and to be taught) in Teaching Sequence 1 in present tense 'as if writing for another teacher' (TA/RJ/2807). Rachel engaged in collaboration and problem-solving, seeking precedents—one a briefly documented example from Bamaga in Queensland (Kalantzis and Cope, 2004; Kalantzis et al., 2005) and one undertaken by the researcher in the year prior to this study (Cloonan, 2005;

Kalantzis and Cope, 2004)—for consideration (TA/RJ/2807). Rachel adopted the use of present tense and drew on sentence stems deployed in the precedents in development of the Learning Element.

The slippage of language between the multiliteracies pedagogies, the 'pedagogical knowledge processes schemas' and other professional terminology used to describe pedagogy such as 'immersion', while initially a challenge, served to clarify Rachel's understandings. Collegiate dialogue and practical illustrations connected to specific teaching contexts also assisted clarification in terminology usage (see discussion in following section). The impact of this engagement was publication of a peer-reviewed, published Learning Element and an article adapted from the peer-reviewed Learning Element which was published in a quarterly journal of a peak, national teacher subject association. This publication activity defines Rachel as a published author with credentials in the field of multiliteracies.

Collaboration and problem-solving, motivated by Rachel's determined engagement with the complexities of different terminology used to label pedagogies in the 'multiliteracies pedagogies schema' and 'pedagogical knowledge processes schema', resulted in jointly-produced expertise.

7.1.3: On Professional Repertoires

The impact of the 'pedagogical knowledge schema' and the Learning Element on expanding Rachel's repertoire of pedagogical deployment in teaching multimodality can be considered in terms of the two Teaching Sequences. Teaching Sequence 1, 'Body Talk: Making and Interpreting Meaning', was mostly taught prior to Rachel's retrospective completion of the Learning Element and Teaching Sequence 2, 'Fairytales', was taught during and after Rachel's completion of the same Learning Element—see table 7.2 and table 7.3 below. The 'multimodal schema' influenced Rachel to attend to teaching a range of modes of meaning and multimodal relationships, an expansion of the literacy teaching repertoire from the print focused literacies of the Early Years Literacy Program. The schema was important in bringing to conscious awareness meaning-making modes previously overlooked as a result of cultural lenses which have privileged linguistic meaning-making (Kress, 2003) perhaps involuntarily as 'the way it is' (Delpit, 1995 p.151).

Table 7.2: Rachel: Deployment of Pedagogical Knowledge Processes in Teaching Multimodality (Predominant mode of focus is shown by print size) Teaching Sequence 1 (Body Talk)

Lesson	Pedagogical knowledge process	Linguistic mode	Audio mode	Visual mode	Gestural mode	Spatial mode
1	Experiencing the Known				X	
2	Experiencing the Known			x	X	
3	Experiencing the New			x	X	
4	Conceptualising by Naming			x	X	
5	Conceptualising by Theorising	x		X	x	

6	Analysing Functionally			X	x	
7	Analysing Functionally			x	X	
8	Analysing Functionally		X			
9	Analysing Functionally	X				
10	Analysing Functionally				X	

Teaching Sequence 2: 'Fairytales'

11	Analysing Functionally				x	X	
12	Analysing Functionally	X				x	
13	Analysing Functionally			X			
14	Applying Appropriately			X	x	x	
15	Experiencing the Known	X			x		
16	Experiencing the New				X		
17	Conceptualising by Naming				X	x	x
18	Conceptualising by Theorising				X	x	x
19	Analysing Functionally				X	x	
20	Applying Appropriately	X			x		
21	Applying Creatively				X		

Comparison of data from the two Teaching Sequences shows that Teaching Sequence 1 was somewhat emergent, and reflective of Rachel's developing knowledge. Addressing individual and combined modes within the context of a study of narratives saw Rachel isolate modes for teaching attention within the context of a study of narratives. Designs of meaning in focus in Rachel's Teaching Sequence 1 included the human gestures (lessons 1–4) and gestures of humanised animal characters in illustrated picture books (lessons 5 and 6). Isolation of individual modes for concentrated study involved a visual animation without audio (lesson 7); and with audio (lesson 8); and gestural in the animation (lesson 10) and in peers' videos (lesson 11) teaching about each mode's meaning-making potential, as well as their intermodal relations (Unsworth, 2006b) in multimodal designs. The linguistic was deployed as a means of response and reflection (lessons 9 and 12) with Rachel undertaking additional language-based reading and writing instruction outside the parameters of the project. The audio in the form of music was analysed for mood creation (lesson 13), and the interplay of musical resources with visuals in a video (lesson 14) was explored. The spatial was not addressed and additional linguistic-focused teaching took place outside the parameters of the project (TA/TI/2807).

This data shows that teaching addressed modes of meaning made ubiquitous by technology: modes that have in recent times been more fully articulated: the visual, gestural and audio (Kress and van Leeuwen, 1996; Martinec, 1999; van Leeuwen, 1999). Linguistic-focused teaching was partitioned, teaching within the project taking the form of teaching through the linguistic. Teaching about the linguistic, teaching emergent readers and writers 'how to' read and write, was also undertaken through the pre-project habituated practices outside the realm of the project. This was a type of insurance, ensuring 'business as usual' for the processes which attract high stakes testing.

Greater confidence was exhibited in Rachel's tighter, more cohesive teaching focus evident in Teaching Sequence 2. Linguistic-focused teaching was re-integrated in a focus on fairytales which foregrounded fewer modes, but developed a depth of modal study, rather than breadth.

> I found talking with other teachers that sometimes people say this is just good teaching practice and that's really true; it is good teaching practice, its what we've always done but, once again I think we're doing it at a more explicit level. I would never have spent three weeks unpacking pictures and fairytales like I have this time but I think the time and effort really shows in the sorts of things the kids are doing. Before I would have maybe spent a session on it and assumed that the knowledge was there and assumed that they'd take it on board but not see the evidence in a really, really deep way like I'm seeing now... they're [the students are] making links in their reading, I'm seeing it across other areas too, in other settings, other activities that they do, they're maintaining that knowledge because it's very strong and they're using that [knowledge of] design in the way they draw their characters too and there's an individualism about the way they work, they bring their own meaning to it ... you see the power of the visual literacy coming through (TA/SFTI/0209).

This depth, as opposed to breadth of modes, was apparent through focus on the contributions of linguistic and visual modes in illustrated picture books (lessons 15 and 16); constructing visual and linguistic in multimodal designs; selecting, constructing and documenting characters, props and settings with consideration also of linguistic, gestural and spatial meaning-making (lessons 17 and 18); teaching about visual perspective (lesson 19); developing visually-based teacher and student co-constructed PowerPoint presentations (lesson 20); and student-constructed visually-based fairytale storyboards (lesson 21). In this Teaching Sequence, Rachel clearly focused on the visual and linguistic modes, and their intersection. The gestural mode had a secondary focus and the audio mode was not addressed. The spatial mode was addressed for the first time by Rachel through exploring props and settings, but as secondary to the visual.

Comparison of data from the two Teaching Sequences shows growth in Rachel's confidence and capacities in purposefully addressing teaching of modes through deployment of pedagogies. Teaching Sequence 2, saw Rachel deploying pedagogical knowledge processes with greater control and clearer purpose in an exploration of visual and linguistic meaning-making in picture story books, see table 7.3 below.

Table 7.3: Rachel: Deployment of Pedagogical Knowledge Processes in Two Teaching Sequences

	Experiencing	Conceptualising	Analysing	Applying
Teaching Sequence 1	22%	14%	57%	7%
Teaching Sequence 2	28.5%	28.5%	14.5%	28.5%

Rachel's deployment of the pedagogical knowledge process of experiencing, limited in Teaching Sequence 1 to addressing the gestural mode, was expanded in Teaching Sequence 2 to address teaching of linguistic and visual modes in illustrated picture books. Deployment of the pedagogical knowledge process of conceptualising, limited in Teaching Sequence 1 to naming body parts and theorising about meanings made by words and pictures in multimodal designs, was, in Teaching Sequence 2, deployed in selecting, constructing and documenting characters, props and settings in linguistic, visual, audio and spatial modes.

In Teaching Sequence 1, the predominant pedagogical emphasis was on the pedagogical knowledge process of analysis, which was deployed in exploring the meaning-making potentials of linguistic, visual, gestural and audio modes. This strong emphasis on analysis may be accounted for by the 'newness' of consideration of non-linguistic modes as literacy meaning-making resources in their own right. Following documentation of the 'Learning Element', Rachel's heavy emphasis on deployment of the pedagogical knowledge process of analysis, focused on linguistic, visual, gestural and audio modes in Teaching Sequence 1, was tempered in Teaching Sequence 2 with one lesson addressed to perspectives of characters and settings in linguistic, visual and gestural modes.

The pedagogical knowledge process of applying was, in Teaching Sequence 1, restricted to matching audio resources with visuals. This lack of explicit scaffolding and documenting of attempts to apply new knowledge, to position students as knowing, transformed individuals, meant that students remained consumers rather than producers of knowledge. When the teaching of individual modes is considered, limited deployment of pedagogical knowledge processes is evident, illustrating a limited pedagogical repertoire in developing knowledge of the modes addressed. In Teaching Sequence 2 this was expanded to address linguistic and visual meaning-making in PowerPoint presentations and storyboards, as a result of Rachel's realisation of under-utilisation of this pedagogical knowledge process in documenting the Learning Element. The heavier emphasis on deployment of the pedagogical knowledge process of applying, engaged students in knowledge production as well as consumption and critique.

Engagement with the pedagogical knowledge processes schema through documenting Teaching Sequence 1 as a Learning Element saw Rachel shift from sampling and experimenting with a range of modes to more purposeful deployment of pedagogies in Teaching Sequence 2, an analysis and multimodal production of 'Fairytales'. Teacher knowledge of the pedagogical knowledge processes provided a means for more deliberate exploration of modes. Engagement with the Learning Element template as a heuristic (Burrows, 2005; Neville, 2005) for teachers' reflection on their pedagogical deployment, through retrospective documentation of Teaching Sequence 1 as a Learning Element, led to greater teacher capacity to identify, articulate and apply pedagogical knowledge processes. Engagement in collaborative reflection on their classroom applications through the filmed artefacts further supported this learning.

Table 7.4: Rachel: Addressing of Mode and Deployment of Pedagogical Knowledge Processes (Predominant mode of focus is shown in italics) Teaching Sequence 1

Lesson	Multimodality emphases	Pedagogical knowledge process
1	*Gestural* Peer and personal expressions, gestures, mirrored reflections	Experiencing the Known
2	*Gestural* in visual Expressions in magazines; bingo cards	Experiencing the Known
3	*Gestural* in visual Expressions and gestures in peer and personal digital photos; Isolated facial features	Experiencing the New
4	*Gestural* in visual Expressions, gestures and stances in peer and personal digital photos; Isolated body parts in peers and personal digital photos	Conceptualising by Naming
5	*Visual* including gestural and linguistic Picture story book characters	Conceptualising by Theorising
6	*Visual* including gestural Picture story book and enlarged story map; Puppet characters	Analysing Functionally
7	*Gestural* in visual Animation	Analysing Functionally
8	*Audio* Speech, music, sound effects interplay in visual animation	Analysing Functionally
9	*Linguistic* Response to audio (speech, music, sound effects) and visual (animation)	Analysing Functionally
10	*Visual* and linguistic Expressions, gestures and stances within filming process	Analysing Functionally
11	*Gestural* in visual Process of viewing film	Analysing Functionally
12	*Linguistic* and gestural Reflection on gestural representation	Analysing Functionally

13	*Audio*	Analysing Functionally
	Musical resources	
14	*Audio* and Gestural in visual	Applying Appropriately
	Musical resources in interplay with visuals on video	

Teaching Sequence 2

15	*Linguistic* and visual	Experiencing the Known
	Illustrated picture books: fairytales	
16	*Visual* and linguistic	Experiencing the New
	Illustrated picture books: fairytales	
17	*Visual*, gestural, spatial and linguistic	Conceptualising by Naming
	Selecting, constructing characters, props, settings: fairytales	
18	*Visual*, gestural, spatial and linguistic	Conceptualising by Theorising
	Documenting characters, props and settings (digital stills)	
19	*Visual*, linguistic and gestural	Analysing Functionally
	Analysing perspectives of characters and settings	
20	*Linguistic* and visual	Applying Appropriately
	Creating a fairytale PowerPoint	
21	*Visual* and linguistic	Applying Creatively
	Developing fairytale storyboards; Effects of music on mood	

Rachel's growing capacity to articulate the language of the 'pedagogical knowledge processes schema' was evident in the last filming session. When asked how the pedagogies were impacting on their work with students, Rachel's reply indicates control over the terminology of pedagogical knowledge processes to meet learning goals.

> I try to make sure I'm connecting with the children's experiences by building on what we've talked about before...continually making those links explicit...even in other subject areas or across the curriculum ...and taking notice of their comments and what they're building on...conceptualising... for example with the deconstructing and reconstructing the pictures and the meaning. I had to give them a language to do that ...the amusement of me laying down taking a photo of [Child X] was to get that angle... explicit teaching and talking about angle, and now one word they really know is angle... ways of using the language and the skills to look at things critically ...like critical framing when we were doing the fairytale pictures getting them to use the things that I'd taught them... then working out well why is this picture a better picture? Should we use this one? What makes that one more powerful? It's getting them to use that language, or use those understandings to frame their ideas... getting them to apply their knowledge... say in a setting of doing a PowerPoint which is a new, different sort of presentation for them (TA/TI/2807).

A comparison with Rachel's knowledge of multiliteracies and capacity to articulate this at the beginning of the project, as evident in the following quote, indicates substantial growth.

> When I first heard about multiliteracies I was quite confident with some parts, like visual literacy and critical literacy... I'd done a little bit of work on them, but I had to find out about the other aspects or literacies. So it's a steep learning curve as to how everything fitted in, in making meaning of the different designs of meaning that can be made, and I wasn't sure where it fitted in the classroom in an integrated way (TA/SFTI/0704).

At the time of the work-based professional learning project, Learning by Design was an emergent theoretical framework which argued a case for teacher documentation and sharing of practice. The process of filming similarly sought to place teaching practice in the public realm—to create a shareable document which lay teacher practice open for scrutiny by other teachers beyond the project-specified days with the intent of developing professional expertise. As a pioneer in this project, Rachel made a contribution to the knowledge bank through development of a Learning Element but could only look to the future to share others' contributions (TA/RJ/0209). Rachel was prepared to do this to further personal professional learning of multiliteracies despite the substantial commitment of time required beyond the project (TA/RJ/2907). In relation to the professional learning of other teachers, Rachel had doubts about achieving such commitment.

Researcher   What are your thoughts on using the Learning Element template?
Rachel   I guess I don't want teachers to think 'this is another thing I'm going to have to do and another thing I'm going to have to learn' but just trying to show that it's an awareness and a focus in the way that you're thinking and what questions you're asking to draw out that awareness. Does that make sense?
Researcher   So it's a frame for working with what the teacher knows and is using?
Rachel   Yes, but you don't want it to be an added extra. You need something that is going to make you aware when you're planning that 'Oh—I can bring in these other elements'. I think that my thing as a teacher is just being conscious when I am planning now, of ways of bringing that out. Does that make sense?
Researcher   Yes. Will you be talking about the examples that you have trialled?
Rachel   Yes, that's right. I'm not saying this is the answer but this is where I am in my thinking and then other people are coming along (TA/SFTI/0209).

Personal professional pride is evident in Rachel's engagement with the Learning Element template. The prompts in the template which raised awareness of the pedagogical knowledge processes were valued, and were something Rachel was prepared to engage with despite their complexity. For others, Rachel sought a planning tool which was easily applied when planning, to support the immediate professional learning of multiliteracies of other teachers—something which accounted for teachers' intense work schedules. Rachel didn't see the likelihood of teachers in general undertaking public documentation of practice for sharing but saw the 'pedagogical knowledge processes schema' as useful in informing classroom applications. School planning practices appear to be habituated, wielding strong influence on curriculum.

> I'm hoping to make this [multiliteracies] an explicit part of the planning across the school and across KLAs [Key Learning Areas], and in our planners I want to make an area so that we look at this across the school and link in (TA/SFTI/0209).

Rachel's professional understandings of the application of multiliteracies teaching and learning to designs of learning across all subject areas challenged the heritage practices of the Victorian Early Years Literacy Program, the prevailing literacy policy at the time of data collection. Teaching engaged with a range of the modes from the 'multimodal schema' challenged placement of literacy and English into a daily block of time.

> When I first thought about multiliteracies it was still probably within the context of an English block of teaching. I think the most powerful thing that I found is how it is in all learning and how we've really got to be aware of that and make those links, so taking it from sort of just looking at it in one area, one subject area across all subject areas would be the most sort of...I didn't think I'd go that far in my learning, and teaching too I guess (TA/SFTI/0209).

This data also indicates a limited expectation of change evident as a result of participation in professional learning, a limited expectation of and an indication of the power of established routines in the work of teaching. Viewing meaning-making not as the exclusive province of the linguistic mode but as enabled by multiple modes of meaning, begged a consideration of designs of meaning taught about outside of the literacy block. Rachel had plans for the future which involved responding to multiliteracies in 'a more broad way':

> ...across the school ... rather than being boxed into subject areas...[considering] use of designs in maths...technology, the visual arts, and different subject areas [so that] the librarian, visual arts teacher, phys ed teacher are all using the same language... assisting students in making connections... offering depth of experience (TA/SFTI/0209).

When juxtaposed with Rachel's early attempts at 'fitting it within the early years block' (TA/SFTI/0205) this displays quite a shift. Features of the framework of the literacy block from the Early Years Literacy Program remained an influence, with Rachel's referring to key organisational structures in documentation of Teaching Sequence 1 in the Learning Element including small group teaching, learning centres, whole grade discussion and whole group sharing (TA/LE). However specific teaching approaches within the organisational structure were not referred to except during lessons which foregrounded linguistic learning (see table 5.1).

The 'multimodal schema' and 'pedagogical knowledge processes schema' had significant impact on Rachel's control over both deployment and articulation of the concepts in the multiliteracies schemas, suggesting greater congruence in Rachel's espoused theories of action and theories-in-use (Argyris and Schön, 1974). The qualitative and quantitative data indicate substantial changes to Rachel's knowledge of and ability to articulate and enact multiliteracies-influenced classroom practices. However, as a result of engagement with the 'multimodal' and 'pedagogical knowledge processes schema', a consistent approach to the teaching metalanguage was required; involving teachers from across the school.

The Learning Element template supported teacher control of pedagogy as displayed in data relating to Teaching Sequence 2. However, Rachel could not envisage the resources being available to support wide scale development of Learning Elements. Rachel, a highly regarded teacher and acting Assistant Principal with responsibilities for school-based and region-based professional learning, was prepared to document teaching practices on the Learning Element template but had lower expectations of other teachers, believing their intense work schedules would militate against such a practice.

7.2: Kim and Meredith's Impact Story

Kim and Meredith, although relative novices on a very established staff, were being groomed for leadership by Rachel—particularly Kim who had undertaken teacher education as a mature-aged student. Like Rachel, they displayed hesitancy in joining the project, in this instance primarily because of their commitment to another innovation, the setting up of a team-teaching relationship, which they were finding very stimulating. In part, however, this was also due to their perception of the exposing nature of the filming medium and to a stated lack of affinity with the Early Years Literacy Program, a program that had been developed by the researcher's work-based team. Despite this hesitancy, they came voluntarily into the project on the urging of Rachel, their acting Assistant Principal (TBC/RJ/2103), because 'we always trust [Rachel's] judgement!'

They both also expressed a professional interest in 'trying something new' (TBC/TI/2807), in spite of the perceived link with the Early Years Literacy Program. Unlike Rachel and Pip, Kim and Meredith were not known to central or regional Early Years team members and did not have responsibilities that included professional learning for other teachers. Their relative lack of experience in facilitating teacher professional learning contributed to their reluctance to take on the role of professional spokespeople. It was their newly formed team teaching relationship that was their highest priority, a commitment manifested in their request to be treated as 'one research case study', and they found sufficient collegiate support in their sense of being a team working together to achieve agreed goals.

7.2.1: On Multimodality

Data collected during interventions designed to support 'planning' for Teaching Sequence 1, shows Kim and Meredith were influenced by the 'multimodal schema' in planning teaching literacy within their social science related unit of work exploring celebrations and festivals.

> I knew we were going to do celebrations and multicultural festivals as an integrated theme, and I was just trying to think of something that has a lot of symbols, and the first thing that popped into my head was cards; cards are just filled with symbols or pictures that represent emotion, love... (TBC/TI/2807).

However the data shows that the first five lessons were focused on social science outcomes and these were pursued through deployment of the linguistic mode. Work on greeting cards was not introduced until lesson 6. In describing teaching acts undertaken, Kim and Meredith commented that:

> We haven't changed our style of planning at all to fit in with what you wanted, you know for the taping; it was what we normally did but then recognising, or identifying which part it fits into (TBC/TI/2807).

Data shows that in these early applications (lessons 1–5) Kim and Meredith taught exclusively through the linguistic mode. Data collected during interventions designed to facilitate teaching 'acts' (Carr and Kemmis, 1986; Kemmis and McTaggart, 2005) show Kim and Meredith emphasising aspects of their newly implemented team teaching arrangements and their deployment of the an 'integrated inquiry' approach (TBC/RJ/0205).

Kim and Meredith's over-riding pedagogical affinity was to integrated, inquiry learning and it was difficult to elicit articulation of any literacy professional learning undertaken as a result of participation in the project. It was also difficult to see any evidence of the enactments of multiliteracies learning, or theory-in-action (Argyris and Schön, 1974) — evidence which showed that 'we are already doing it' (TBC/RJ/0205). The data illustrates that the emphasis on greeting cards within the inquiry unit into celebrations and festivals was planned following engagement with the 'multimodal schema', yet this focus was not enacted until lesson 7 of Teaching Sequence 1. An excerpt from Rachel's film commentary on Kim and C's classroom applications suggests that Rachel may have been instrumental in prompting Kim and Meredith to begin work on the visual mode.

> Kim and Meredith and I were talking about ways of showing the different cards and I remembered when I first came here a few years ago, there was this wonderful machine that we had in the library that you could put a book on and it projected the full colour page up. So we rediscovered that together... Once we found out how to use the projector Kim and Meredith decided to use that as a 'whole class shared reading'. First of all their focus was looking at the front of the card and trying to determine what the features on that card showed, was it for a wedding or what celebration it suited. They covered up the actual key word on the card, to get the children to focus on those [visual] features at first, and then when they looked at it the second time they looked at the inside the card, the language, what sort of language was it, looking at the different features of the language within each card (TAonTBC/SFTI/0704).

Kim and Meredith moved from teaching exclusively through the linguistic mode, to teaching about the visual and the linguistic modes through collaboration with Rachel. Rachel was also instrumental in Kim and Meredith learning to use previously unused technology in the 'whole class shared reading' teaching approach in the Early Years Literacy Program.

The data illustrates that during interventions designed to facilitate observation and reflection (Carr and Kemmis, 1986; Kemmis and McTaggart, 2005) in cycle one, collaborative viewing of the initial filmed artefacts and the ensuing reflective debriefing (Argyris and Schön, 1974; Schön, 1987), Kim and Meredith passionately clarified and extended Rachel's descriptions, impressing on the team the finer details of their teaching purposes and the ways of extending students' responses they felt were missing from Rachel's commentary in the film edited by the researcher (TBC/RJ/2807).

> ... but it was throughout the four or five weeks of the integrated unit that we were doing it, the pictures or the cards became more complex as well. At first we had just the birthday cake, but when it got to the one that was the love heart—it was an engagement card—but when we made our list we realised that a love heart can be found on an anniversary card, a valentines day card, a wedding card... it takes a lot of work, because it's a birthday card and you might say 'what is it?'; 'it's a birthday card; 'how do you know?; 'I just know it' and it takes a lot of prior work for them to feel that they can say 'I think it's a birthday card BECAUSE...there's eight candles and I think it might be for a girl because the candles are pink, and she might be eight years old because there are eight candles' (TBC/TI/2807).

This quote from the data gives a flavour of the objections Kim and Meredith had to the way their work had been portrayed. Kim and Meredith's objections concerned condensation of the detail of teaching and lack of detail on the emphases of lessons and the outcomes being pursued. The recall stimulated by the viewing of film artefacts of their classroom practice enabled the team to collectively 'relive an original situation with vividness and accuracy' (Bloom, 1953, p. 161), enabling collaborative scrutiny of the classroom applications and the reflective commentary by team members.

The data shows that, as a result of Kim and Meredith's dissatisfaction with the filmed artefacts, they undertook a new professional role, that of professional spokespeople providing commentary on their teaching applications in future films in the series, (TBC/RJ/2807). This was enabled by reflection and tolerance of dissonance. This a hallmark of a teachers' inquiry community, a community which regards 'dissonance and questioning as signs of teachers' learning rather than their failing' (Cochran-Smith and Lytle, 1999, p. 22)

Undertaking the role of professional spokespeople involved Kim and Meredith in overcoming considerable discomfort associated with the scrutiny involved in the revealing process of filming. Passivity, through delegating responsibility for the role to Rachel, had resulted in a filmic artefact of their practices which they saw as an inadequate representation. Undertaking the role of professional spokespeople involved taking responsibility for future commentary and involved a greater commitment and accountability to the project. This is a significant professional shift for those working in environments where:

> [t]eachers have not been encouraged to work together on voluntary, self-initiated projects or speak out with authority about instructional, curricular, and policy issues (Cochran-Smith and Lytle, 1990, p. 9)

The data shows that Kim and Meredith's renewed commitment to the project involved an opening up of the discursive space around their engagement with and application of the multiliteracies schemas beyond, 'we are already doing it' (TBC/RJ/0205). The following excerpt is from an interview undertaken after the collective viewing, in the midst of the reflective debriefing.

Researcher	Do you want to tell us how what you always did—because that's what you just said, that this is what you would have always done, how in any way did it change as a consequence of this project?
Kim & Meredith	We had the main questions that we would like them [students] to answer... 'What is a celebration?' 'What is a festival?' 'How do people celebrate?' What do we want the kids to achieve by participating in this unit, what were they going to learn, so that's what those questions were a reflection of.
Researcher	Those questions are about the social science part of it, but you added another level ... the designs of meaning...
Kim & Meredith	Mmm...Our next point was to look at just symbols and logos around our community, and identify them around our classroom. Then we looked at Clip-Art on the computers, and what can we use if we are making a wedding card or a birthday card, and we made lists around our room on things you'd find on a wedding card.
Researcher	You started talking about images...
Kim & Meredith	Yes, and I suppose that is the multimodal? ...[W]e thought well....we can't really do this part of this without the kids developing an understanding of what they understand about symbols and how they interpret them, how they are used in our language (TBC/TI/2807).

Through commitment to sustained dialogue, Kim and Meredith began to engage in finer articulation of their classroom applications, and through collaborative dialogue shifted from defending their habitual practices to considering habitual and emergent practices in terms of the multiliteracies schemas—in this instance, the 'multimodal schema'. This is a movement towards exemplifying the disposition of a lifelong and lifewide learner (Aspin and Chapman, 2001), including preparedness to reveal understandings and practices and to transparently grapple with issues of professional learning. It is also an instance of teacher learning as 'breaking professional silence', as they thought about, discussed and 'read the texts' of teaching (McDonald, 1992, p. 43).

These sensibilities are unlike the prevailing culture in many schools wherein the development of teacher practice is not open to the scrutiny of colleagues and expectations are that teachers gain the knowledge required for their professional practice during teacher training and develop further practical knowledge predominantly through teaching experience (Elmore, 2002). Teacher culture which viewed theoretical learning as completed once formal teacher education was completed was felt keenly by Kim and Meredith, more recent graduates than many on the established school staff.

Researcher	In terms of professional development, what do you two think you have gained, what do you think others might need, what would help other teachers do the sorts of things that you do?

Kim & Meredith	It's a difficult one because I don't see that I do things... we are not in other [class]rooms—and you can't say that I do things differently than somebody else.
Researcher	But you've engaged in professional development as part of this project...
Kim & Meredith	Yes... I think it's sort of being able to identify and put things into some sort of perspective so that we are looking at the multiliteracies and knowing what we are doing it and where it fits into the curriculum, and to share that—I suppose that needs to be shared with staff in small doses...
Researcher	Hmm, there's more of that coming in now, with our reviews... There are professional standards...My personal opinion is that some teachers need to lighten up, and accept that there are people around them who can give them information that might help, and they are not there—as a teacher you are not there to know everything... those people that need to lighten up, I suppose, for lack of a better description, are the people that need to know all of the answers and need to have total control, and you see what we DON'T have is total control.
Researcher	That's a big problem isn't it?
Kim & Meredith	And sometimes it's hard for people to let go of that because they haven't got control and at the end of the day they haven't produced what they have said they are going to produce.
Researcher	They are not open to being learners...?
Kim & Meredith	And some people value I think too, the pen and paper test a lot, whereas you get so much too out of the conversations that you have. And I mean to be able to even record what the children are saying might be a really rich form of assessing and sort of have that sense of what they are thinking and how they are analysing things and the complexity of their thinking. And there have been times when we have taped [Child X and Y] who are fairly new to the country, their English is fairly good, yet they find it very difficult to write or express their thoughts in our grammar... so I gave them a tape recorder and they were talking about what they did on the weekend, and everybody else was writing about what they did on the weekend.
Researcher	You allowed multimodal forms as a way of doing the same task, so some students wrote, others spoke. That's complex...
Kim & Meredith	Mmmm. And they can all feel successful...The management is challenging, we had to be prepared to have children all over the place because we were looking at so many different aspects like the ICT; the aspect about the actual language; the oral language aspect, the written aspect, the visual, so we had children working on different tasks at the same time (TBC/TI/0108).

There is a sense of conflict evident between the values and practices of Kim and Meredith and those of other teachers at the school. This conflict explains somewhat the initially defensive attitude of Kim and Meredith in project participation. As relatively recently teacher education graduates (eight years' experience) in a school where many members of staff had twenty of thirty years' experience (TA/RJ/2003), sharing experience in a knowledgeable way with other staff was not always appreciated (TBC/RJ/2907). Rather than appreciating professional shared learning in a distributed leadership model, where the responsibility for sustaining improvement is shared broadly among school community members (McLaughlin and Talbert, 2001), less experienced staff adopting professional learning leadership roles attracted negative reactions from more experienced staff.

This exchange points to Kim and Meredith's valuing of diversity of student meaning-making capacities (van Haren, 2007) in this case of students' knowledge as displayed through oral language in lessons 1-5 of Teaching Sequence 1 (written question and answer; oral and written brainstorm; written [and for some students oral] survey, oral definition of celebrations—values which the above extract shows were at odds with the prevailing values of some of their colleagues. Participation in the project with educators from outside the school and collaboration and mentoring from Rachel, their acting Assistant Principal, served to support their professional learning, to assist in identifying current practices as multimodal examples of teaching, and extend their classroom applications to include a broader range of modes of meaning.

These differences in values resound with the theories of 'insider' and 'outsider' mindsets in approaches to digital literacies (Bigum and Lankshear, 1998; Lankshear and Knobel, 2003; Lankshear and Knobel, 2006). Kim and Meredith did not display an openness to digital sensibility until lesson 7, however in their classroom enactments they increasingly rejected the 'digital outsider' mindset which values the stable order of hierarchical authority and control of knowledge and competence rather than distributed social power and agency. As the project proceeded Kim and Meredith increasingly displayed 'digital insider' qualities in their classroom, seeing value in collective expertise, distributed authority and value in dispersal of information: a 'production house' environment (Neville, 2006), where what teachers 'DON'T have is total control' (TBC/SFTI/0109).

The data collected in Teaching Sequence 2 (lessons 11-19), following the expanded commitment of Kim and Meredith to the research project, shows a broadening of the modes taught to include the linguistic, audio, visual, gestural and spatial modes of meaning (see discussion below). Lesson 7 served as a turning point, with Kim and Meredith connecting multimodality as a means of catering for diverse student abilities (TBC/TI/0108). Unlike Rachel, Kim and Meredith had extensive opportunities for application of multiliteracies-influenced classroom teaching and learning, and the data shows an increasingly broad range of application—see table 7.7.

Kim and Meredith approached multimodality teaching as teaching through modes to support social science outcomes, and as deploying multiple modes as a way of catering for multiple entry points for diverse students (van Haren, 2007). Depth of pedagogical learner knowledge (Darling-Hammond, 1998; Shulman, 1999) was espoused as of paramount importance to Kim and Meredith, evident in comments made throughout the project, typified by 'we know our kids, not just know them...da da da is consolidating level 2, but I think we have got a fairly good knowledge of where our kids are, and what they can do and where they can go to and how far, and what support they require' (TBC/TI/2807).

Kim and Meredith showed great respect for students as learners:

> ... the kids surprise you, they do pick up an enormous amount and they have an incredible understanding that sometimes we don't always give them credit for (TBC/SFTI/0109).

However they resisted the 'telling of information' or the multimodal metalanguage advocated in the pedagogical knowledge process of conceptualising, with teaching involving an emphasis on 'finding out what the kids could tell us, not us delivering that information' (TBC/TI/2807).

In their case there was no strong evidence in the data illustrating teaching which foregrounded teaching about modes (including the linguistic) as well as teaching through modes. This was unlike Rachel, who taught about mode, but due to limited time spent with students, did not connect strongly with students' diverse capacities and interests; and Pip (see discussion below) who taught both through and about mode; and used mode to connect with diverse student capacities. In relation to multimodal teaching emphases, Kim and Meredith's focus in Teaching Sequence 1 was within the context of integrated inquiry, and focused initially on linguistic-related organisational and contextual dimensions of meaning. Teaching expanded to include the visual and tended to emphasise the contextual dimension of meaning with a lesser focus on organisation of 'conceptual' visual representations (Kress and van Leeuwen, 1996). As shown in data from Teaching Sequence 1 discussed in Chapter Six, Kim and Meredith's prompting drew attention to the cultural context of multimodal designs, such as giving and receiving greeting cards as part of celebrations and the demographics and sensibilities of the card recipients.

7.2.2: On Pedagogy

Where Rachel had discovered the transferability of multiliteracies across subject areas, particularly addressing visual designs in mathematics (TA/RJ/2807), Kim and Meredith began with an integrated approach but struggled in identifying and articulating the multimodal learning within their integrated practice. Rachel was able to articulate and teach about modes of meaning, foregrounding these in planning. Kim and Meredith continued to struggle with identifying and articulating teaching about modes of meaning, as evident in the following extract.

Researcher	The Learning Element—how useful do you think it is going to be or not be?
Kim & Meredith	We started looking at it, and it started to be difficult for us because to write because you look at the card or the greeting aspect of what we have done, and that's only then a very small component. The whole topic, we have been doing it for weeks and it is an integrated topic, and we have included data charts, so mathematics as a part of it, so they have gained knowledge through those areas as well.
Researcher	Would you have to include all of that to capture the richness?
Kim & Meredith	Mmmm, how do we do that on that particular format? I suppose they are the things that we need to grapple with...

Researcher	The format is a Word document...with spaces for writing lessons according to the pedagogies...
Kim & Meredith	I suppose it is looking at all the tiny little links so that it makes sense, because there are so many parts to it. Because we don't ever look at it as 'lesson 1' or 'activity 1'...sometimes one runs into the other
Researcher	So you had your social science goals, and you had literacy goals for the designs of meaning?
Kim & Meredith	When we look at our initial planning, we look at the social science, for example in this particular unit, and we look at where does the opportunity for mathematics fit in? Where does the science fit in? All these components so that that all of it is tied together.
Researcher	This project is about literacy, the part that takes up the multimodality... but, the cards are only one part of an integrated disciplinary program.
Kim & Meredith	Mmm, because if you had to address everything separately, there aren't enough hours in the day ...
Researcher	Can you record just the multimodal learning part? Give it to somebody else, or once you cut it up, do you miss what you're doing with the integration?
Kim & Meredith	Hmmm, but, like we have to cover 'data' sometime between now and the end of the year, what better way than to do graphs—it's real, it links with what we are doing. 38 kids in our grade celebrate birthdays...
Researcher	So can you record that for somebody else to use... can we take a thread?
Kim & Meredith	You can give little bits of it but in the end, it ends up being who we are, and how we work and how we do things and ...it will be very different to how...others with same outcomes deliver their lessons... it's dependent on their styles and their children.

Like Rachel, Kim and Meredith were challenged in retrospectively documenting lessons on the Learning Element template, seeing their practice as heavily contextualised and individual. Kim and Meredith valued documenting what they had done, in the way they had done it, and critiqued the ability of the Learning Element template to capture, 'the richness of the discussions we have [with the children]' and about the children, we discuss the children constantly at every opportunity' (TBC/TI/0109).

Clearly, pedagogical affinity with integrated inquiry learning and habituated planning practices were obstacles for Kim and Meredith in the documentation process. Departure from accustomed ways of documenting classroom applications resulted in a struggle, with attempts to dialogue around reconsideration of lessons in terms of their underpinning pedagogical knowledge processes somewhat stalled, as apparent in the above example. Shifts in the audience that Kim and Meredith were writing for—from planning for school-based implementation to sharing Learning Elements on the Web—also created difficulties. 'This is not what we do. We usually do our planning for ourselves. We would never do this [amount of detail/kind of documentation]...' (TBC/RJ/2907). To Kim and Meredith, it seemed that the benefits of the Learning Element template were far outweighed by the difficulty created by trying to incorporate this into their existing practice.

Kim and Meredith's confidence in 'tagging' learning activities as pedagogical knowledge processes grew in contexts of collaboration as they undertook the documentation of the multimodality aspect of the integrated unit on the Learning Element template, a documentation task which engaged Kim and Meredith in reflecting on the pedagogical knowledge processes underpinning taught and to-be-taught lessons.

> We were looking at this piece of work with the others [case study teachers]; a piece we were going to do or try, and it was very easy to fit into those different modules [pedagogical knowledge processes] (TBC/TI/2807).

Here it can be seen that a disposition towards collaborative reflection and self-revelation is becoming apparent, with the problem-solving collegiality offered by the professional learning team countering physical, classroom-based and intellectual isolation (Gabelnick et al., 1990) that can lead to a disposition to defend and conceal, rather than reveal and explore, classroom applications and teacher knowledge.

7.2.3: On Professional Repertoires

The impact of the 'pedagogical knowledge processes schema' and the Learning Element template on expanding Kim and Meredith's repertoire of pedagogical deployment in teaching multimodality can be considered in terms of the two Teaching Sequences: Teaching Sequence 1, taught prior to Kim and Meredith's retrospective completion of the Learning Element; and Teaching Sequence 2, taught after Kim and Meredith's completion of the same Learning Element—see table 7.5 and table 7.6. below.

Table 7.5: Kim and Meredith: Deployment of Pedagogical Knowledge Processes in Teaching Multimodality (Predominant mode of focus is shown by print size)
Teaching Sequence 1

Lesson	Pedagogical knowledge process	Linguistic mode	Audio mode	Visual mode	Gestural mode	Spatial mode
1	Experiencing the Known	X				
2	Experiencing the Known	X				
3	Experiencing the New	X				
4	Conceptualising by Naming	X				
5	Conceptualising by Naming	X				
6	Conceptualising by Theorising	x		X		
7	Conceptualising by Theorising	x		X		
8	Analysing Critically	x		X		
9	Applying Appropriately	X		x		
10	Applying Creatively	x		X		

Teaching Sequence 2

11	Experiencing the Known	X				
12	Analysing Critically	x	X	x		
13	Experiencing the New	x	X			
14	Analysing Functionally	X				
15	Applying Appropriately			X		x
16	Conceptualising by Naming	X				
17	conceptualising by theorising		X			
18	Applying Creatively				x	X
19	Applying Appropriately	X	x	x	x	x

Comparison of data from the two Teaching Sequences shows that in Teaching Sequence 1 the 'multimodal schema' had no apparent impact on Kim and Meredith's first five lessons, which exclusively addressed the linguistic mode. While Kim and Meredith did not claim affinity with the teaching approaches of the Early Years Literacy Program, their literacy related teaching was print-focused. However, the focus was learning through the linguistic, with social science learning foregrounded. This differs from Rachel's teaching about mode. Where Rachel was on a learning trajectory, which focused initially on teaching about isolated modes of meaning within the context of an English block of teaching and led to a realisation of potential for multimodal teaching in other subject areas, Kim and Meredith were on a learning trajectory which focused initially on teaching subject matter as integrated, and the linguistic mode used in service of other subject areas within this integrated approach.

Other teaching, conducted with an integrated, inquiry approach but not documented in the Learning Element, also deployed mode as a vehicle for other subject learning—for example, teaching about 'data' in mathematics lessons through visual representation. In describing their approach to teaching multimodality, Kim and Meredith replied, 'it's integrating it across everything we do... it's more than just a one off ... it's the multiliteracies of mathematics... of science ... it's every other part of the curriculum' (TBC/SFTI/0109).

In lessons 6–10, Kim and Meredith's learning became evident as they expanded their teaching foci to address the meaning-making resources of the visual and linguistic modes of meaning in greeting cards and the interrelationships between the visual and the linguistic. Designs of meaning in focus in Kim and Meredith's Teaching Sequence 1 included written question and answer; oral and written brainstorm; written survey, oral definition of celebrations (lessons 1–5); and brainstormed symbols, slogans, and jingles and greeting cards—child-made, teacher-made, and cards generated using 'Clip Art' and 'Publisher' (lessons 6–10). This was a shift towards teaching the visual, the most prevalent and well-theorised mode of meaning outside the linguistic (Kress and van Leeuwen, 1996). The audio, gestural and spatial modes were not addressed in the teaching of the first ten lessons.

The data shows a marked increase in the diversity of designs of meaning in focus in Teaching Sequence 2, a study of 'Entertainment' in which students selected a musical number and designed a set for a school concert performance, reflecting a willingness by Kim and Meredith to enact an extended repertoire. Designs included oral and written brainstorming and listing; 'Y chart' analysis; and editing of lyrics downloaded from the internet (lessons 11, 14, 16, 19), displaying a continued emphasis on the linguistic mode. The linguistic was deployed as a reflective means for considering types of entertainment and the effect of other modes (the audio). It was also taught about, as evidenced in conceptualising the use of lists and labels. Linguistic was also the emphasis of the actual performance, with dialogue and lyrics a major focus of teaching. Teaching focused on audio designs in the form of songs and soundtracks (lessons 12, 13, 17); visual designs in set plans (lesson 15); and the spatial in construction of dioramas for planning stage design (lessons 18 and 19), reflecting a broader approach to designs of meaning. Teaching addressed modes less well theorised as meaning-making resources, particularly the audio and spatial (van Leeuwen, 1999, 2006).

Comparison of data from the two Teaching Sequences shows growth in Kim and Meredith's confidence and capacities in purposefully addressing teaching of modes through deployment of pedagogies—see table 7.6 below. In planning an item for a school concert, Teaching Sequence 2 saw Kim and Meredith deploying pedagogical knowledge processes with greater control and clearer purpose in an exploration of visual, linguistic, audio and spatial meaning-making.

Table 7.6: Kim and Meredith: Deployment of Pedagogical Knowledge Processes in Two Teaching Sequences

	Experiencing	Conceptualising	Analysing	Applying
Teaching sequence 1	30%	40%	10%	20%
Teaching sequence 2	22%	11%	33.5%	33.5%

Kim and Meredith's deployment of the pedagogical knowledge process of experiencing, used in Teaching Sequence 1 to address social science learning through the linguistic mode (including written question and answer; oral and written brainstorm; written survey), was again used in Teaching Sequence 2 to involve students in 'experiencing the known' social science knowledge through linguistic brainstorming of types of entertainment (lesson 11). Kim and Meredith also deployed 'experiencing the new', engaging students with songs in the audio mode (lesson 13).

In Teaching Sequence 1, the pedagogical knowledge process of conceptualising was deployed in 'naming' celebrations and identifying those in which the giving of greeting cards was involved; and 'theorising' about the meaning-making potential of symbols (and to a lesser extent slogans and jingles), particularly on greeting cards. In Teaching Sequence 2, the pedagogical knowledge process of conceptualising was deployed in listing materials required for diorama construction, through the linguistic mode; and theorising about the effect of music on mood (lessons 16/17).

Unlike Rachel, Kim and Meredith showed reluctance to plan for concept-naming using specialised multimodal language, reflecting the aversion shown by educators with strong affiliation to progressivist pedagogies to overt instruction and a valuing of student inquiry, or children 'finding out' (Kalantzis et al., 2005; New London Group, 2000) The following example shows how Kim and Meredith would stop short of using specialised language of perspective with students, placing a higher value on the pedagogy of experiencing:

> When we were making the dioramas the children at first found it very difficult where to place things, and we tried to help them find out for themselves where to place bigger objects, where to paste smaller objects, also size, we had tiny trees and huge monkeys, and we were just saying to the kids, 'Is that what we normally see? What changes could you make to your diorama?' 'Oh the trees need to be bigger' or 'the trees need to be pushed back', so its just that understanding, again that experience, or experiencing, giving them those experiences where they could move things, see if it works for them and if it didn't work for them asking them 'well what can you do to make it work?' (TBC/SFTI/0109).

Although essential for knowledge development, because it is the process by which experience becomes knowledge (Halliday, 1994), the specialised multimodal metalanguage, in this case of perception and depth, was not shared directly with students.

The pedagogical knowledge process of analysis, limited in Teaching Sequence 1 to a focus on visual and linguistic features of greeting cards, was expanded in Teaching Sequence 2. In lesson 12, involving a concert performance, students were involved in 'analysing critically' in the audio mode as well as, although to a lesser extent, the linguistic and visual modes. In lesson 14 they were involved in 'analysing functionally' through linguistic responses to music.

In Teaching Sequence 1 the pedagogical knowledge process of applying was deployed to highlight the visual (and the linguistic) in making cards co-constructed by teachers and students and independently produced by students; and in Teaching Sequence 2 'applying appropriately' through the visual planning of a diorama (lesson 15) and 'applying creatively' through the spatial mode in the construction of dioramas (lesson 18); and 'applying appropriately' the linguistic mode (and to a lesser extent the audio, spatial, visual and gestural modes) in rehearsal and performance of a concert song (lesson 19).

Like Rachel's experimentation with mode in Teaching Sequence 1, Kim and Meredith's later classroom applications in Teaching Sequence 1 and in Teaching Sequence 2 showed sampling of modes for different purposes. As a result of engagement with the 'pedagogical knowledge processes schema', Kim and Meredith, like Rachel, were more focused on depth of teaching rather than breadth, as evidenced in the following quote. In their case this was in the context of integrated inquiry which sought to link teaching of different subject areas through topic-based work.

> We started out with a lot of ideas and we thought we would do a lot of different activities... [A]s we started to get into it we realised that to do the work at the depth we wanted to do it we really needed to be more focused on fewer tasks but do them well, look at the task and peel back the layers and develop the understandings we wanted the children to achieve and where we wanted them to go rather do a whole lot of tasks, just touch on the surface and then go onto the next task (TBC/SFTI/0109).

By concentrating on depth rather than breadth of experience, Kim and Meredith found they were able to 'get the children really thinking deeper about what they're doing... children had a lot deeper understanding of what they're building... they became very picky—critical—about what they wanted to choose, really critical... they can question more [and] back up their beliefs, they have [greater] reasoning (TBC/SFTI/0109). Placing value on peeling back the layers, seeking depth over breadth and developing students' critical skills is evidence of a critical disposition, born of reflection on teaching, developing 'the disposition toward reflection [which] is central to expert teaching' (Sternberg and Horvath, 1995, p. 15).

While it was not overtly articulated, following documentation of the Learning Element, shifts in focus from foregrounding the integration of disciplines in planning to consideration of the modes and pedagogies deployed to support literacy and social science learning are apparent in Kim and Meredith's classroom applications.

Unlike Rachel, Kim and Meredith, as class teachers with major responsibility for the learning of the combined class, had broad scope and opportunities to apply multiliteracies schemas. In Teaching Sequence 2, Kim and Meredith's classroom increasingly took on a production house quality (Neville, 2006). Expansion of modes and designs of meaning in literacy teaching programs resulted in challenging organisational and technical issues for Kim and Meredith. There was a sense of needing to use flexibility and responsiveness in the flow of teaching, in terms of extending planned sessions to allow more time if 'something is working, we'd prefer to keep going with it rather than dropping it' (TBC/TI/2807), but also because 'sometimes your direction changes completely because of the experiences the children have' (TBC/SFTI/0109).

Table 7.7: Kim and Meredith: Addressing of Mode and Deployment of Pedagogical Knowledge Processes (Predominant mode of focus is shown in italics) Teaching Sequence 1

Lesson	Multimodality emphases	Pedagogical knowledge process
1	*Linguistic* Written question and answer	Experiencing the Known
2	*Linguistic* Oral/written brainstorm	Experiencing the Known

3	*Linguistic* Written survey	Experiencing the New
4	*Linguistic* Oral definition of celebrations	Conceptualising by Naming
5	*Linguistic* Oral/written classification of celebrations	Conceptualising by Naming
6	*Visual* and linguistic Brainstorm of symbols, slogans, jingles	conceptualising by theorising
7	*Visual* and linguistic Features of greeting cards	Conceptualising by Theorising
8	*Visual* and linguistic Features of greeting cards	Analysing Critically
9	*Linguistic* and visual Making cards - written and child illustrated	Applying Appropriately
10	*Visual* and linguistic Making cards–ClipArt, Publisher	Applying Creatively

Teaching Sequence 2

11	*Linguistic* Oral/written brainstorm	Experiencing the Known
12	*Audio*, linguistic and visual Considering songs for performance	Analysing Critically
13	*Audio* and linguistic Listening to songs from favourite movies	Experiencing the New
14	*Linguistic* Responses to music using Y charts	Analysing Functionally
15	*Visual* and spatial Planning a diorama of a concert set	Applying Appropriately
16	*Linguistic* Developing lists and labels	Conceptualising by Naming
17	*Audio* Effects of music on mood	Conceptualising by Theorising
18	*Spatial* and visual Construction of dioramas	Applying Creatively
19	*Linguistic*, audio, spatial, visual, gestural Rehearsal and performance of item	Applying Appropriately

Expertise in articulating the terminology of the pedagogical knowledge processes began to be apparent, although partial, as Kim and Meredith continued to struggle with the terminology. This is evident in the following interview extract about their work on 'Entertainment' and came late in the filming process.

Kim & Meredith	We decided to look at movies because the children could relate to them more than just listening to songs, so they were able to make those connections with the movie and the song. ... [W]e modelled how to do a Y chart... what it felt like, what it sounded like and what it would look like... that was where we did the directed teaching, where we were telling them, 'Ok, this is what we need to do'. ... We had to show them what we meant by designing their set... they had to draw their set for their diorama... develop a list of materials... they made links between their diagram and their list... we talked about listing... we talked about the importance of labelling.
Researcher:	In terms of the conceptual stuff then, how do you decide...
Kim & Meredith	I have different names for them, which is the 'conceptual'?
Researcher:	All the explicit language and concepts, for example 'lyrics', teaching that kind of stuff, 'point of view'. How do you plan for that?
Kim & Meredith	I think it's really hard to plan what you're going to cover fully... the group of children you're working with helps you, they do all the planning for you, again sometimes you assume that a child understands a word when they may not and we try to instil in our kids that if they don't understand something to let us know...we used the term 'lyrics', and immediately the hand went up, 'what do you mean by 'lyrics'? And then we explain that words to a song we usually call 'lyrics'.
Researcher	'Lists' and 'labels'...these are concepts...
Kim & Meredith	Doing the lists and labels we were re-visiting things that the children had done before so we weren't taking them completely into the unknown... it was highlighting the importance of making a list and how to label their diagrams and the importance of making the links between the diagram and what they needed, and what they needed to put in their lists to be able to make their diorama basically. During that process too where they were designing their diorama and doing their drawings there was a lot of talk about things like perception and depth and how, where are we going to put certain things like, if we had a tall building did we want it to be in the foreground or did we want it to be in the background? Would we have a tall building at the back if we wanted it to look as if it were far away?
Researcher	Can you just tell us about the whole reason, the whole purpose of this teaching and where you're going with it?
Kim & Meredith	Designing the dioramas is the first step towards doing something very real ...designing the set for their concert so all of the concepts they come up with and all of the ideas that they come up with they're going to be working on in the real thing and the arts teacher is also going to be working with us to help us make the dioramas become a reality.
Researcher	You talked about your kids' experiences you talked about the conceptual stuff. Have you done any work in the 'Entertainment' unit on critical framing?
Kim & Meredith	The critical framing was an integral part virtually from the beginning... we were looking at what is the purpose, who's our audience going to be? And making those links back to the cards. What was the purpose? Our audience?
Researcher	You may have touched on this too but, what about the transforming of practice or applying the knowledge they learn in one situation to another?

Kim & Meredith	I'm just trying to think, transferring that knowledge, when we talked about, reflected back to what we did with the cards and talking about well, why are we doing what we're doing with the videos? Why would we be designing these things in the way that we're doing it? So they did make those links but I don't think it was as overt.
Researcher	Do you feel there's anything else you would like to add to that or do you think we've done that [the pedagogical knowledge processes]?
Kim & Meredith	Yeah I feel that we've done that. Because I'm not very good with the terms (TBC/SFTI/0109)

Like Rachel, Kim and Meredith experienced difficulty in mastering the language of the 'pedagogical knowledge processes schema'. Slippage between the multiliteracies schema and the 'pedagogical knowledge processes schema' is evident in the teachers' and the researcher's use of terminology. The data does indicate a shift apparent in their dispositions: a new preparedness for self-revelation. Kim and Meredith remained confident that 'we were doing it anyway' but were aware of slippage in their use of terminology and openly sought clarification of terms and concepts.

Kim and Meredith's learning trajectory was substantial when project entry understandings are considered.

> [W]e had no idea what it [multiliteracies] involved, or even to a point what multiliteracies really was... we had heard the term (TBC/TI/2803).

> I didn't have a really big idea of what multiliteracies were. I'd heard the word and you conjure up things like, computers and all those sorts of things, but really I didn't have my head around what it really did mean (TBC/SFTI/0108).

In the later filmed segments, Kim and Meredith began to use the first person pronoun, 'I' in reference to themselves as learners and teachers. This is further evidence of preparedness to reveal themselves as professionals with emergent knowledge.

As was the case with Rachel's learning trajectory, documentation of the Learning Element, facilitated by expert input, collaborative dialogue and collaborative reading and viewing, enabled deeper engagement with the pedagogical knowledge processes around the multimodal learning aspects of their unit of work. Unlike Rachel, Kim and C's capacity to articulate the language of the 'pedagogical knowledge processes schema' was tentative, as evident in the last filming session. Key learnings for Kim and Meredith included identification and shifts towards articulation of 'tacit' knowledge—knowledge that practitioners hold but cannot easily articulate, or 'a certain knowledge that [one] cannot tell' (Polanyi, 1966, p. 8)—of the 'multimodal schema' and 'pedagogical knowledge processes schema'.

Kim and Meredith's practitioner identities were primarily classroom-based and their collegiate reference group was school-based, as evident in the following excerpt.

Researcher	Is there anything from this whole experience of the way you do this, that would be transferable?

Kim & Meredith	I suppose looking at the different levels of thinking and how you can actually draw that out for the children. I don't know how you could communicate that, but then maybe looking at it or practising it—we have looked at our own practice, and looked at well, this is where it fits in, this is what we are doing. And talking, talking, we are great talkers... also knowing what people's beliefs are and their vision of teaching.
Researcher	So it really is important, that engagement, the conversation?
Kim & Meredith	I think professional conversation is really important, because I know that we have actually taken things say to the staffroom, where we were actually working on an analysis of the task, something very practical to share and then talk about what the kids were doing—maybe having people coming in and seeing what you are doing...?
Researcher	That doesn't seem to happen much... So what do you think this experience did give you, being part of this group?
Kim & Meredith	Mmm, and I think too, now that we have gone more into it, I think we understand that we are probably doing a lot of this anyway, but we never ever had a real 'tag' to put with it, and now we can almost say well, yes, I can almost see how this fits in to that particular mode, or this particular mode, whereas before we wouldn't have been aware of the terminology... How do you put it into words? I have a clearer... It has probably given names to things that I do. I would not have called it 'situated practice' or 'visual mode' that is just something that we do, so this reassured me that the way I am planning is somewhere along the right track....
Researcher	So has it built your confidence?
Kim & Meredith	It also gets you to tease it out a little bit more too. Like ask that more potent question... And also too knowing that we are going to be able to share it, and I don't mean share it with a great big group of people but I think you probably share it as a class or a team... Kim is on the Multiliteracies Project Team and has taken it back to this particular project team and I've got one of the other grade 1–2 teachers and we are looking at another piece of work and how we can incorporate multiliteracies. But also sharing what you have gotten through this with the rest of the staff (TBC/SFTI/0109).

Creation of teaching documentation in response to the multiliteracies schemas enabled Kim and Meredith to instigate collaborative school-based discussion, a bridge to counterpoint professional isolation resulting from individual teaching spaces—isolation which is a major factor affecting the role of teacher and teacher professionalism and which presents difficulty in developing shared knowledge and standards of practice (Darling-Hammond, 1998).

The excerpt above shows that Kim and Meredith did not confidently take on the role of teacher–author in sharing their documentation with colleagues outside the school, in the broader profession. Like Rachel and Pip, the impact of this engagement was publication of a peer-reviewed, web-published Learning Element. However, unlike Rachel and Pip, Kim and Meredith declined an offer to further develop their Learning Element for inclusion in a peer-reviewed journal for a peak national teacher association. Development of a Learning Element had the benefit of assisting in identifying tacit knowledge and local sharing. For Kim and Meredith this was a more localised move towards teacher authorship and supporting other teachers' professional learning. Aspects of the role of published author, like that of filmed practitioner and spokesperson, appeared more difficult for Kim and Meredith to incorporate, as teachers whose major concerns are classroom responsibilities.

7.3: Pip's Impact Story

Pip, newly returned to classroom duties after re-deployment from a regionally-based ICT/Early Years Literacy consultancy role, displayed interest in the project due to its potential for foregrounding professional strengths and interests in technologies in literacy teaching, a way of engaging students in their literacy learning (TD/SFTI/1004). Like Kim and Meredith, Pip had major responsibility for a class (Years 3 and 4 students) but, like Rachel, Pip also had welfare and within-school and regionally-based professional learning responsibilities. Pip did not anticipate substantial consequences due to project involvement, being 'used to all that kind of professional stuff that goes with being a curriculum consultant and an early years trainer and talking to large groups' (TD/TI/2907).

7.3.1: On Multimodality

As in Rachel's case, the data illustrates Pip's heightened awareness as a result of the expert input related to the meaning-making resources of modes other than the linguistic in the midst of practical application, in this case the reading, analysis and construction of web resources.

Data collected during interventions designed to support 'planning' (Carr and Kemmis, 1986; Kemmis and McTaggart, 2005), for Teaching Sequence 1, highlights Pip's desire to improve the literacy capacities of all students in the class, particularly disengaged boys with an aversion to writing (TD/SFTI/1004). Unlike other case study teachers, Pip was very confident with, passionate about, and eager to incorporate technology into literacy learning. Pip also openly displayed the disposition of a learner, 'If there's something I don't know, I say to the children, 'I don't know. Let's look it up on the internet' (TD/SFTI/1004).

Expert input on the 'multimodal schema', consideration of students' disengagement with writing, and personal interest and expertise influenced Pip's decision to explore and create webpages (TD/RJ/1004). In the course of classroom action, the shift from print-based texts to the web environment led to a focus on the visual as well as the linguistic mode, particularly on the organisational dimension of meaning (Cope and Kalantzis, 2000a), as evident in the following interview excerpt.

Researcher	The video shows you looked at the elements of webpages.
Pip	We started off reading them and as we were reading them we discovered that some were easier to read, some of the links were easier to use. They [the students] looked at background colours, font size, font colours, images, some were really slow loading. They loved the animated ones.
Researcher	So reading is very complex, the way you're approaching it.
Pip	Exactly. Also making the connection between what's written and the actual use of the background or perhaps the use of the graphics... Kids are quite critical whether the actual graphics were appropriate to what was written in terms of the content. They like the content to be matching fairly closely.
Researcher	Have you got an example?
Pip	One of the sites we looked at was a Grade 3/4 site and they'd been to an athletics day. They had a lovely little graphic of an animated 'Sonic', a little cartoon character... and while they loved that, they said 'well that's not really appropriate for a report about an athletics day'. I said 'what could we have used instead?' and Child X said, 'They should have just taken a digital photo and downloaded it onto the computer and they could have had the actual photo of what happened on the day rather than putting in this really cute little animated guy that had nothing to do with school athletics'.
Researcher	It would be more appropriate?
Pip	Yes, initially they thought that's great because he's really cute and he looks like he's running across the page but once we actually started to analyse 'was it a good thing or a bad thing', they said 'no it wasn't appropriate to the content'.
Researcher	So a lot of analysis about the multimodal....
Pip	Exactly and looking at just even the way the actual ... I guess it is the visual relationships too, the way the text is presented on the page, sometimes there's quite a large section of writing with nothing to break it up which when you are looking at a screen and having to scroll down the page makes it a bit laborious. They liked sites where there was small amount of text but with some kind of a horizontal line or something to break up each section so that when you are scanning, physically having to go down a large webpage, it made it easier to be able to follow ...
Researcher	The total design ...
Pip	The total design ... like the navigation bars, which ones are easy to use? The preference seems to be for like an index type thing down the left hand side rather than at the very bottom of the page...you've got to go all the way down to actually get to those bars. We looked at what makes it easy for us as readers to access a page.
Researcher	Would you normally have done that with a piece of written text, like would you have said, 'Let's look at the front cover, the title, the chapter...?
Pip	We would have but this was a whole new level because you have got the animation and you've got a completely different layout to what a book has and each page can be quite different too.
Researcher	Did you do any comparisons between, say a book and website?
Pip	We looked at the links, how when you click on a link it is similar to turning a page. We used that analogy (TD/TI/2907).

As discussed in Chapter Six, the data indicates that, in the visual mode in Teaching Sequence 1, there is concentration of teacher prompts on the organisational dimension of meaning (54%). While Rachel's focus on literature tended to concentrate on narrative visual representation (Kress and van Leeuwen, 1996), greater focus was evident on conceptual representation (Kress and van Leeuwen, 1996) in Pip's focus on web design. Pip focused attention on hyperlinks and navigations icons as salient visual organisational elements, and deployed conceptual visuals such Venn diagrams and concept maps to develop classificational taxonomies.

While Pip was, like Kim and Meredith, immersed in explorative classroom action with emergent multimodal metalanguage, Pip was comfortable with identifying and emphasising specialised multimodal metalanguage with students.

Researcher	The video shows you've worked up a vocabulary; there's some quite complex technical terms.
Pip	We had to really push it forward because we had the filming crew coming and we hadn't done a lot with it... it was the language that they discovered... children are just like using it... are getting very skilled at using the appropriate language and are able to rattle off 'www dot' or whatever it happens to be... [I introduced the term] 'hyperlink', they hadn't really used it before, but they were using things like 'links'. Child X when he was talking about digital photos said, 'Well you just download it to the computer' like it wasn't something that I'd even gone through with them. We did talk about 'fonts' and 'background colours', 'graphics', 'images' and 'animation', but a lot of it they picked up along the way as they'd see different examples. So we are developing a class glossary.
Researcher	I suppose you'd be continually adding to that too?
Pip	We've made two [A3] pages of our glossary words, but certainly each time we find a new word we're working out what it means and adding to the glossary, so it's going to be ongoing. I imagine it will continue for most of the year, because there's going to be so much scope with what we're doing with the webpages, leading on to developing our own class newspaper or newsletter, which will link again to the webpage (TD/TI/2907).

The filming schedule and the impending screening of the films on the Schools Television network pressured Pip to respond to the multiliteracies schemas with practical enactments. While the metalanguage was somewhat incidental and emergent from the classroom acts, Pip emphasised the language of the internet through isolating terms and building a class glossary. Like Rachel, Pip found the students well able to use specialised multimodal metalanguage.

Incorporating multimodal texts required Pip to reflect on and reframe the strategies habitually used in print-based teaching practices in applying these to multimodal teaching situations. An example of this was the use of a PMI (Plus/Minus/Interesting) thinking tool to generate analysis.

> [T]hey're [the students] used to using PMI, which is the plus, minus and interesting way of looking at [texts], we've done it with books and with book characters, it was very easy to transfer that to a webpage (TD/SFTI/0105).

Like Rachel, Pip considered definitions of teaching approaches in light of the nature of multimodal texts. During an interview, Pip was describing a small group teaching session focused on hyperlinking. When asked 'What teaching approach did you use to teach the small group about hyperlinking?' Pip replied with a self-reflective question, 'Would that be shared reading or shared writing?' This self-reflection was followed by a description of the following lesson.

> We introduced the hyperlinking with a small group and we had a shared writing session around my laptop computer. We were looking at linking our personal profile to our passion projects. For some children it was quite easy, they went through their personal profile and found the particular bit of text that was going to match their passion project, for example one boy had written about mythological creatures, so he straight away worked out that he needed to hyperlink from the word 'mythological' which he was able to do (TD/SFTI/0105).

The shift of literacy teaching context from the page to the online environment prompted reflection on the nature of reading and writing, a consideration of what hyperlinking involves and how it might be compared with the practices of print-based reading and writing. Restricted access to technological resources within the online environment limited Pip's deployment of the modes of meaning to the linguistic and visual, with a much lesser emphasis on the audio, despite earlier plans, as evident in the following excerpt.

Researcher	In terms of the modes of meaning, what plans do you have? I know you've explored a lot of the linguistic and the visual.
Pip	Yes. And what we wanted to do was to also add digital video footage and audio sound to our personal profiles. We found with the technology that we had available to us we weren't actually able to use the children's own sound, or their own video footage of themselves, so we used what Microsoft PowerPoint provided for us, so the children were able to add animated clipart and also audio sound to go with that, so we had teaching groups, or a group working with me each day, and we went through the process of how do you add animation and how to you add the relevant sound (TD/SFTI/0105).

Lack of available resources, in this case, impacted on the extent of modes taught within the purposeful context of the online environment. Classroom and resource management increasingly became an issue, as the project 'gained its own momentum' (TD/TI/2907) and the production house environment (Neville, 2006) became evident as children were 'working in the library, in other rooms, three quarters of the grade on computers around the school; [and the challenge of having to] remember which room they're in' (TD/SFTI/0909).

Of the case study teachers, Pip was the closest to being a digital native (Prensky, 2001), with well developed technological knowledge. However, like the other case study teachers, Pip grappled with the foregrounding and backgrounding of literacy learning and subject matter, as evidenced in the following excerpt.

> I was really aware that we still have to be focusing on literacy skills... that was one of the things that stuck in my mind. While it is fine to integrate literacy and use, for example, a theme on 'The Sea' during your literacy block, your actual reading and writing focus must remain on reading and writing and not on 'The Sea' or whatever it happens to be. So it might be that you actually choose to research, using your research skills, about 'The Sea'. I was really conscious of that, making sure that the focus was on literacy and using our literacy just in different ways (TD/SFTI/0105).

Pip clearly differentiated literacy learning foci from the foci of the subject matter students were learning, be it through their 'passion projects' or in general topic-based work.

In relation to multimodal teaching emphases, Pip's focus in Teaching Sequence 1, was within the context of exploration and creation of personal webpages, and focused initially on linguistic-related organisational dimensions of meaning. Over the course of Teaching Sequence 1, Pip showed a strong preference for prompting towards the organisational dimension of meaning in teaching associated with the linguistic and visual modes. As shown in data from Teaching Sequence 1 discussed in Chapter Six, Pip's prompting drew attention to the navigational aspects of web-based multimodal designs.

Teaching expanded to include the visual which tended also to emphasise the organisational dimension of meaning of 'conceptual' visual representations (Kress and van Leeuwen, 1996) and maintained a strong emphasis on the organisational dimension of meaning of linguistic representations.

7.3.2: On Pedagogy

Like the other case study teachers, Pip initially found the structure and language of the Learning Element template different to previous planning formats (TD/RJ/2907).

Researcher	How are you finding the Learning Element?
Pip	It's different in terms of not having used it before and the language... it is a different language than what I am used to.
Researcher	What do you mean by a different language?
Pip	I guess it is different terminology... like the 'knowledge processes' etc, just the way it is structured or worded is different to what I have used before... like our planning is not quite as structured.
Researcher	Does it matter?
Pip	I don't think it matters; I think it's got to work for you; at this stage I need to just get into it, get more familiar with it. Like most things, the more you do it...
Researcher	What do you hope to gain?

Pip	Well it is a way of tying it all together I think in a more meaningful way in that it actually shows the multiliteracies nature of it as opposed to perhaps the way that I would regularly plan.
Researcher	The pedagogy...?
Pip	Yes. And the multimodal—I am still coming to terms with writing that up too. Because I am using a technology, I have got to keep coming back to—the technology was never the focus, it was still the literacy that is the focus, and actually being able to actually articulate that... That the technology was just a tool that was going to enhance and enrich the literacy experiences, not the other way around.

Cohesion of multiliteracies schemas in meeting teaching purposes is an issue in Pip's reflections. Clarity of purpose is clear, as evidenced in the foregrounded focus of literacy, with a lesser emphasis on technology. Pip displayed preparedness to persist with the Learning Element template in the search for a planning format which captured comprehensively the multiple aspects the theory was prompting: teaching multimodality and deployment of pedagogical knowledge processes.

Like Rachel, the impact of this engagement was publication of a peer-reviewed, published Learning Element and an article adapted from the peer-reviewed Learning Element which was published in a quarterly journal of a peak, national teacher subject association.

Pip, like Kim and Meredith with full classroom responsibilities, displayed and emphasised the importance of foregrounding 'pedagogical learner knowledge' (Darling-Hammond, 1998; Shulman, 1999), or:

> ...knowing your children really well and being able to identify with them as a person, so you're in touch with them, with where they need to go, with their learning, but also what they're bringing into the classroom, their prior knowledge and their life experiences. It's also taking them beyond what they know already by being more critical and analysing their world and things around them ... learn and they move on (TD/SFTI/0105).

Pip related this pedagogical point: the importance of 'experiencing the known and the new', developing the knowledge of students as meaning-makers. Pip believed that project participation had developed awareness of 'the range of learning needs and styles but actually looking at the way the children bring meaning. I've had to reflect on that a lot more. It's taking my understanding to a deeper level' (TD/TI/2907). Pip noted connections between teacher learning and student learning, displaying a great respect for students as learners. Increasingly, Pip displayed a digital insider mindset (Prensky, 2001), with control shared with students, and students identifying themselves as 'experts within the room' in aspects of technology.

7.3.3: On Professional Repertoires

The impact of the 'pedagogical knowledge schema' and the Learning Element on expanding Pip's repertoire of pedagogical deployment in teaching multimodality can be considered in terms of the two Teaching Sequences:

Teaching Sequence 1, taught prior to Pip's retrospective completion of the Learning Element entitled 'Web Passion'; and Teaching Sequence 2, taught after Pip's completion of the same Learning Element.

Table 7.8: Pip: Deployment of Pedagogical Knowledge Processes in Teaching Multimodality (Predominant mode of focus is shown by print size) Teaching Sequence 1

Lesson	Pedagogical knowledge process	Linguistic Mode	Audio Mode	Visual mode	Gestural mode	Spatial mode
1	Experiencing the Known	X		x		
2	Experiencing the Known	X				
3	Experiencing the New	X		x		
4	Conceptualising by Naming	X				
5	Conceptualising by Naming	x		X		
6	Conceptualising by Theorising			X		
7	Analysing Functionally	x		X		
8	Analysing Functionally	x				
9	Analysing Functionally	X				
10	Analysing Critically	X		x		
11	Analysing Critically	X		x		
12	Applying Appropriately	X		x		
13	Applying Creatively	x	x	X		
14	Applying Creatively	x	x	X		

Teaching Sequence 2

Lesson	Pedagogical knowledge process	Linguistic Mode	Audio Mode	Visual mode	Gestural mode	Spatial mode
15	Experiencing the Known	X		x		
16	Experiencing the New	x	x	X		
17	Conceptualising by Naming	X	x	x		
18	Conceptualising by Theorising	x	x	X		
19	Analysing Functionally	X	x	x		
20	Analysing Critically	X				
21	Applying Appropriately	X		x		
22	Applying Creatively	x		X		

The 'multimodal schema' influenced Pip to attend to teaching the linguistic and visual modes of meaning, and their multimodal relationships, an expansion of the literacy teaching repertoire from the print-focused literacies of the Early Years Literacy Program. Cursory attention was given to the audio mode. Pip addressed modes of meaning made ubiquitous by technology—modes that have in recent times been more fully articulated (Kress and van Leeuwen, 1996).

Comparison of data from the two Teaching Sequences in table 7.8 above shows that in Teaching Sequence 1 the impact of the 'multimodal schema' on Pip's documented classroom practices was limited to expanding oral and written linguistic literacy teaching to include visual meaning resources. Pip displayed skill in teaching *through* and *about* the linguistic and visual modes. This skill became more pronounced over the two Teaching Sequences.

Individually and in combination in Teaching Sequence 1, Pip addressed the linguistic and visual modes within the context of a study of web design and passion projects. Audio teaching was limited to inserting audio 'effects' into PowerPoint presentations. A strong focus on teaching *about* the linguistic was apparent (writing concept maps, personal profiles, writing about a 'passion', reading an author's website and writing an author profile in lessons 1–3 and 8), as well as *through* the linguistic such as researching for information on the internet in lessons 4 and 9.

Pip's early deployment of the visual mode was to teach *through* the visual, for example to use the visual incidentally to show knowledge of websites in lessons focused on writing concept maps (lesson 1); and to use the visual features of a webpage as a means to listening to an author read stories (lesson 3). Pip's teaching *about* the visual, indicated recognition of the visual as a mode of meaning-making (lessons 5, 6), an influence of the 'multimodal schema'. Later in the sequence Pip addressed the meaning-making affordances of both the linguistic and the visual, teaching through and about them (lessons 9–14), incidentally incorporating the audio for presenting information but not teaching *about* it (lessons 13, 14). Addressing of the audio mode was limited. The gestural and spatial modes were not addressed in Teaching Sequence 1.

In Teaching Sequence 2, an exploration of print and online newspapers, Pip continued to emphasise teaching *about* both the linguistic and visual within the contexts of newspapers. Teaching addressed prior knowledge of linguistic and visual knowledge of newspapers (lessons 15–16); the linguistic, visual and audio features of newspapers, including concepts such as mastheads, datelines, bylines, captions and photographs (lessons 17–18); comparisons of print and online newspapers including design structure and its relation to purposes and audiences (lessons 19–20); and the creation of a class newspaper involving design of mastheads, logos, barcodes, prices, interviewing, genre selection and reporting (lesson 21). While teaching of the audio mode was increasingly incorporated, it was not taught *about*.

A juxtaposition of emphasis between the two modes, linguistic and visual, was evident as Pip emphasised mode one and then the other, exploring them individually and their intermodal relations (Unsworth, 2006b). Teaching addressed audio only as a means for delivering linguistic information in online newspapers, or linguistic *through* audio. The gestural and the spatial modes were not addressed by Pip.

Comparison of data from the two Teaching Sequences shows Pip's relatively confident and purposeful teaching of modes through deployment of pedagogies was fine-tuned in Teaching Sequence 2: a study of print and online newspapers—see table 7.9 below.

Table 7.9: Pip: Deployment of Pedagogical Knowledge Processes in Two Teaching Sequences

	Experiencing	Conceptualising	Analysing	Applying
Teaching Sequence 1	21%	21%	37%	21%
Teaching Sequence 2	25%	25%	25%	25%

Like Rachel, but to a lesser extent, Pip emphasised the pedagogical knowledge process of analysis in Teaching Sequence 1, reflecting the usefulness of this pedagogy in exploring the 'newness' of the visual as a meaning-making resource. In both Teaching Sequences, Pip deployed all the pedagogical knowledge processes in teaching addressed to either the linguistic and/or the visual mode. Teaching Sequence 2, which saw a greater focus on the visual as a meaning-making mode in its own right, as well as in a secondary capacity in teaching the linguistic, also saw each of the pedagogical knowledge processes deployed in the teaching of each mode.

For example, Pip's deployment of the pedagogical knowledge process of experiencing, used in Teaching Sequence 1 to address the linguistic mode, was expanded in Teaching Sequence 2 to address the teaching of linguistic and visual modes and, to a lesser extent, the audio in print and online newspapers (lessons 15–16). Deployment of the pedagogical knowledge process of conceptualising, used mainly in Teaching Sequence 1 to name and theorise about the linguistic mode in website features, was, in Teaching Sequence 2, deployed in naming and theorising about the multimodal realisation of online and print newspapers, specifically the linguistic and visual modes (lessons 17–18). As discussed in the previous section, multimodal metalanguage was emphasised in an ongoing way through development of a class glossary.

The pedagogical knowledge process of analysis, predominantly deployed in Teaching Sequence 1 to address the linguistic mode, but with a lesser emphasis on the visual, was similarly deployed in Teaching Sequence 2 to focus on functions of linguistic, and to a lesser extent the visual and audio modes (lesson 19), as well as audience preferences through the linguistic mode (lesson 20).

The pedagogical knowledge process of applying, deployed in Teaching Sequence 1 to emphasise the linguistic, but with a lesser emphasis on the visual in the publication and presentation of personal profiles and passion projects on a class webpage, was deployed in Teaching Sequence 2 in addressing both the linguistic and visual modes in creating a newspaper (lessons 21–22). In Pip's case, Teaching Sequence 2 showed a fine tuning of emphasis between the teaching of the linguistic and visual. Teaching in both Teaching Sequences was tightly focused on students' literacy development, encouraging traditional literacies of reading and writing in the online environment enabled by technology, with the visual increasingly treated as a mode of meaning in its own right.

Table 7.10: Pip: Addressing of Mode and Deployment of Pedagogical Knowledge Processes (Predominant mode of focus is shown in italics) Teaching Sequence 1

Lesson	Multimodal emphasis	Pedagogical knowledge process
1	*Linguistic* and visual Concept map showing knowledge of websites	Experiencing the Known
2	*Linguistic* Personal details	Experiencing the Known
3	*Linguistic* and visual Listening and responding to stories on website	Experiencing the New
4	*Linguistic* and visual Navigating websites	Conceptualising by Naming
5	*Visual* Website features	Conceptualising by Naming
6	*Visual* Structure and layout of website	Conceptualising by Theorising
7	*Visual* and linguistic Features of a search engine	Analysing Functionally
8	*Linguistic* Writing about a 'passion'	Analysing Functionally
9	*Linguistic* Researching for information on websites	Analysing Functionally
10	*Visual* and linguistic Critiquing features on websites	Analysing Critically
11	*Linguistic* and visual Critiquing features on websites	Analysing Critically
12	*Linguistic* and visual Comparing websites and books	Applying Appropriately
13	*Visual*, linguistic, (and audio) Publishing profiles	Applying Creatively
14	*Linguistic*, visual (and audio) Publishing and presenting passion projects	Applying Creatively

Teaching Sequence 2

15	*Linguistic* and visual Exploration of print newspapers	Experiencing the Known
16	*Visual* and linguistic (and audio) Exploration of online newspapers	Experiencing the New
17	*Linguistic*, visual (and audio) Naming features of a newspaper	Conceptualising by Naming
18	*Visual* and linguistic (and audio) Realisation of features in different newspapers	Conceptualising by Theorising
19	*Linguistic*, visual, (and audio) Functions of features; print and online	Analysing Functionally
20	*Linguistic* Consideration of audience preferences	Analysing Critically
21	*Linguistic*, visual Creation of class newspaper	Applying Appropriately
22	*Visual*, linguistic Creation of class newspaper	Applying Creatively

Pip's reflection, recorded during the last filming session, on the impact of the pedagogical knowledge processes in work with students, displays control over the terminology.

> We've got a wide range of children within this room. Three quarters of the children are boys and also a huge range of abilities and ... prior experiences and things that they bring with them from home. So as a way of connecting to them and making their learning more meaningful to them and engaging them and motivating them, technology and computers was a fantastic link, but linking it to what they already knew... Not all children have access to a computer at home, so there's been lots of planning for that concept naming and being able to understand that this is a 'hyperlink', or this is a 'font'...identifying these features and concepts that they need to be able to use and need to be able to name... being able to articulate what the concept is and then learn what does this do... The critical framing or the critical analysis has been a really big part of looking at the webpages [and] newspapers for example and identifying features, they've been quite critical as to why they've chosen a particular background colour or animation or does that font work with that particular coloured background. The children are very good at that now and they use the language very easily, very comfortably... We've applied what we've learnt in creating our own webpages, each child now has their own personal profile, which is on the school intranet... including the hyperlink to their passion project... So they've come in with what they know and we're building on that and hopefully transforming their practice (TD/SFTI/0909).

As was the case with other case study teachers, Pip's knowledge of multiliteracies on entry to the project was vague.

> It's a term that's been around a long time and I guess I'd heard about it. I didn't know much about it at all. My initial understanding, I think, was probably the changing nature of literacy, particularly now with email, mobile

phones and SMS messages, how that's changed. So I really didn't know anything about, or hadn't considered, the multimodal nature of the learning involved with multiliteracies (TD/SFTI/I004).

The contrast between these two excerpts highlights growth in expertise in use of terminology of the pedagogical knowledge processes and confidence in framing classroom enactments through the theoretical terminology.

Pip was transparent in reflecting on personal professional growth and the qualities of productive professional learning, as shown in the following two excerpts, recorded at different points over the life of the project.

Researcher	What are you looking for in any professional development?
Pip	Something that is going to be readily able to be taken back and used with the children and something that is going to enhance their learning. I mean there is so much PD [Professional Development] that we do... unless it actually goes back into the classroom and it makes a difference in terms of our teaching, it is really a waste of the school's money.
Researcher	Can you give an example of something you think is effective?
Pip	I guess what we have been doing now is terribly effective, because we have had to use it l...I mean we had a film crew coming so there were certain things we had to get done... there wasn't anything probably terribly new, that I wasn't already doing, like it is just the way I teach... but it allowed me to articulate that perhaps better, or be more explicit as to why I was planning a certain activity or to what the outcomes were going to be... and not just perhaps focusing on the alphabetical text (TD/TI/2907).

The connection between the project requirements and classroom applications was seen as a stimulus for classroom applications. At the time of this interview, midway through the project, Pip appreciated the efficacy of the project's model of professional learning but didn't acknowledge the experience as resulting in significant personal professional learning. Learnings were limited to articulating tacit knowledge and broadening the modes of meaning taught about. In a later interview, Pip saw the experience as more significant.

Researcher	What have you learnt through the project?
Pip	Its been a huge learning process for me and a great experience for me to be involved in the multiliteracies project... being able to interact with my peers, not just in our local area but in a much broader environment and with academics as well so that we're getting the theoretical background to underpin what we're doing in the classroom.
Researcher	What outcomes has it had for you?
Pip	I guess it's that whole ... it is taking my understanding to a deeper level. I was always aware of the range of learning needs, I guess, and learning styles within the classroom but actually looking at the way the children bring meaning. I've had to reflect on that a lot more... the way that I'm more strategically planning

for those particular purposes, looking at the multiliteracies and the way children learn have been really powerful for me as a teacher (TD/SFTI/0909).

Membership of, and accountability to, a professional learning community, in this instance between shared analysis of practice-based documentary data (film segments and Learning Elements) contributed to a sense of team, an interdependent collegiality between interschool team members (McLaughlin and Talbert, 1993), with a positive impact on the quality of teaching. Engagement with theory and theorists was seen as having a positive impact.

The increased significance of project involvement emanated from a greater connection with students and purposeful planning and teaching towards student learning outcomes. One of Pip's starting points was the disengagement of many students in the class, three-quarters of whom were male, in print-based learning, particularly writing.

Researcher	So are boys more engaged using technology, do you think?
Pip	I've only got eight girls but the girls love it as well. I mean, I think there's that general perception there [that boys enjoy technology] but I think all children do and the girls certainly get as much out of it as the boys do.
Researcher	So what difference has it made, engaging your children with the online environment; has it made a difference?
Pip	I think it has made a huge difference for some of them...as I said, the girls, but the boys in particular because some of them are a little – not turned off – but I mean writing is not a pleasurable thing for them. But the machine is. And if they make a mistake, it is – 'fix it', like that...I think the multiliteracies is a really powerful way of engaging the children in their own learning...it's made me more aware of some the theories behind it and how we can actually use that teaching and learning more effectively to hook in with the children and what they know already and then move them on (TD/SFTI/0909).

Developing expertise in deploying and articulating teaching in terms of the multiliteracies schemas and attention from having undertaken their deployment and articulation in the public realm through the filming and authorship of a Learning Element and article for a peer-reviewed teacher association magazine, built Pip's confidence further. A further boost came after Pip applied for, and won, a *National Award for Quality Schooling Literacy and Numeracy* from the Department of Education, Science and Training, Australia—an award that is bestowed on an individual teacher in the year of project participation. An excerpt from the report, describing the focus of the award, positions involvement in the project as central to the success, is shown below.

> Producing the *School's Television* programme has been one of the keys to teaching multiliteracies at Rosegardens primary School. [Pip] has... highlighted the importance of differences within English language usage, and the uses of the visual as a cross-cultural medium of communication. Improvements in literacy and cross-cultural communication, and better integration of students with

learning disabilities have been outcomes of [Pip's] use of ICT to enhance learning (Reference Report)

In the year following the project, Pip was named the sole teacher representative on the Federal Government's 'National Inquiry into the Teaching of Literacy' (TD/RJ/011204). In 2005, Pip was promoted to school principal of Rosegardens Primary School, declaring that 'All of these things would not have come about if I hadn't been in the Multiliteracies videos, I am so grateful for this opportunity' (TD/RJ/email correspondence/181205). Project involvement is credited for professional growth as a national educational leader and spokesperson.

Having discussed the impact of project participation on case study teachers, concluding comments and recommendations will now be addressed in the final chapter.

Chapter 8
Conclusions

This study sought to analyse the impact of interventions designed to support teacher professional learning for literacy education within a communications environment marked by new social and multimodal affordances. The outcomes relate to six main areas of intervention: 1) my role as an educational consultant; 2) the role of the filming co-production; 3) the role of the Early Years Literacy Program; 4) the role of the 'multimodal schema'; 5) the role of the 'pedagogical knowledge processes schema'; and 6) the role of participatory action research methodology.

8.1: Role and Impact of Researcher as Educational Consultant

As outlined in Chapter Five, 'Breakthroughs to New Practices', and Chapter Seven, 'Teacher Impact Stories', the researcher, within the context of her role as education project and policy consultant with the Early Years Branch and Schools Television Unit, Department of Education, Victoria, intervened to impact on the habitual practices expected of this role in the co-production of training/educational films intended to support teacher learning. One of the impacts of the role was on me, as I sought to create and enact renewed principles and approaches in the production of films; principles which positioned me less as a technician or implementer of policy through customary practices and more as an agent of change and transformation in teachers' professional learning and the development of resources. The role itself thus had an impact both on me as a practitioner and on the practices I deployed. Bringing an open, rather than a fixed view of possibilities, I allowed myself to be transformed. I learnt the importance of the consultant's role in mentoring and scaffolding other teachers. I convinced colleagues of the importance of teacher engagement through professional learning and of the significance of capturing, on film, authentic vignettes of classroom application and teacher reflection. As a result, the process of film-making, teacher learning and research, as well as the produced films, grew in importance for all the participants associated with my project.

Greater project officer engagement and collaboration in the design and methodology of the project, as outlined in Chapter Three, which were in contradistinction to the habitual practices deployed in film co-productions within the Early Years Literacy Strategy, resulted in more meaningful collaborations among the various stakeholders—the bureaucracy, school and tertiary representatives—as evidenced in the 'Breakthroughs to New Practices' and the 'Teacher Impact Stories'.

Mentoring and scaffolding others required growth in my own learning; engaging with theory, collaboratively collecting data, and reflecting. As the films and researcher–teacher interviews demonstrate, the result included a reciprocal flow of theoretical and practical knowledge rather than a theorist-to-teacher or consultant-to-teacher flow of knowledge.

As the literacy film task progressed, I re-shaped my departmental consultant role so that it embraced more explicitly a mindset, sensibilities and capacities which reflected the changes in the social dynamics that were emerging. On reflection, I am conscious that there are further shifts I could have made in the way I organised my interaction with the various participants and in the way we used the film medium. For example, filming the interactions between theorists and teachers would have created distinctive and useful artefacts for reflection beyond relying on face to face exchanges. It would also have been useful to produce film interviews of the theorists talking about their learning over the course of the project, not only illuminating the way aspects of the theory developed during this project but also substantiating the collaborative nature of the relationship. This way my interview questions, which framed the professional learning goals, could have been included in the data set more explicitly, rather than being edited out. That way my presence as an 'actor' in the process would have been made visible and the films would not simply present an interchange of ideas with my voice embedded in the 'hidden camera' representation.

8.1.1: Findings and Recommendations: Educational Consultants

1. Educational consultants, working in the contemporary changing social milieu and communications environment can broker ongoing relationships between the academy, schools and bureaucracies, promoting in-

novative flows and fostering multiple agency in the development of professional learning, theory and practice. Educational consultants, therefore, should be cognisant of such powerful potential when fulfilling their roles and responsibilities and include broader goals in their change strategies.
2. The engagement of teachers as agentive and collaborative learners and their positioning as creators of knowledge and generators of data, supports professional learning and classroom performance. Educational consultants should, therefore, engage teachers in ongoing, collaborative, reflective documentation which situates practice in relation to theoretical frameworks.
3. Engagement, high expectations, flexibility, scaffolding and mentoring are all key factors in the transformation of teacher learning and performance. Educational consultants, therefore, need to factor these into their teacher professional learning plans and strategies.
4. A collaborative mindset enables educational consultants to engage more meaningfully and productively with teachers and academic theorists when introducing new theory and practice about teaching. Such an orientation should, therefore, be encouraged as foundational to the successful introduction of new educational policies.

8.2: Role of the Film Co-production between Early Years Branch and Schools Television Unit

In my role as a literacy education project and policy consultant I consciously decided to reconsider the nature, impact and authenticity of a filmed resource. As the sections outlining the Early Years Literacy Strategy and the Research Design demonstrate, the consequential processes for resource development challenged the customary hierarchical and authoritative direction of flows of knowledge from bureaucracy to consultant, from consultant to teacher and from theorist to teacher.

The process outlined in the reporting of the case studies in Chapters Five and Seven required heightened levels of project officer engagement in what had previously been deemed as 'technical aspects of film-making', so as to shoot and edit films whose content was more representative of teachers, their practices and learning. These so called 'technical' aspects of making educational policy films, usually overlooked in ways similar to the overlooking of modes of meaning other than the linguistic, in fact were transformed into meaning-making aspects. Rather than, hearing the 'voice of God', narration style, in the presentation of education departmental policy objectives, where control of what will be presented is in the edit suite, or in the scripted teacher voices, teacher viewers of such films deserve to see veracity in teacher–student interactions—teacher–theorist, teacher–teacher and teacher–theorist–consultant reflections through authentic illustrative examples.

As the teaching choices testify, this somewhat radical approach to government departmental film-making encouraged teachers to be authentic, rather than scripted and managed, in teaching episodes and in voicing their reflections. Theorists were filmed in the teachers' schools and at home rather than a studio—'natural' settings unlike the newsroom-connotative artificiality of a desk in a studio. Their expertise was presented as emergent and open to teacher interpretation. Tackling the topic of teacher professional learning as a series filmed over time, rather than a 'one-off' resource, offered a sense of a journey of possibilities, rather than an exemplary solution.

The evidence in the teacher interviews suggests that the resolute and highly coordinated nature of the film schedule, with its pre-determined deadlines, provided a strong stimulus for teachers to undertake multiliteracies theory-informed classroom enactments. The intended distribution of the films resulted in the creation of permanent records of grounded classroom designs, or illustrative teaching texts available for review by those involved, and for a broad audience. As the teachers' voices explain, the 'playback' of the films impacted powerfully. Seeing themselves in the medium of film promoted strong teacher engagement with the project and resulted in a developing sense of maturity, which became more evident as the series was progressively developed over four episodes. The role of the films also impacted on the students involved and the communities from which they were drawn, with the 'star' quality, the publicity and broad interest resulting in increased engagement, heightened performance and developing a sense of confidence.

There is also evidence that the films have powerfully impacted on the broader education community; they were transmitted to over 1300 Victorian government schools as well as numerous Catholic and independent schools, with repeat screenings as a result of viewer demand. Copies have been distributed to all regional offices in Victoria and have been deployed by numerous Australian state bureaucracies. The films have been drawn on as resources at conferences with principal, teacher and parent groups and continue to be used in universities across Australia and in teacher professional learning programs. The series of films is held in high esteem, evidenced by its receipt of the 2004 Australian Teachers of Media award for 'Best Educational Resource', ahead of numerous commercial and state and national government-developed resources.

Given, however, the recent advent of 'You Tube' and 'Teacher Tube', where access to appropriate technology enables recording, and internet connection with sufficient bandwidth enables global distribution of film, new film possibilities are now available, giving more immediate voice to a broader number of people; they can turn anyone into a film-maker. The Schools Television Unit was disbanded on this premise. Whereas interviewing, shooting, editing and distribution were facilitated by the researcher, these roles are now increasingly available to teachers; an indication of the speed and magnitude of change.

8.2.1: Findings and Recommendations: Future Filming

1. The deadlines, permanency, publicity and the community interest associated with filming contribute to the accelerated development of teacher confidence, expertise and performance. The use of filming should be further explored as a productive stimulus for theory-influenced classroom applications and articulation.
2. The involvement of educators in the 'technical' aspects of filming resulted in heightened levels of engagement and more authentic teacher interviews and vignettes of teaching and learning. Teacher professional learning programs should include more systematic understandings of the power of educational film-making as a means of documenting educational practices.
3. Teachers' capacities as reflective practitioners are fostered by personal and collaborative self-viewing of their performance in learning situations, and this then flows through to student engagement and performance. Teachers and students should engage with images and sounds of themselves in the filmic medium over sustained periods in order to evaluate and reflect upon their teaching and learning experiences and its relationship to their learning goals.

8.3: Role of the Victorian Early Years Literacy Program

The broadly resourced and recommended Victorian state Early Years Literacy Program, formed the policy milieu within which the project was conducted and continued to impact on the teachers' classroom applications throughout the life of the project. The take-up of the policy, however, was not uniform.

As the case studies revealed, 'modelled' and 'shared' reading and writing approaches were incorporated, extended and innovated upon by case study teachers undertaking multimodality teaching. Examples of these hybrid teaching approaches included shared reading of websites; shared writing of websites focusing on elements such as inserting hyperlinks, text and visuals; and shared viewing of animations and videos. Other teaching approaches from the Early Years Literacy Program were not referred to within the context of the work-based filming project; these included 'guided reading' and 'interactive writing', probably due to their close alignment with print meaning-making.

The teacher interview and documentation data suggests that the interplay of the Early Years Literacy Program and the multiliteracies schemas created tensions between the print-based focus of the organisational structures of the Early Years Literacy Program, a reading hour and a writing hour, and the multiliteracies schemas, which were increasingly seen as applicable across learning areas. The data suggests that teachers addressed this differentially. In the case of teachers with a weaker affiliation with

Early Years Literacy Program, the 'multimodal schema' was deployed across the curriculum, with challenges apparent in identifying aspects of the 'multimodality teaching and learning triptych'—see discussion below—within this broad context. In the case of a teacher with expert knowledge of the Early Years Literacy Program, responsibilities for regional professional training, and limited time teaching school entrants, additional linguistic-focused teaching was initially undertaken outside the parameters of the project. Teaching engaged with a range of modes from the 'multimodal schema' challenged placement of literacy and English into a daily block of time and resulted in re-integration of the linguistic.

In another case a teacher with a blend of expertise in digital technologies and the Early Years Literacy Program integrated multimodal literacy and various disciplinary areas, mindful of foregrounding literacy, not so much through a timed allocation of protected time through a literacy block of time, but through controlling teaching emphases across disciplinary content and modes of meaning.

In two cases where teachers had major responsibility for grades, the multiliteracies schemas resulted in a 'production house' approach. In the case where limited time was available for teaching the group, the teacher recommended a whole of school approach across different subject areas. All cases displayed increased awareness of literacy learning opportunities present in all learning, beyond the Early Years Literacy Program.

8.3.1: Findings and Recommendations: Literacy Policy Development

1. Literacy policy directives worked as both constraining and enabling mechanisms in meeting teacher professional learning and performance as well as learner performance. Literacy policy directives require a flexible orientation to their implementation to ensure that directives enable teachers to interpret policy appropriately within given contexts and to be free to innovate and respond to the needs of their learners in a rapidly changing environment.
2. Given that 'alphabetic' literacy in English remains the dominant understanding of the term 'literacy' within education department policies, the emerging new multimodal literacies remain theoretically, and in practice, illusive to teachers currently in classrooms. Teachers need to gain a firmer grasp of theories of multimodal design and future literacy policy needs to be developed, explicitly advising on the teaching, learning and assessment of multimodal meaning-making.

8.4: Role of the 'Multimodal Schema'

As the data in Chapter Six suggests, multiliteracies theory, presented in the form of the 'multimodal schema', had an impact of expanding the perception of the modes of meaning that needed to be addressed as literacy resources for all participating teachers. Modes that would previously have been positioned as extra-linguistic, auxiliary or as belonging to another part of the curriculum were seen to be fundamental parts of the teaching of literacy. This transformation could be plotted in the data, as teachers could be seen to visibly revise the purposefulness of their teaching focus during the course of two Teaching Sequences—see table 8.1 below.

Table 8.1: Teaching Focus: Mode Rachel-Pip (% of lessons)

Teaching focus: Mode	Rachel	Kim & Meredith	Pip	Total
Linguistic				
Teaching sequence 1	(2/14) 14%	(5/10) 50%	(10/14) 71%	45%
Teaching sequence 2	(2/7) 29%	(4/9) 45%	(5/8) 62.5%	46%
Visual				
Teaching sequence 1	(2/14) 14%	(5/10) 50%	(4/14) 28%	29%
Teaching sequence 2	(5/7) 71%	(1/9) 11%	(3/8) 37.5%	38%
Gestural				
Teaching sequence 1	(7/14) 50%	0	0	18%
Teaching sequence 2	0	0	0	0
Audio				
Teaching sequence 1	(3/14) 22%	0	0	8%
Teaching sequence 2	0	(3/9) 33%	0	12%
Spatial				
Teaching sequence 1	0	0	0	0
Teaching sequence 2	0	(1/9) 11%	0	4%

As the case study illustrates, engagement with the 'multimodal schema' made it essential that teachers should be explicit about their teaching of mode and multimodality. As evidenced in table 8.1, engagement with the 'multimodal schema' prompted teachers to design and document teaching which addressed different modes of meaning and directed them to engage with deep grammatical knowledge of modes and multimodality. The 'multimodal schema' provided a scaffold for teaching of multimodality and a language with which to discuss such teaching. Collaboration between theorists, teachers and the educational consultant/researcher around the 'multimodal schema' prompted teachers to engage at a greater theoretical level with modes of meaning other than linguistic and resulted in the useful deployment of modes other than linguistic in the planning of their lessons.

The data, as presented in table 8.1, illustrates that while the linguistic mode continued to be most heavily emphasised by teachers, this was followed by the visual mode, the most theoretically developed mode after the linguistic. The testimonies from the teachers suggest that they felt themselves to be on more substantial theoretical ground teaching the visual mode than they did in teaching the other modes, where they appeared to feel ill at ease. The data illustrates that, in relation to these other modes, most of the attention to gestural and audio-focused teaching was limited to one case study, with much of the gestural-related teaching remaining strongly embedded in the visual mode, with a case to be made that the visual was even more highly represented. The spatial and audio modes were minimally addressed. So, although the 'multimodal schema' developed teacher awareness of previously overlooked meaning-making affordances of modes other than linguistic and this awareness resulted in teaching foregrounding particular modes of meaning or aspects of intermodal relationships, it is clear that professional learning programs will have to target the acceptance of the lesser used modes.

The case study evidence reveals that teaching enactments addressed 'modes across the curriculum'. As described in Chapter Six, patterns identified in teachers' approaches to the teaching of multimodality can be categorised in terms of *teaching* multimodality and mode; *teaching through* multimodality and mode; and *teaching about* multimodality and mode—a 'multimodality teaching and learning triptych' reminiscent of Halliday's language learning triptych (Halliday, 1980). Teaching mode and multimodality highlighted the contribution of different modes as meaning-making resources. Teaching through mode and multimodality supported learning about other curriculum areas or other modes. Teaching about mode and multimodality addressed individual modes and their interplay as meaning-making resources.

The interview, Learning Element and filming data suggests that teaching modes and multimodality, teaching through mode and multimodality, and teaching about mode and multimodality often required teachers to learn how to use technology to allow their own engagement with multimodal texts and their engagement with students. These data sources also showed evident differences between the meaning attributed to the term 'metalanguage' by the teachers and theorists, with much teaching emphasising context-bound meaning-making elements and behaviours, rather than more global, 'meta' meaning-making functions of the design elements.

The case studies indicate that in deployment of a multimodal metalanguage of isolated and combined modes of meaning, teachers drew on tacit knowledge of design, and vernacular and technical language in a pastiche-like articulation of designs and their affordances. As illustrated in Chapter Six, attempts to glean an emergent lexicon for multimodality using the 'dimensions of meaning schema' faced the challenge of examples which stopped short of teaching about each mode present in designs.

Chapter Six revealed patterns in addressing dimensions of meaning, including narrative-related teaching with school entrants which tended to emphasise the representational dimension of linguistic, visual/gestural and audio meanings; a social science-related integrated inquiry which tended to emphasise teaching through the linguistic mode and the 'contextual' dimension of linguistic and visual meanings; and a focus on website exploration and creation which tended to emphasise the 'organisational' dimension of linguistic and visual meanings—see table 8.2 below.

ROLE OF THE 'MULTIMODAL SCHEMA'

Table 8.2: Focus of Teaching Prompts: Dimension of Mode Teaching Sequence 1

Dimension of meaning focus of prompts	Linguistic	Audio	Visual	Gestural	Total
Number	170	26	95	70	361
% of set	47%	7%	26%	20%	100%
Representational	5%	34%	18%	70%	
Social	3%	58%	14%	10%	
Organisational	57%	8%	54%	11%	
Contextual	33%	0	13%	0	
Ideological	2%	0	1%	8%	

Overall, the data makes clear that a growing emphasis was given to teaching that meaning is represented in multiple modes, reflecting the teachers' own developing awareness; and to the organisational dimension of meaning, particularly the organisation of the linguistic and visual modes of meaning in multimodal texts. This suggests that deployment of specialised metalanguage has not yet reached a purposeful level of expertise.

8.4.1: Findings and Recommendations: Multimodality

1. The 'multimodal schema' was powerful in expanding an understanding and articulation of different modes of meaning and their teaching as literacy resources. The 'multimodal schema' can be purposefully deployed in literacy professional learning to expand teaching repertoires as it provides a theoretical framework that informs teachers of the meaning-making affordances of modes of meaning other than linguistic.
2. A 'multimodality teaching and learning triptych' was evident in effective literacy teaching repertoires: teaching mode and multimodality; teaching through mode and multimodality, and teaching about mode and multimodality. Teachers need to explore the power of a 'multimodality teaching and learning triptych' in articulating and scaffolding purposeful choices in the teaching of multimodal literacy in diverse classroom contexts.
3. The 'dimensions of meaning schema' was useful in revealing patterns in multimodality teaching choices, and a lack of explicit expertise in deploying a metalanguage for different modes of meaning-making. The 'dimensions of meaning schema', and its associated theoretical contributions, needs be explored further in the professional learning context, as a tool to generate and document the manner in which multimodal metalanguage is understood and used in learning experiences, either of isolated and/or combined modes of meaning.

8.5: Role of 'Pedagogical Knowledge Processes Schema'

The case study experiences demonstrate that the multiliteracies-informed Learning by Design framework presented in the form of the 'pedagogical knowledge processes schema' influenced the case study teachers to become more pedagogically purposeful and to address gaps and over-reliance over the two Teaching Sequences of the project—see table 8.3 below.

Table 8.3: Teacher Deployment of Pedagogical Knowledge Processes

Pedagogical Knowledge Process	Rachel	Kim & Meredith	Pip	Total
Experiencing				
Teaching sequence 1	22%	30%	21%	23.5%
Teaching sequence 2	28.5%	22%	25%	25%
Conceptualising				
Teaching sequence 1	14%	40%	21%	23.5%
Teaching sequence 2	28.5%	11%	25%	21%
Analysing				
Teaching sequence 1	57%	10%	37%	37%
Teaching sequence 2	14.5%	33.5%	25%	25%
Applying				
Teaching sequence 1	7%	20%	21%	16%
Teaching sequence 2	28.5%	33.5%	25%	29%

As evidenced in the 'Breakthroughs to New Practices' and 'Teacher Impact Stories', engagement with the 'pedagogical knowledge processes schema' compelled teachers to be explicit about their selection and deployment of pedagogy. Teacher testimonies, documentation and filming indicate that the 'multimodal schema' prompted teachers to engage theoretically with, and to document, plan, choose, articulate and practically demonstrate pedagogy. The 'pedagogical knowledge processes schema' acted as a scaffold for teaching of mode and multimodality, although its broader application also allowed other teaching foci.

Case study teacher interview and teacher documentation suggests that collaboration between theorists, teachers and the researcher around the 'pedagogical knowledge processes schema' promoted engagement with pedagogies. Through engagement, habitual pedagogical reliance, affinities and oversights became apparent and were tempered. Participating teachers acknowledged through interview that through collaborative engagement with, and documentation on the Learning Element template, they reviewed, refined and re-framed practices. The heuristic of the Learning Element template for documenting a range of taught and future lessons challenged pedagogical affinities as teachers isolated a manageable, cohesive thread of multimodality teaching for documentation, particularly within an integrated curriculum.

Documenting teaching according to pedagogical knowledge processes on the Learning Element template proved useful in making problematic habitual planning and teaching practices, supporting articulation of tacit pedagogical knowledge, resulting in greater self-awareness, ability to articulate and purposefulness in teaching. Teachers were compelled to justify their teaching choices, promoting reflective practice. This was most obvious in teachers accustomed to broader professional roles who displayed a ready engagement and preparedness to embrace the agency offered by the Learning Element template and to further develop these into peer-reviewed articles. In cases where teachers were less accustomed to responsibilities beyond the classroom, and lacked precedent in using such templates, engagement and growth were more of a struggle, as teachers worked to see the relevance of their role, which was perceived primarily as classroom-based. Interview data indicates that collaborative effort and feedback supported teacher learning of the pedagogical knowledge processes and development of Learning Elements.

Teacher testimony and documentation practices suggest that while the Learning Element template offers multiple potentials as a planning, documentation, reflective heuristic and publication tool, teachers did not see the relevance of all of these affordances. Within a context of paucity of multiliteracies-influenced classroom exemplars at the time of the research, unlike the expanding knowledge bank of Learning Elements available online at the time of writing, the affordances were not clearly apparent to case study teachers, who were positioned as pioneers and innovators.

Aggregated data about practices indicates that deployment of the pedagogical knowledge processes in teaching mode and multimodality revealed preferences for teaching mode and multimodality; teaching through mode and multimodality; and teaching about mode and multimodality.

Engagement with the Learning Element template resulted in increased purposefulness and skill in addressing and articulating teaching of mode and multimodality—see table 8.4 below.

Table 8.4: Pedagogical Effect on Mode

	linguistic	audio	visual	gestural	spatial
Experiencing					
Teaching sequence 1	16%	0	0	8%	0
Teaching sequence 2	13%	4%	8%	0	0
Conceptualising					
Teaching sequence 1	8%	0	13%	2.5%	0
Teaching sequence 2	8 %	4%	13%	0	0
Analysing					
Teaching sequence 1	16%	5%	8%	8%	0

Teaching sequence 2	17%	4%	4%	0	0
Applying					
Teaching sequence 1	8%	2.5%	5%	0	0
Teaching sequence 2	13%	4%	8%	0	4%

As table 8.4 indicates, most purposeful was the deployment in teaching the linguistic mode. The pedagogical knowledge processes of experiencing, analysing, and applying were deployed consistently in teaching the linguistic mode, with a curious, lesser emphasis on the deployment of the pedagogical knowledge process of conceptualising. While this can be partially explained by evidence of additional linguistic-focused conceptualising undertaken outside the parameters of the project, there was also a tendency to not use linguistic metalanguage with young students.

Teachers heavily deployed the pedagogical knowledge processes of conceptualising and analysing in teaching the visual mode, with teachers expressing amazement and surprise at students' capacities to deploy specialised language. Much of the attention on the gestural mode was embedded in visual representation, with slippage between these two modes apparent, making categorisation of deployment of the pedagogical knowledge process of analysis in the teaching of the gestural mode arguably pertaining to the visual mode. As evidenced in teacher testimony, the interplay of the two multiliteracies schemas had the effect of teaching which enhanced students' multimodal literacy outcomes.

Teaching addressed to visual, gestural and audio modes was somewhat arbitrary, displaying lack of purposefulness in attending to the 'multimodal teaching and learning triptych'. However the pedagogical knowledge process of analysis was deployed in teaching the visual (including the gestural) and audio modes of meaning—modes gaining in prevalence through digitisation. Expanded capacities were more obvious as the project proceeded.

8.5.1: Findings and Recommendations: Pedagogical Knowledge Processes

1. The 'pedagogical knowledge processes schema' was influential in scaffolding the purposeful deployment, articulation and reflection of pedagogical choices related to multimodal literacy teaching. The use of the 'pedagogical knowledge processes schema' needs to be further explored as a tool for scaffolding professional learning and enacting literacy pedagogy in order to reveal the pattern of choices teachers make and the impact this has on learner outcomes.
2. The teachers' engagement with the 'pedagogical knowledge processes schema' revealed habitual practices and preferences in multimodality teaching and learning, such as a disinclination to deploy specialised multimodal metalanguage with all students. The co-deployment of the 'pedagogical knowledge processes schema' combined with the 'multimodal

schema' needs to be further explored in promoting reflective literacy professional learning and practice.
3. The use by teachers of the Learning Element template, as a means of documenting their teaching and learning choices, was significant in achieving increased purposefulness, skill and explicitness in addressing multimodality teaching and learning, with planning and documentation providing a valued reference point for teacher reflection. The effective use of the Learning Element template, to purposefully scaffold professional learning as a means of extending teachers' literacy pedagogical repertoires, should be further explored with the support of robust expert mentoring and peer collaboration.

8.6: Role of Participatory Action Research Methodology

The role of participatory action research methodology was to involve case study teachers as researchers of their own practice. The case study experiences demonstrate that, as a result, teachers engaged with multimodal and pedagogical theory in the form of schemas, and undertook individual, context-specific school-based enactments within a context of collaboration. Data was collectively produced in the form of filmed classroom enactments, reflective interviews, and documentation on the Learning Element template. Teachers worked collaboratively with each other, with theorists, the researcher, and with colleagues outside the project team to review and reflect on the data, and re-frame and extend understandings and repertoires of practice.

Observation, filming and teacher testimony reveals that teachers' capacities as reflective practitioners were positively impacted upon through examination of the data—the teacher's own and one another's data—in light of the theoretical schemas. Teachers considered the data's impact on learners and on themselves; engaged collaboratively in reflective discussion; and sustained data examination and engagement throughout the production of four films and the development of published Learning Elements.

The case study experiences outlined in Chapter Seven reveal that embedding of staged filming and collective reflection within a spiral of action research cycles contributed to sustained teacher learning within the life of the project, based on collaborative reflection and publicly transparent action. 'Planning' involved theoretical engagement with the multiliteracies schemas; classroom 'action' could be transparently and collectively 'observed'; and subsequent 'reflection' and interactive feedback was directly related to filmic reference points. The impact was the opening of a professional discursive space featuring scrutiny, interpretation, dissonance, revelations of unfamiliarity and uncertainty, analysis, and clarification which supported development of expertise in articulating and deploying practices in the frameworks of the multiliteracies schemas. Classroom 'planning' was re-framed in light of collaborative reflection and engagement with theory, and resulted in refined articulation of and expanded teacher repertoires in deployment of the 'multimodal' and 'pedagogical knowledge processes schemas'.

Teacher testimony and observation revealed that participatory action research, with embedded public sharing of expertise, impacted on teacher roles, identities and sensibilities. Completed films and Learning Elements are evidence that teachers undertook knowledge creation as media spokespeople and became published authors, requiring reflection on habitual understandings of their roles and their expansion. This was most easily achieved in cases of experienced teachers accustomed to undertaking responsibilities beyond the classroom and school.

Participating teachers acknowledged in the interviews that participatory action research methodology impacted on their dispositions, their 'tendencies to act in a particular manner... [which] are predictive of patterns of action' (Borko et al., 2007, p. 361). The case study experiences illustrate that participatory action research methodology impacted on teachers' expectations of themselves and their students as learners; their preparedness for collaboration with colleagues; their sense of responsibility for learning across the profession; their openness to collegiate scrutiny; their engagement in problem-solving; and their acceptance of the ambiguities of a research context.

The evidence in Chapters Five and Seven indicates that participatory action research methodology impacted on nurturing a disposition for intense engagement with learning, featuring high expectations of teacher and student learning alike, enabling an active seeking of literacy teaching practices which address the affordances of the changed communications environment; a disposition attuned to students' broad semiotic capacities, including, but not exclusively, their linguistic strengths.

8.6.1: Findings and Recommendations: Participatory Action Research Methodology

1. Participatory action research methodology was found to empower teacher learning through engagement with theory; the undertaking of context-specific enactments; the collective production and examination of data; and subsequent reframing of practice. This methodology needs to be explored further as means for involving teachers as researchers of their own practice.
2. The collaboratively produced documentation of teaching and learning experiences in the form of filmed classroom enactments, reflective interviews, and documentation on the Learning Element template proved illuminating as sources of data on effective practice and was thereby a stimulus for professional learning. Film representations of teaching and learning experiences that embody teacher-created knowledge need to be further explored as powerful multimodal data sources in future research.

3. Teacher disposition played a demonstrated role in the efficacy of the specific interventions deployed, both in terms of teacher professional learning and the design and delivery of learning experiences. Future research needs to explore further the inter-relationships between teacher disposition, teacher learning and student outcomes.

8.7: Recommendations: Future Research Agendas

This research was commenced five years ago. In the ensuing time, the trend towards a communications environment characterised by multimodal design and shifts in social dynamics has been unrelenting. What was a pioneering effort in engaging with twenty-first century literacy learning, has now become an imperative. The connections between literacy and technological competencies and workforce and citizenry literacy repertoires are increasingly emphasised. Rapid educative responses are required. Extensive further research will be required if theoretical and school responses are to keep abreast with social engagement with digital multimodal designing. The findings of this research project indicate five future research agendas:

1. This research went some way towards exploring multimodal metalanguage deployment in pedagogical situations. There remains a pressing need for further research, which will contribute to the development of a metalanguage related to alternative modes of meaning, and which will enable teachers to deploy such metalanguage.
2. The inter-relationships between pedagogy and modes of meaning have undergone some exploration in this research, with some patterns of alignment evident between particular modes and pedagogies. Possible alignments between particular modes and pedagogies and the nature of such relationships requires further investigation.
3. This research has proved the importance of the research role for educators—whether theorist, teacher or bureaucrat—documenting and tracking applications and outcomes in addressing learner diversity. Further investigation is required into relationships of research and reflective practice and the impact it has on teaching.
4. While pedagogy and ongoing assessment move some way to valuing multimodality literacy, they remain secondary unless they find themselves in high stakes assessment agendas. There exists a clear research need to develop the models and means to incorporate multimodal competencies into high stakes assessment as well as ongoing assessment.
5. Underlying the outcomes of this research was the role of teacher disposition as an influential factor in teacher learning, teacher practice and student learning. Future research needs to investigate in detail the correlation between positive teacher disposition and positive learner outcomes.

CONCLUSIONS

In the midst of an epochal shift in the communications environment, characterised by rapid shifts and transformations of knowledge, the need for judicious educative responses is acute. Agentive, collaborative teacher professional learning, resonating with the affordances of the changed communications environment, is positioned as an effective mechanism for renewal of literacy education.

Bibliography

Alvermann, D. E., and Hagood, M. (2000). Critical Media Literacy: Research, Theory, and Practice in 'New Times'. *Journal of Educational Research, 93*(3), pp. 193–205.

Argyris, C., and Schön, D. (1978). *Organisational Learning: A Theory of Action Perspective.* San Francisco: Jossey-Bass.

Argyris, C., and Schön, D. A. (1974). *Theory in Practice: Increasing Professional Effectiveness.* San Francisco: Jossey-Bass.

Aspin, D., and Chapman, J. (2001). *Lifelong Learning: Concepts, Theories and Values.* Paper presented at the Standing Conference on University Teaching and Research in the Education of Adults (SCUTREA), 31st Annual Conference, University of East London.

Atkinson, R., and Hansen, D. (1966–1967). Computer-Assisted Instruction in Initial Reading: The Stanford Project. *Reading Research Quarterly, 2,* 5–26.

Australian Government. (2000). *National Inquiry into School History.* Retrieved 4 August, 2006, from http://www.dest.gov.au/sectors/school_education/publications_resources/nationalinquiry_into_school_history/chapter_5.htm.

Beavis, C. (1997). Computer Games, Culture and Curriculum. In I. Snyder (Ed.), *Page to Screen: Taking Literacy into the Electronic Era*, pp. 234–55. London & New York: Routledge.

Beck, U., Giddens, A., and Lash, S. (1994). *Reflexive Modernization: Politics, Tradition and Aesthetics in the Modern Social Order.* Cambridge: Polity Press.

Bernstein, B. (1971). *Class, Codes and Control.* London: Routledge and Kegan Paul.

Bigum, C., and Lankshear, C. (1998). *Literacies and Technologies in School Settings: Findings from the Field.* Keynote address to 1998 ALEA/ATEA National Conference. Retrieved 4 November, 2005, from http://www.schools.ash.org.au/litweb/bigum.html.

Blackmore, J. (1993). *The Colonising Discourses of Devolution and Restructuring in Educational Administration: Why Now and Who Gains?* Paper presented at the AARE Conference, Perth, Australia.

Bloom, B. S. (1953). Thought Processes in Lectures and Discussions. *Journal of General Education, 7,* 160–69.

Board of Studies Victoria. (1995). *Curriculum and Standards Framework.* Melbourne: Department of Education, Employment and Training.

Board of Studies Victoria. (2000). *Curriculum and Standards Framework II.* Melbourne.

Bodgen, R., and Bilken, S. (1992). *Qualitative Research in Education.* Boston: Allyn and Bacon.

Bond, D. (2000). Negotiating a Pedagogy of Multiliteracies: the Communication Curriculum in a South African Management Development Programme. In B. Cope and M. Kalantzis (Eds.), *Multiliteracies: Literacy Learning and the Design of Social Futures,* pp. 311–20. London: Routledge.

Borko, H., Liston, D., and Whitcomb, J. (2007). Apples and Fish: The Debate over Teacher Dispositions. *Journal of Teacher Education, 58*(5), 359–64.

Brown, A., and Campione, J.C. (1994). Guided Discovery in a Community of Learners. In K. McGilly (Ed.), *Classroom Lessons: Integrating Cognitive Theory and Classroom Practice,* pp. 229–70. Cambridge, MA: MIT Press.

Bruce, B. (2003). *Literacy in the Information Age Inquiries into Meaning Making with New Technologies.* Delaware: International Reading Association.

Bruner, J. (1983). *Child's Talk: Learning to Use Language.* Oxford: Oxford University Press.

Buckingham, D. (1996). *Understanding Children's Emotional Responses to Television.* Manchester: Manchester University Press.

Buckingham, D. (2000). *After the Death of Television: Growing Up in the Age of Electronic Media.* London: Polity.

Buckingham, D. (2002). *Small Screens: Television for Children.* Leicester: Leicester University Press.

Buckingham, D., and Sefton-Green, J. (1994). *Cultural Studies Goes to School: Reading and Teaching Popular Media.* London: Taylor and Francis.

Buckingham, D., Grahame, J., and Sefton-Green, J. (1995). *Making Media—Practical Production in Media Education.* London: English and Media Centre.

Burn, A., and Parker, D. (2003a). *Analysing Media Texts.* London: Continuum.

Burn, A., and Parker, D. (2003b). Tiger's Big Plan: Multimodality and the Moving Image. In C. Jewitt and G. Kress (Eds.), *Multimodal Literacy.* New York: Peter Lang.

Burns, R. (2000). *Introduction to Research Methods.* Sydney: Pearson Education.

Burrows, P. (2005). Learning by Design: A Marriage of Theory and Practice. In M. Kalantzis and B. Cope (Eds.), *Learning by Design.* Melbourne: Victorian Schools Innovation Commission in association with Common Ground Publishing.

Caldwell, B., and Haywood, D. (1998). *Future of Schools (Student Outcomes and the Reform of Education.* London and Bristol, PA: Falmer Press.

Campbell, D. (2003). Foreword. In *Case Study Research Design and Methods,* pp. ix–xi. Thousand Oaks, California: Sage Publications Inc.

Carr, W., and Kemmis, S. (1986). *Becoming Critical: Education, Knowledge and Action Research* (Third ed.). London: Falmer Press.

Castells, M. (1996a). *The Information Age: A Science of Learning in the Classroom.* Oxford: Blackwell.

Castells, M. (2001). *The Internet Galaxy: Reflections on the Internet, Business, and Society.* Oxford: Oxford University Press.

Castells, M. (1996b). *The Rise of the Network Society.* Malden, MA: Blackwell.

Casti, J. (1994). *Complexification: Explaining a Paradoxical World through the Science of Surprise.* New York: Harper Collins.

Cazden, C. (1988). *Classroom Discourse: The Language of Teaching and Learning.* Portsmouth, NH: Heinemann.

Cazden, C. (2000b). Four Innovative Programmes: a Postcript from Alice Springs. In B. Cope and M. Kalantzis (Eds.), *Multiliteracies: Literacy Learning and the Design of Social Futures,* pp. 321–32. London: Routledge.

Cazden, C. (2000a). Taking Cultural Differences into Account. In B. Cope and M. Kalantzis (Eds.), *Multiliteracies: Literacy Learning and Design of Social Futures.* London: Routledge.

Chall, J., Jacob, V., and Baldwin, L. (1990). *The Reading Crisis: Why Poor Children Fall Behind.* Cambridge, MA: Harvard University Press.

Chandler-Olcott, K., and Mahar, D. (2003). Tech-Saviness Meets Multiliteracies: Exploring Adolescent Girls' Technology-Mediated Literacy Practices. *Reading Research Quarterly.*

Clay, M. (1993a). *An Observation of Early Literacy Achievement.* Auckland: Heinemann.

Clay, M. (1991). *Becoming Literate: The Construction of Inner Control.* Auckland: Heinemann Education.

Clay, M. (1993b). *Reading Recovery: A Guidebook for Teachers in Training*. Auckland: Heinemann Education.

Clay, M. (1992). A Vygotskian Interpretation of Reading Recovery. In C. Cazden (Ed.), *Whole Language Plus: Essays on Literacy in the United States and New Zealand*, pp. 114–35. New York: Teachers College Press.

Clay, M., Gill, M., Glynn, T., McNaughton, T., and Salmon, K. (1983). *Record of Oral Language and Biks and Gutches*. Auckland: Heinemann Publishers.

Cloonan, A. (2002). *Report into Multiliteracies and the Victorian Early Years Literacy Program*: Unpublished report to the Early Years Team, Department of Education and Training, Victoria.

Cloonan, A. (2005). Professional Learning and Enacting Theory (Or Trying to be a Lifelong/Lifewide Teacher–Learner while Hanging on to Your Sanity). In M. Kalantzis and B. Cope (Eds.), *Learning by Design*. Melbourne: Victorian Schools Innovation Commission in association with Common Ground Publishing.

Cochran-Smith, M., and Lytle, S. (1993). *Inside/Outside: Teacher Research and Knowledge*. New York and London: Teachers College Press.

Cochran-Smith, M., and Lytle, S. (1999). Relationships of Knowledge and Practice: Teacher Learning in Communities. In A. Iran-Nejad and P. Pearson (Eds.), *Review of Research in Education*, Vol. 24, pp. 249–305. Washington, DC: American Educational Research Association.

Cochran-Smith, M., and Lytle, S. (1990). Research on Teaching and Teacher Research: The Issues that Divide. *Educational Researcher, 19* (2), 2–11.

Cochran-Smith, M., and Lytle, S. (1999). The Teacher Research Movement: A Decade Later. *Educational Researcher* (October), 15–25.

Coiro, J., Knobel, M., Lankshear, C., and Leu, D. (2007). *Central Issues in New Literacies and New Literacies Research*. Retrieved 26 July, 2007, from http://www.newliteracies.uconn.edu/pub_files/Handbook_of_Research_on_New_Literacies.pdf.

Cole, M. (1996). *Cultural Psychology: A Once and Future Discipline*. Cambridge, MA: Harvard University Press.

Comber, B., and Kamler, B. (2004). Getting Out of Deficit: Pedagogies of Reconnection. *Teaching Education, 15* (3), 293–310.

Comber, B., Kamler, B., Hood, D., Moreau, S., and Painter, J. (2004). Thirty Years into Teaching: Professional Development, Exhaustion and Rejuvenation. *English Teaching: Practice and Critique, 3* (2), 74–87.

Cope, B., and Kalantzis, M. (2000a). Designs for Social Futures. In B. Cope and M. Kalantzis (Eds.), *Multiliteracies: Literacy Learning and the Design of Social Futures*, pp. 203–34. London: Routledge.

Cope, B., and Kalantzis, M. (Eds.). (1993). *The Powers of Literacy: Genre Approaches to Teaching Writing*. London and Pittsburgh: Falmer Press.

Cope, B., and Kalantzis, M. (Eds.). (2000b). *Multiliteracies: Literacy Learning and the Design of Social Futures*. London: Routledge.

Cormack, P., and Comber, B. (1996). Writing the Teacher: The South Australian Junior Primary English Teacher 19620150199 5. In B. Green and C. Beavis (Eds.), *Teaching the English Subjects:(Dis)continuities in Curriculum History and English Teaching in Australia*. Geelong: Deakin University Press.

Crèvola, C., and Hill, P. (1997). *The Early Literacy Research Project: Success for All in Victoria Australia*. Paper presented at the Annual Meeting of the American Educational Research Association, Chicago.

Crowther, F., Kaagan, S., Ferguson, M., and Hann, L. (2002). *Developing Teacher Leaders: How Teacher Leadership Enhances School Success*. California: Corwin Press.

Culican, S., Emmitt, M., and Oakley, C. (2001). *Literacy and Learning in the Middle Years: Major Report on the Middle Years Literacy Research Project*. Burwood: Deakin University. Undertaken for Department of Education, Training and Youth Affairs through the Department of Education, Employment and Training, Victoria as part of Successful Interventions: A Secondary Literacy and Numeracy Initiative.

Curriculum Development Centre. (1987). *Overview of the Early Literacy Inservice Course*. Canberra: Curriculum Development Centre.

Darling-Hammond, L. (2003). Keeping Good Teachers: Why it Matters, What Leaders Can Do. *Educational Leadership, 60* (8), 6–13.

Darling-Hammond L. (1998). *Teacher Learning that Supports Student Learning*. Retrieved 29 November, 2004, from http://www.ascd.org/publications/ed/darlinghammond.html.

Darling-Hammond, L. (2000). *Teacher Quality and Student Achievement: A Review of State Policy Evidence*. Retrieved 8 June, 2006, from http://epaa.asu.edu/epaa/v8n1.

Darling-Hammond, L., and McLaughlin. M. (1995). Policies that Support Professional Development in an Era of Reform. *Phi Delta Kappan, 76* (8), 597–604.

Darling-Hammond, L., and Sykes, G. (Eds.). (1999). *Teaching as the Learning Profession: Handbook of Policy and Practice*. San Francisco: Jossey-Bass.

Delpit, L. (1995). *Other People's Children: Cultural Conflict in the Classroom*. New York: New Press.

Denzin, N., and Lincoln, Y. (2000). Introduction. In N. Denzin, and Y. Lincoln (Eds.), *Handbook of Qualitative Research*, pp. 1–28. Thousand Oaks, California: Sage Publications.

Department of Education and the Arts. (2006). *New Basics Project: Productive Pedagogies*. Retrieved 16 May, 2006, from http://education.qld.gov.au/corporate/newbasics/html/pedagogies/pedagog.html.

Department of Education and Training. (2002a). *Assessment of Reading (Prep–2) Report*. East Melbourne: Department of Education and Training Victoria.

Department of Education and Training. (2002b). *Early Numeracy Research Project (1999–2001) Summary of the Final Report*. Retrieved 4 August, 2006, from http://www.sofweb.vic.edu.au/eys/num/enrp.htm.

Department of Education and Training. (2002c). *Literacy and Technology Case Study Report*. Retrieved 16 August, 2007, from http://www.sofweb.vic.edu.au/eys/eystech/index.htm.

Department of Education and Training. (2002d). *Teaching ESL Students in the Early Years*. Retrieved 16 August, 2007, from http://www.sofweb.vic.edu.au/eys/pd/schoolstv/term1.htm.

Department of Education and Training. (2002e). *Teaching Writers: What About Handwriting?* Retrieved 16 August, 2007, from http://www.sofweb.vic.edu.au/eys/pd/schoolstv/term3.htm.

Department of Education and Training. (2003a). *Accountability: Statewide Minimum Standards for Reading*. Retrieved 16 August, 2007, from http://www.sofweb.vic.edu.au/eys/lit/account.htm.

Department of Education and Training. (2003b). *Blueprint for Government Schools Future Directions for Education in the Victorian Government School System*. Retrieved 18 July, 2006, from http://www.det.vic.gov.au/det/resources/pdfs/blueprint/Blueprint_complete.pdf.

Department of Education and Training. (2003c). *Early Years Schools Television 2003 Literacy and Numeracy*. Retrieved August 16, 2007, from http://www.sofweb.vic.edu.au/eys/pd/schoolstv/index.htm.

Department of Education and Training. (2005). *Schools Television*. Retrieved 8 August, 2006, from http://www.sofweb.vic.edu.au/schoolstv%5Fnotice/.

Department of Education and Training. (2006). *The Principles of Learning and Teaching P–12 Background Paper*. Retrieved May 16, 2006, from http://www.sofweb.vic.edu.au/pedagogy/plt/index.htm.

Department of Education Employment and Training. (1999). *The Middle Years: A Guide for Strategic Action in Years 5-9*. Melbourne: Department of Education, Victoria.

Department of Education Employment and Training. (2000a). *Public Education The Next Generation: Report of the Working Party*. Retrieved 2

August, 2006, from http://www.sofweb.vic.edu.au/publiced/pdfs/PEdNGen.pdf.

Department of Education Employment and Training. (2000b). *Your Invitation to a Conversation about Public Education: The Next Generation.* Retrieved 2 August, 2006, from http://www.sofweb.vic.edu.au/publiced/index.htm.

Department of Education Employment and Training. (2001a). *Knowledge, Innovation, Skills and Creativity: A Discussion Paper on Achieving the Goals and Targets for the Future in Victoria's Education and Training System.* Melbourne: Department of Education, Employment and Training, Victoria.

Department of Education Employment and Training. (2001b). *The Middle Years Research and Development (MYRAD) Project.* Retrieved 19 July, 2006, from http://www.sofweb.vic.edu.au/mys/research/#myrad.

Department of Education, N. Z. (1985). *Reading in the Junior Classes.* Wellington, New Zealand: Ministry of Education.

Department of Premier and Cabinet. (2001). *Growing Victoria Together: Innovative State. Caring Communities.* Retrieved 2 August, 2006, from http://www.dpc.vic.gov.au/CA256D800027B102/Lookup/GVTBooklet/$file/DPCbrochure.FA.pdf.

Dewey, J. (1956). *The School and Society.* Chicago: University of Chicago Press.

Dewey, J. (1990). *The School and Society and the Child and the Curriculum.* Chicago: University of Chicago Press.

Dillon, J., Osborne, J., Fairbrother, R., and Kurina, L. (2000). *A Study into the Professional Views and Needs of Science Teachers in Primary and Secondary Schools in England.* London: Council for Science and Technology.

Directorate of School Education. (1995). *Course Advice.* Melbourne: Curriculum and Development Section.

DuFour, R., and Eaker, R. (1998). *Professional Learning Communities at Work: Best Practices for Enhancing Student Achievement.* Bloomington, Indianapolis: National Education Service.

Durrant, C., and Green, B. (2000). Literacy and the New Technologies in Schools Education: Meeting the L(IT)eracy Challenge? *The Australian Journal of Language and Literacy, The Australian Literacy Educators Association, 17* (2), 89–108.

Education Queensland. (2000a). *Queensland State Education 2010.* Brisbane: Queensland Department of Education.

Education Queensland. (2000b). *Report of the Literacy Review for Queensland State Schools.* Retrieved 3 August, 2006, from http://education.qld.gov.au/curriculum/learning/literate-futures/pdfs/lf-review.pdf.

Education Queensland. (2002). *Literate Futures: Reading*. Brisbane: Queensland Department of Education.
Education Queensland. (2003). *New Basics Project: Productive Pedagogies*. Brisbane: Queensland Department of Education.
Education Queensland. (2005). *New Basics Project*. Brisbane: Queensland Department of Education.
Education Victoria. (1997a). *Classroom Helpers: A Course for Parents, Helpers and Aides*. Melbourne: Addison Wesley Longman.
Education Victoria. (1997b). *Developing Literacy Partnerships: Early Years Literacy Program*. Melbourne: Addison Wesley Longman.
Education Victoria. (1997c). *Guided Reading: A Companion Video to Professional Development for Teachers*. Melbourne: Addison Wesley Longman.
Education Victoria. (1997d). *Learning Centres: A Companion Video to Professional Development for Teachers*. Melbourne: Addison Wesley Longman.
Education Victoria. (1997e). *Professional Development for Teachers: Keys to Life*. Melbourne: Addison Wesley Longman.
Education Victoria. (1997f). *Professional Development for Teachers: Readers*. Melbourne: Addison Wesley Longman.
Education Victoria. (1997g). *Teaching Readers in the Classroom: Keys to Life*. Melbourne: Addison Wesley Longman.
Education Victoria. (1997h). *Teaching Readers in the Early Years*. Melbourne: Addison Wesley Longman.
Education Victoria. (1998a). *Professional Development for Teachers, Stage 2 Writing*. Melbourne: Addison Wesley Longman.
Education Victoria. (1998b). *Teaching Writers in the Classroom, Stage 2*. Melbourne: Addison Wesley Longman.
Education Victoria. (1999a). *Professional Development for Teachers, Stage 3 Speaking and Listening*. Melbourne: Addison Wesley Longman.
Education Victoria. (1999b). *Teaching Speakers and Listeners in the Classroom, Stage 3*. Melbourne: Addison Wesley Longman.
Education Victoria. (1999c). *Teaching Speakers and Listeners: A Companion Video to Professional Development for Teachers*. Melbourne: Addison Wesley Longman.
Ehrich, L., and Hansford, B. (1999). Mentoring: Pros and Cons for HRM. *Asia Pacific Journal of Human Resources, 37* (3), 92–108.
Eiser, J. (1994). *Attitudes, Chaos, and the Connectionist Mind*. Oxford: Basil Blackwell.
Elliot, J. (1991). *Action Research for Educational Change*. Milton Keynes: Open University Press.
Elmore, R. (1996). Getting to Scale with Good Educational Practice. *Harvard Educational Review, 66*, 1–26.
Elmore, R. (2002). *Bridging the Gap between Standards and Achievement: Report on the Imperative for Professional Development in Education*. Washington DC: Albert Shanker Institute.

Erickson, F. (1986). Qualitative Methods in Research on Teaching. In M. Wittrock (Ed.), *Handbook of Research on Teaching* (3rd Ed.), pp. 119–61. New York: Macmillan.

Fairclough, N. (1992). Discourse and Text: Linguistic and Intertextual Analysis within Discourse Analysis. *Discourse and Society, 3,* 193–217.

Fairclough, N. (2000). Multiliteracies and Language. In B. Cope and M. Kalantzis (Eds.), *Multiliteracies Literacy Learning and the Design of Social Futures.* London: Routledge.

Fals Borda, O. (1979). Investigating Reality in Order to Transform it: The Colombian Experience. *Dialectical Anthropology, 4,* 33–55.

Fletcher, S. (2000). *Mentoring in Schools: A Handbook of Good Practice.* London: Kogan Page.

Flick, U. (1992). Triangulation Revisited: Strategy of Validation or Alternative. *Journal for the Theory of Social Behaviour, 22* (2), 175–97.

Furhman, S. (Ed.). (2001). *From the Capitol to the Classroom: Standards-based Reform in the States. One Hundredth Yearbook of the National Society for the Study of Education.* Chicago, Illinois: NSSE.

Gabelnick, F., MacGregor, J., Matthews, R., and Smith, B. (1990). *Learning Communities: Creating Connections among Students, Faculty and Disciplines.* San Francisco: Jossey-Bass.

Gardner, H. (1991). *The Unschooled Mind: How Children Think and How Schools Should Teach.* New York: Basic Books.

Gardner, H. (2002). Who Owns Intelligence? In M. Singh (Ed.), *Global Learning,* pp. 181–96. Melbourne: Common Ground.

Garet, M. S., Porter, A., Desimone, L., Birman, B.F., and Yoon, K.S. (2001). What Makes Professional Development Effective? Results from a National Sample of Teachers. *American Educational Research Journal, 38,* 915–45.

Gee, J. P. (1990). *Social Linguistics and Literacies: Ideology in Discourses.* London: Falmer.

Gee, J. P. (1992). *The Social Mind: Language, Ideology and Social Practice.* New York: Bergin and Garvey.

Gee, J. P. (1996). *Social Linguistics and Literacies: Ideology in Discourses* (2nd ed.). London: Taylor and Francis.

Gee, J. P. (2000). New People in New Worlds: Networks, the New Capitalism and Schools. In B. Cope and M. Kalantzis (Eds.), *Multiliteracies: Literacy Learning and the Design of Social Futures.* London: Routledge.

Gee, J. P. (2005). Meaning Making, Communities of Practice, and Analytical Toolkits. *Journal of Sociolinguistics, 9* (4), 590–94.

Gee, J. P., Hull, G., and Lankshear, C. (1996). *The New Work Order: Behind the Language of Fast Capitalism.* Sydney and Boulder, CO: Allen & Unwin and Westview Press.

Geertz, C. (1973). *The Interpretation of Cultures.* New York: Basic Books.

Good, T. (1987). Two Decades of Research on Teacher Expectations: Findings and Future Directions. *Journal of Teacher Education, 38* (4), 32–47.

Goodrum, D., Hackling, M., and Rennie, L. (2001). *The Status and Quality of Teaching and Learning of Science in Australian Schools. A research report prepared for the Department of Education, Training and Youth Affairs*. Canberra: Department of Education, Training and Youth Affairs.

Green, B., and Bigum, C. (1993). Aliens in the Classroom. *Australian Journal of Education, 37* (2), 119–41.

Greenwood, D.J. & Levin, M. (2000). Reconstructing the relationship between universities and society through action research. In N.K. Denzin & Y.S. Lincoln (Eds.), *Handbook of qualitative research* (2nd ed.), pp. 85–106). Thousand Oaks, CA: Sage Publications.

Grimmett, P. (1988). The Nature of Reflection and Schön's Conception in Perspective. In P. Grimmett and G. Erickson (Eds.), *Reflection in Teacher Education*, pp. 5–15. New York: Teachers College Press.

Grimmett, P., and MacKinnon, A. (1992). Craft Knowledge and the Education of Teachers. In G. Grant (Ed.), *Review of Research in Education 18*. Washington, D.C.: American Educational Research Association.

Grisham, D. (2000). *Teacher Voices: Research as Professional Development*. Retrieved 3 August, 2007, from http://www.readingonline.org/editorial/edit_index.asp.

Grossman, P. (1994). Teachers' Knowledge. In T. Husen and T. Postlethwaite (Eds.), *International Encyclopaedia of Education*. Oxford: Pergamon.

Grundy, S. (2006). Personal Conversation with the author. Melbourne.

Guba, E. (1981). Criteria for Assessing the Trustworthiness of Naturalistic Inquiries. *Educational Communication and Technology Journal, 29*, 75–92.

Hale, R. (1999, November). *To Mix or Mis-match? The Dynamics of Mentoring as a Route to Personal and Organisational Learning*. Paper presented at the European Mentoring Conference, Cambs.

Halliday, M. A. K. (1980). Three Aspects of Children's Language Development: Learning Language, Learning Through Language and Learning About Language. In J. Webster (Ed.), *The Language of Early Childhood*, pp. 308–26. London and New York: Continuum International Publishing Group.

Halliday, M. A. K. (1994). *An Introduction to Functional Grammar* (2nd ed.) London: Edward Arnold.

Halliday, M. A. K. (1978). *Language as Social Semiotic*. London: Edward Arnold.

Halliday, M. A. K. and Hasan, R. (1985). *Language, Context and Text: Aspects of Language in a Social-Semiotic Perspective.* Geelong: Deakin University Press.

Hargreaves, A., and Fullan, M. (2000). Mentoring in the New Millennium. *Theory Into Practice, 39* (1), 50–57.

Harre, R., and Gillett, G. (1994). *The Discursive Mind.* Beverley Hills: Sage Publications.

Hattie, J. A. (2003, October). *Teachers Make a Difference: What is the Research Evidence?* Paper presented at the Building Teacher Quality Research Conference, Melbourne.

Heath, S. B. (1983). *Ways with Words: Language, Life and Work in Communities and Classrooms.* Cambridge: Cambridge University Press.

Hill, P. and Crèvola, C. (1998a). Characteristics of an Effective Literacy Strategy. *Unicorn, 24* (2), 74–85.

Hill, P. and Crèvola, C. (1998b). *Developing and Testing a Whole-School Design Approach to Improvement in Early Literacy.* Paper presented at the 11th International Congress for School Effectiveness and Improvement, Manchester, UK.

Hill, P. and Crèvola, C. (1999a). *Key Features of a Whole-school, Design Approach to Literacy Teaching in Schools.* Retrieved 1 August, 2006, from http://www.pdn.asn.au/confs/2001/Brierley/WholeSchoolapproachtoliteracy.pdf.

Hill, P. and Crèvola, C. (1997a). *The Literacy Challenge in Australian Primary Schools.* IARTV Seminar Series, (No 69).

Hill, P. and Crèvola, C. (1997b). *The Role of Leadership and Professional Development in a Design Approach to School Improvement.* Retrieved 26 July, 2005, from http://www.leadership.sa.edu.au/papers.phill.html.

Hill, P. and Crèvola, C. (1999b). The Role of Standards in Educational Reform for the 21st Century. In D. D. Marsh (Ed.), *The 1999 ASCD Yearbook: Preparing our Schools for the 21st Century*, pp. 117–42. Alexandria,: Association of Supervision and Curriculum Development.

Hill, P. and Rowe, K. J. (1996). Multilevel Modelling in School Effectiveness Research. *School Effectiveness and School Improvement, 7* (1), 1–34.

Hill, P., Rowe, K. J., Holmes-Smith, P., and Russell, V. J. (1996). *The Victorian Quality Schools Project: A Study of School and Teacher Effectiveness Report to the Australian Research Council (Volume 1 Report).* Melbourne: Centre for Applied Educational Research, Faculty of Education, The University of Melbourne.

Hobsbawm, E. (1994). *The Age of Extremes: The Short Twentieth Century, 1914–1991.* London: Michael Joseph.

Holdaway, D. (1979). *The Foundations of Literacy.* Sydney: Ashton Scholastic.

Husserl, E. (1970). *The Crisis of European Sciences and Transcendental Phenomenology.* Evanston: Northwestern University Press.

Internet World Stats. (2006). *Internet Usage Statistics–The Big Picture: World Internet Users and Population Stats*. Retrieved 26 July, 2007, from http://www.internetworldstats.com/stats.htm.

James, R., and Beckett, D. (2000). Higher Education and Lifelong Learning: an Australian Experience. In H. Schuetze and M. Slowey (Eds.), *Higher Education and Lifelong Learners: International Perspectives on Change*, pp. 173–194. London: Routledge-Falmer.

Jewitt, C. and Kress, G. (2003). *Multimodal Literacy*. New York: Peter Lang.

Kalantzis, M. (2005). *Elements of a Science of Education*. Paper presented at the AARE.

Kalantzis, M., and Cope, B. (2004). *Designs For Learning*. Retrieved 12 August, 2007, from http://www.wwwords.co.uk/pdf/.

Kalantzis, M., and Cope, B. (2008). *Learning by Design*. Retrieved 20 October, 2009, from http://newlearningonline.com/learning-by-design/the-learning-element.

Kalantzis, M., and Cope, B. (unpublished paper). A Grammar of Multimodal Meaning.

Kalantzis, M., and Cope, B. (2000). A Multiliteracies Pedagogy: A Pedagogical Supplement. In B. Cope, B. and M. Kalantzis (Eds.), *Multiliteracies: Literacy Learning and Design of Social Futures*. London: Routledge..

Kalantzis, M., and Cope, B. (2004). *Designs for Learning*. Retrieved 12 August, 2007, from http://www.wwwords.co.uk/pdf.

Kalantzis, M., Cope, B., and the Learning by Design Project Group. (2005). *Learning by Design*. Melbourne: Victorian Schools Innovation Commission in association with Common Ground Publishing.

Kemmis, S. (2005). *Participatory Action Research and the Public Sphere*. Paper presented at the PRAR Conference at Utrech University, 20 November.

Kemmis, S. (December 5th 2000). *Educational Research and Evaluation: Opening Communicative Space*. Retrieved 10 July, 2006, from http://www.aare.edu.au/00pap/radford.htm.

Kemmis, S., and McTaggart, R. (2005). Participatory Action Research. In N. Denzin and Y. Lincoln (Eds.), *The Sage Handbook of Qualitative Research*. Thousand Oaks, California: Sage Publications.

Knobel, M., and Lankshear, C. (2007). *A New Literacies Sampler*. New York: Peter Lang Publishing.

Kosky, L. (2003). *Framework for Reform*. Retrieved 18 July, 2006, from http://www.det.vic.gov.au/det/resources/detreports.htm.

Kress, G. (2000a). Design and Transformation: New Theories of Meaning. In B. Cope and M. Kalantzis (Eds.), *Multiliteracies: Literacy Learning and the Design of Social Futures*. London: Routledge.

Kress, G. (2000b). Multimodality. In B. Cope and M. Kalantzis (Eds.), *Multiliteracies: Literacy Learning and the Design of Social Futures*. London: Routledge.

Kress, G. (2003). *Literacy in the New Media Age*. London: Routledge.

Kress, G., and van Leeuwen, T. (1996). *Reading Images: The Grammar of Visual Design*. New York: Routledge.

Kress, G., Jewitt, C., Ogborn, J., and Tsatsarelis, C. (2001). *Multimodal Teaching and Learning: The Rhetorics of the Science Classroom*. New York: Continuum.

Kristeva, J. (1984). *Revolution in Poetic Language*. New York: Columbia University Press.

Kuzel, A. J. (1992). Sampling in Qualitative Inquiry. In B. F. Crabtree and W. L. Miller (Eds.), *Doing Qualitative Research*, pp. 31–44. Newbury Park, California: Sage Publications.

Labbo, L. (2000). *Toward a Vision of the Future Role of Technology in Literacy Education.*: Commissioned by the Office of Educational Technology, US Department of Education, Forum on Technology in Education—Envisioning the Future, Washington DC, December, 1999.

Labbo, L. (2003). The Symbol Making Machine: Examining the Role of Electronic Symbol Making in Children's Literacy Development. In L. Richards and M. McKenna (Eds.), *Teaching Multiple Literacies in K-8 Classrooms: Cases, Commentaries and Practical Applications*. Mahwah, NJ: Lawrence Erlbaum.

Ladson-Billings, G. (1991). *Returning to the Sources: Implications for Educating Teachers of Black Students*. New York: AMS Press.

Lankshear, C. (1999). *Digital Rhetorics: Literacies and Technologies in Classrooms—Current Practices and Future Directions*. Retrieved 4 November, 2005, from http://education.curtin.edu.au/iier/qjer/qjer15/lankshear.html.

Lankshear, C., and Knobel, M. (2003). *New Literacies*. Buckingham: Open University Press.

Lankshear, C., and Knobel, M. (2006). *New Literacies: Everyday Practices and Classroom Learning* (2nd ed.). Maidenhead and New York: Open University Press.

Lankshear, C., Bigum, C., Durrant, C., Green, B., Honan, E., Morgan, W., et al. (1997). *Digital Rhetorics: Literacies and Technologies in Education—Current Practices and Future Directions*. Retrieved 14 December, 2005, from http://www.griffith.edu.au/school/cls/clearinghouse/content_1997-rhetorics_.html.

Lankshear, C., Snyder, I., and Green, B. (2000). *Teachers and Technoliteracy*. Sydney: Allen & Unwin.

Lash, S., and Urry, J. (1994). *Economics of Time and Space*. Beverley Hills: Sage.

Lather, P. (1986). Issues of Validity in Openly Ideological Research: Between a Rock and a Soft Place. *Interchange, 17* (4), 63–84.

Lave, J., and Wegner, E. (1991). *Situated Learning: Legitimate Peripheral Participation*. Cambridge: Cambridge University Press.

Law, J. (2004). *After Method Mess in Social Science Research*. London: Routledge.

Law, J. (2003). *Making a Mess with Method.* Retrieved August 16, 2007, from http://www.lancs.ac.uk/fss/sociology/papers/law-making-a-mess-with-method.pdf.

LeCompte, M., and Schensul, J. (1999). *Analysing and Interpreting Ethnographic Data.* Walnut Creek, California: Alta Mira Press.

Leu, D. J., Ataya, R., and Coiro, J. (2002). *Assessing Assessment Strategies among the 50 States: Evaluating the Literacies of our Past or our Future?* Paper presented at the National Reading Conference December. Miami, Florida.

Leu, D. J. Jr. (2000). Literacy and Technology: Deictic Consequences for Literacy Education in an Information Age. In M. Kamil, P. Mosenthal, P. Pearson and R. Barr (Eds.), *Handbook of Reading Research*, Vol. 3, pp. 743–64. Mahwah, NJ: Erlbaum.

Lincoln, Y., and Guba, E. (1985). *Naturalistic Inquiry.* Thousand Oaks, California: Sage Publications.

Locke, T., and Andrews, R. (2004). ICT and literature: a Faustian compact? In R. Andrews (Ed.), *The Impact of ICT on Literacy Education*, pp. 124–52). London.

Luke, A. (2003a). Making Literacy Policy and Practice with a Difference. *Australian Journal of Language and Literacy, 26* (3), 58–81.

Luke, A. (2006). Editorial Introduction: Why Pedagogies? *Pedagogies: An International Journal, 1* (1), 1–6.

Luke, A., and Freebody, P. (2000). *Literate Futures: Report of the Literacy Review for Queensland State Schools.* Brisbane: Department of Education Queensland.

Luke, A., Lingard, R., Green, B., and Comber, B. (1999). The Abuses of Literacy. In J. Marshall and P. Peters (Eds.), *Educational Policy*, pp. 763–87. London: Edward Elgar.

Luke, C. (1995). Multimedia Multiliteracies. *Education Australia* (30), 14–17.

Luke, C. (2000). Cyber-schooling and Technological Change. In B. Cope and M. Kalantzis (Eds.), *Multiliteracies Literacy Learning and the Designs of Social Futures.* London: Routledge.

Luke, C. (2003b). Pedagogy, Connectivity, Multimodality, and Interdisciplinarity. *Reading Research Quarterly, 38* (3), 397–403.

Luria, A. (1976). *Cognitive Development: Its Cultural and Social Foundations.* Cambridge, MA: Harvard University Press.

Martin, J. R., Matthiessen, M. I. M., and Painter, C. (1997). *Working with Functional Grammar.* London and New York: Hodder Headland Group.

Martinec, R. (1999). Cohesion in Action. *Semiotica, 1/2*, 161–80.

Martinec, R. (2000a). Construction of Identity in Michael Jackson's *Jam. Social Semiotics, 10* (3), 313–29.

Martinec, R. (2000b). Types of process in action. *Semiotica, 130* (3/4), 243–68.

McDonald, J. (1988). The Emergence of the Teacher's Voice: Implications for the New Reform. *Teachers College Record, 89*, 471–86.

McDonald, J. (1992). *Teaching: Making Sense of an Uncertain Craft.* New York: Teachers College Press.

McLaughlin, M., and Talbert, J. (1993). *Contexts that Matter for Teaching and Learning: Strategic Opportunities for Meeting the Nation's Educational Goals*: Stanford University: Centre for Research on the Context of Secondary School Teaching.

McLaughlin, M., and Talbert, J. (2001). *Professional Communities and the Work of High School Teaching.* Chicago, IL: Chicago University Press.

McNeill, D. (1992). *Hand and Mind: What Gestures Reveal About Thought.* Chicago: University of Chicago Press.

Meiers, M., and Ingvarson, I. (2005). *Investigating the Links between Teacher Professional Development and Student Learning Outcomes, Vol. 1.* Retrieved 8 June 2006, from http://www.dest.gov.au/sectors/school_education/publications_resources/profiles/teacher_prof_development_student_learning_outcomes.htm.

Miles, M., and Huberman, A. M. (1994). *An Expanded Sourcebook Qualitative Data Analysis* (2nd ed.). Thousand Oaks, California: Sage Publications.

Miller, L., and Silvernail, D. (1994). Wells Junior High School: Evolution of a Professional Development School. In L. Darling-Hammond (Ed.), *Professional Development Schools: Schools for Developing a Profession.* New York: Teachers College Press.

Minichiello, V., Aroni, R., Timewell, E., and Alexander, L. (1995). *In-depth Interviewing* (2nd ed.). Frenchs Forest, Sydney: Pearson Education Australia Pty. Ltd.

Ministerial Council on Education Employment Training and Youth Affairs. (2005). *Pedagogy Strategy: Learning in an Online World.* Carlton South: Curriculum Corporation.

Monk, D. H. (1992). Education Productivity Research: An Update and Assessment of its Role in Education Finance Reform. *Education Evaluation and Policy Analysis* (14), 307–32.

Montessori, M. (1989). *Education for a New World.* Retrieved 6 June, 2006, from http://www.moteaco.com/clio/world.html.

Montessori, M. (1964). *The Montessori Method.* New York: Schocken Books.

Muijs, D., and Reynolds, D. (2000). School Effectiveness and Teacher Effectiveness in Mathematics. Some Preliminary Findings from the Evaluation of the Mathematics Enhancement Programme (Primary). *School Effectiveness and School Improvement, 11* (3), 273–303.

Neville, M. (2005). Innovation in Queensland Education. In M. Kalantzis and B. Cope (Eds.), *Learning By Design.* Melbourne: Common Ground Publishing.

Neville, M. (2006). *Teaching Multimodal Literacy Using the Learning by Design Approach to Pedagogy: Case Studies from Selected Queensland Schools.* Unpublished MEd thesis, RMIT University, Melbourne.

New London Group. (1996). A Pedagogy of Multiliteracies: Designing Social Futures. *Harvard Educational Review, 66*, 60–92.

New London Group. (2000). A Pedagogy of Multiliteracies: Designing Social Futures. In B. Cope and M. Kalantzis (Eds.), *Multiliteracies: Literacy Learning and the Design of Social Futures*, pp. 182–202. London: Routledge.

Newfield, D., and Stein, P. (2000). The Multiliteracies Project: South African Teachers Respond. In B. Cope and M. Kalantzis (Eds.), *Multiliteracies: Literacy Learning and the Design of Social Futures*, pp. 182–202. London: Routledge.

Nolan. (1994). *Cognitive Practices: Human Language and Human Knowledge.* Oxford: Blackwell.

Nye, B., Konstantopoulos, S., and Hedges, L. (2004). How Large are Teacher Effects? *Educational Evaluation and Policy Analysis, 26* (3), 237–57.

Pandian, A., and Balraj, S. (2005). Approaching Learning by Design as an Agenda for Malaysian Schools. In M. Kalantzis and B. Cope (Eds.), *Learning by Design.* Melbourne/Altona: Victorian Schools Innovation Commission.

Papert, S. (1993). *The Children's Machine: Rethinking School in the Age of the Computer.* New York: Basic Books.

Patton, M. Q. (1990). *Qualitative Evaluation and Research Methods* (2nd ed.). Newbury Park, California: Sage Publications.

Polanyi, M. (1966). *The Tacit Dimension.* New York: Doubleday.

Prensky, M. (2001). Digital Natives, Digital Immigrants. *On the Horizon, 9* (5).

Reinking, D., McKenna, M., Labbo, L., and Kieffer, R. (1998). *Handbook of Literacy and Technology: Transformations in a Post-typographical World.* Mahwah, NJ: Erlbaum.

Reinmann, P., and Goodyear, P. (2004). *ICT and Pedagogies Stimulus Paper.* Sydney: Ministerial Council for Education, Employment, Training and Youth Affairs (MCEETYA) Task Force Review of National Goals: Australia's Common and Agreed Goals for Schooling in the Twenty-first Century.

Rowan, L., and Bigum, C. (2004). *Beyond Pretence: New Sensibilities for Computing and Communication Technologies in Teacher Education.* Retrieved 30 November, 2005.

Rowe, K. (2003). *The Importance of Teacher Quality as a Key Determinant of Students' Experiences of Schooling: A Context and Discussion Paper Prepared on Behalf of the Interim Committee for a NSW Institute of Teachers.* Melbourne: ACER.

Russell-Bowie, D. (2006). *MMADD about the Arts! An Introduction to Primary Arts Education.* Frenchs Forest: Pearson Education Australia.

Scarbrough, H. (2001). From Knowledge Management to Knowledge Sharing. *BHERT News*, 18–20.

Schalock, D. (1979). Research on Teacher Selection. In D. C. Berliner (Ed.), *Review of Research in Education Vol. 7*. Washington D.C: American Educational Research Association.

Scheerens, J., and Bosker, R. J. (1997). *The Foundations of Educational Effectiveness*. Oxford: Pergamon.

Scheerens, J., Vermeulen, C. J. A. J., and Pelgrum, W. J. (1989). Generalizability of Instructional and School Effectiveness Indicators across Nations. *International Journal of Educational Research, 13* (7), 789–99.

Schön, D. (1987). *Educating the Reflective Practitioner: Towards a New Design for Teaching and Learning in the Professions*. San Francisco: Jossey-Bass.

Schön, D. (1983). *The Reflective Practitioner: How Professionals Think in Action*. London: Temple Smith.

Sergiovanni, T. (1994). *Building Community in Schools*. San Francisco: Jossey-Bass.

Shulman, L. (1987). Knowledge and Teaching: Foundations of the New Reform. *Harvard Educational Review, 57* (1), 1–22.

Shulman, L. (1999). Foreword. In L. Darling-Hammond and G. Sykes (Eds.), *Teaching as the Learning Profession: Handbook of Policy and Practice*, pp. xi–xiv. San Francisco: Jossey-Bass.

Shulman, L. (2005). *The Signature Pedagogies of the Professions of Law, Medicine, Engineering, and the Clergy: Potential Lessons for the Education of Teachers*. Paper presented at the Math Science Partnerships (MSP) Workshop: Teacher Education for Effective Teaching and Learning, February 6–8. California: National Research Council's Center for Education.

Snyder, I. (1996). Integrating Computers into the Literacy Curriculum: More Difficult Than We Think. *Australian Journal of Language and Literacy, 19* (4), 330–44.

Snyder, I. (Ed.). (1998). *Page to Screen: Taking Literacy into the Electronic Era*. London, New York: Routledge.

Soar, R., Medley, D., and Coker, H. (1983). Teacher Evaluation: a critique of currently used methods. *Phi Delta Kappan, 65* (4), 239–46.

Southwest Educational Development Laboratory. (2002). *Instructional Coherence: The Changing Role of Teacher*. Retrieved 5 July, 2006, from http://www.sedl.org/pubs/teaching99/3.html.

Stake, R. (1995). *The Art of Case Study Research*. Thousand Oaks, California: Sage Publications.

Stake, R. (2005). Qualitative Case Studies. In N. Denzin and Y. Lincoln (Eds.), *The Sage Handbook of Qualitative Research*, pp. 443–66. Thousand Oaks, California: Sage Publications.

Sternberg, R., and Horvath, J. (1995). The Prototype View of Reflective Teaching. *Educational Researcher, 24* (6), 9–17.

Stewart, T. (1998). *Intellectual Capital: The New Wealth of Organizations*. New York: Bantam Books.

Stigler, J. W., and Hiebert, J. (1997). Understanding and Improving Classroom Mathematics Instruction: An Overview of the IMMS Video Study. *Phi Delta Kappan*, 4–21.

Street, B. (1984). *Literacy in Theory and Practice*. Cambridge: Cambridge University Press.

Supovitz, J. (2001). Translating Teaching Practice into Improved Student Achievement. In S. Fuhrman (Ed.), *From the Capitol to the Classroom. Standards-based Reforms in the States: The One Hundredth Yearbook of the National Society for the Study of Education, Part Two*, pp. 81–98. Chicago: University of Chicago Press.

Tapscott, D. (1998). *Growing Up Digital: the Rise of the Net Generation*, http://www.growingupdigital.com.

Taylor, S., and Bogdan, R. (1984). *Introduction to Qualitative Research Methods: The Search for Meaning*. New York: Wiley and Sons.

Taylor, S., and Bogdan, R. (1998). *Introduction to Qualitative Research Methods* (3rd ed.). New York: John Wiley.

Thompson, C., and Zeuli, J. (1999). The Frame and the Tapestry: Standards-based Reform and Professional Development. In L. Darling-Hammond and G. Sykes (Eds.), *Teaching as the Learning Profession: Handbook of Policy and Practice*, pp. 341–75. San Francisco: Jossey-Bass.

University of South Australia, and South Australian Department of Education and Children's Services. (2005). *Mapping Multiliteracies: Children of the New Millennium. Report of the Research Project 2002–2004*. Retrieved 7 December, 2005, from http://www.earlyyears.sa.edu.au/publish/modules/publish/content.asp.

Unsworth, L. (2002). Changing Dimensions of School Literacies. *The Australian Journal of Language and Literacy, 25* (1), 62-77.

Unsworth L. (2006a). *E-literature for Children: Enhancing Digital Literacy Learning*. Oxford: Routledge.

Unsworth, L. (2001). *Teaching Multiliteracies across the Curriculum: Changing Contexts of Text and Image in Classroom Practice*. Philadelphia: Open University Press.

Unsworth, L. (2006b). Towards a Metalanguage for Multiliteracies Education: Describing the Meaning-Making Resources of Language-Image Interaction. *English Teaching: Practice and Critique*, 5 (1), 55–76.

van Haren, R. (2007). *Diversity and the Learning by Design Approach to Pedagogy (unpublished Masters thesis)*. The Royal Melbourne Institute of Technology University: Melbourne.

van Haren, R. (2005). Effective Teaching and Learning: Pedagogy and Multiliteracies. In M. Kalantzis and B. Cope (Eds.), *Learning by Design*. Melbourne/Altona: VSIC/Common Ground.

van Leeuwen, T. (1999). *Speech, Music, Sound*. London: Macmillan.

van Leeuwen, T. (2005). *Introducing Social Semiotics*. New York: Routledge.

van Leeuwen, T. (2006). *The Discursive Construction of Social Space.* Paper presented at the Multimodal Texts and Multiliteracies: Semiotic Theory and Practical Pedagogy National Conference of the Australian Systemic Functional Linguistics Association, Armidale, University of New England.

Victorian Curriculum and Assessment Authority. (2004a). *Curriculum Framework for Victorian Schools (draft).* East Melbourne: Victorian Curriculum and Assessment Authority.

Victorian Curriculum and Assessment Authority. (2004b). *Victorian Curriculum Reform 2004 Consultation Paper.* Retrieved 24 November 2004, from http://www.vcaa.vic.edu.au/prep10/crp/consultpaper.pdf.

Victorian Curriculum and Assessment Authority. (2005a). *Interdisciplinary Learning Strand Information and Communications Technology.* Retrieved 18 December, 2006, from http://vels.vcaa.vic.edu.au/downloads/vels_standards/velsrevisedict.pdf.

Victorian Curriculum and Assessment Authority. (2005b). *Victorian Essential Learning Standards Level 1 Revised Edition.* Retrieved 16 December, 2006, from http://vels.vcaa.vic.edu.au/downloads/vels_standards/velsrevlvl1.pdf.

Victorian Curriculum and Assessment Authority. (2005c). *Victorian Essential Learning Standards website.* Retrieved 15 May, 2007, from http://vels.vcaa.vic.edu.au/essential/index.html.

Victorian Curriculum and Assessment Authority. (2005d). *Victorian Essential Learning Standards: Overview.* East Melbourne: Victorian Curriculum and Assessment Authority.

Virilio, P. (1997). *Open Sky.* London: Verso.

Vygotsky, L. (1978). *Mind in Society: The Development of Higher Psychological Processes.* Cambridge, MA: Harvard University Press.

Wark, M. (1994). *Virtual Geography: Living With Global Media Events.* Bloomington, Indianapolis: Indiana University Press.

Wenger, E. (1999). *Communities of Practice: Learning, Meaning and Identity.* Cambridge: Cambridge University Press.

Wenger, E., McDermott, R., and Snyder, W. M. (2002). *Cultivating Communities of Practice: A Guide to Managing Knowledge.* Cambridge, MA: Harvard Business School Press.

Wenglinsky, H. (2000). *How Teaching Matters: Bringing the Classroom Back into the Discussions about Teacher Quality.* Princeton, NJ: Educational Testing Service.

Wertsch, J. (1985). *Culture, Communication and Cognition: Vygotskian Perspectives.* Cambridge: Cambridge University Press.

Wilson, J., and Murdoch, K. (2004). *What is Inquiry Learning?* Retrieved 21 June, 2006, from http://www.nationalpriorities.org.uk/Resources/Priority/Noumea/InquiryLearning.pdf.

Woodcock, R. W. (1987). *Woodcock Reading Mastery Tests—Revised.* Circle Pines, MN: American Guidance Service.

Yin, R. (2003). *Case Study Research: Design and Methods*. Thousand Oaks, California: Sage Publications Inc.

www.ingramcontent.com/pod-product-compliance
Lightning Source LLC
Chambersburg PA
CBHW070828300426
44111CB00014B/2483